CONTENTS

INTRODUCTION   1
    History of the Hoverfly Recording Scheme   1
    Coverage   2

STATUS OF HOVERFLIES IN BRITAIN   5
    Species recorded from Ireland but not Britain   5
    Species believed to have become established, or to have increased   5
    Species believed to be migrants, partial migrants or vagrants   5
    Species believed to be extinct in Britain   6
    Species which have declined significantly   6
    Rarity and threat   8
    Biodiversity Action Plans   8
    Habitat-indicator statuses   9

NOTES ON THE DISTRIBUTION MAPS AND SPECIES ACCOUNTS   13
    The maps   13
    Nomenclature   13
    Species accounts   13
    Phenology histograms   13

MAPS AND SPECIES ACCOUNTS   15

ACKNOWLEDGEMENTS   151

REFERENCES   155

SPECIES INDEX   159

INTRODUCTION

The hoverflies are a family of attractive, and often brightly coloured flies which are familiar to most people because they are frequently seen visiting flowers in parks and gardens. They have received a generally 'good press' as beneficial insects because the larvae of many of the common garden species feed on aphids. However, because many possess wasp-like black and yellow striped patterns, or mimic bees, they are often mistaken for Hymenoptera, and during mass movements of some of the common migratory species have occasionally figured in the press as 'a plague of wasps'. They are often the first group to be tackled by budding dipterists and the availability of a well illustrated identification guide (Stubbs & Falk 1983) has greatly boosted interest in the group over the last decade. With 266 British species, many (but by no means all) of which are easily identified, they are an ideal group to study. They are also extremely diverse in form, life-style and habitat preference, which means that an interesting range of species can be found in most localities and habitats. These factors have encouraged an active recording scheme which has collated information about the distribution and natural history of these fascinating insects.

History of the Hoverfly Recording Scheme

The Hoverfly Recording Scheme was launched in 1976 (Stubbs 1990), under the umbrella of the Central Panel of Diptera Recording Schemes, with John Ismay as the first national organiser. In 1980 Philip Entwistle took over as scheme organiser and he subsequently initiated the *Hoverfly Newsletter* which first appeared in October 1982 including six distribution maps. In 1983 a preliminary atlas, containing 30 hand-plotted maps, was produced by the Biological Records Centre (BRC) (Entwistle & Stubbs 1983). Also in 1983 *British Hoverflies*, a well illustrated and 'user friendly' identification guide, was published (Stubbs & Falk 1983), which opened up hoverfly recording to many more people. Another significant publication was *Hoverflies* in the *Naturalists' Handbooks* series (Gilbert 1986). This provides an excellent summary of biology and many useful hints on observing, studying and recording hoverflies, but it should not be relied upon, on its own, for identification. What had been considered a rather specialised and difficult group became by far the most popular group of flies.

Calls for records to be submitted to BRC for the production of a provisional atlas were made at Dipterists Day in 1985 and 1986 and, together with the records that had been accumulated by Ismay and Entwistle, around 80 000 records arrived at BRC of which 54 500 were input to computer file. In 1987

Philip Entwistle retired as Recording Scheme organiser and *Hoverfly Newsletter* editor. The latter job was taken over by Graham Rotheray, and the workload of dealing with records was spread by establishing a network of local advisors to check and forward records to BRC.

In 1988 a new journal, *Dipterists Digest*, was launched which has proved an important vehicle for papers on the natural history of hoverflies in Britain, Ireland and the near continent. The first issue featured a hoverfly on the front cover and papers concerning hoverflies have always provided a substantial portion of the contents.

Between 1987 and 1991 the Recording Scheme underwent a period of inactivity with no national organiser and with no prospect of BRC having resources to progress the provisional atlas. Then, in late 1990, Stuart Ball and Roger Morris took over as national organisers, with Roger Morris in charge of day-to-day liaison with contributors and record checking, and Stuart Ball in charge of data processing. In Autumn 1991 the records that had been computerised by BRC were loaded into a copy of the *Recorder* database and the process of checking them began. The considerable backlog of information on cards and other paper forms which had been submitted to BRC, but not input to computer, was another rather daunting task. By 1992 the records input by BRC had been checked against the original cards and progress was being made on trawling new records, both on cards and on disk from various databases.

In 1992 David Iliff took over as editor of *Hoverfly Newsletter* and in March 1993 the Central Panel started a series of annual training events with a weekend workshop on hoverfly identification at Preston Montford Field Studies Centre. In 1994 the Central Panel reformed itself as an independent society, 'Dipterists Forum', affiliated to the British Entomological and Natural History Society. Its objectives include publication of newsletters, such as *Hoverfly Newsletter*, to foster the study of Diptera and to publish the resulting works in its journal, *Dipterists Digest*.

Information about hoverfly biology has continued to increase, especially knowledge of larvae. Graham Rotheray was particularly active in the latter field and published a summary of the current state of our knowledge in *Colour guide to hoverfly larvae* (Rotheray 1994). In 1996 Alan Stubbs produced a Supplement to *British Hoverflies* including information on the 15 species added to the British list since the original publication in 1983 and updated keys to some genera (Stubbs 1996).

Table 1. Number of records submitted, by year of observation

Year	Records	Cumulative	Cumulative % (of dated records)
19th Century	664	664	0.18%
1900–1909	913	1 577	0.42%
1910–1919	1 330	2 907	0.78%
1920–1929	4 124	7 031	1.89%
1930–1939	3 678	10 709	2.88%
1940–1949	4 077	14 786	3.98%
1950–1959	3 910	18 696	5.03%
1960–1969	9 369	28 065	7.55%
1970–1974	11 554	39 619	10.65%
1975–1979	20 888	60 507	16.27%
1980–1984	51 433	111 940	30.10%
1985–1989	126 853	238 793	64.22%
1990–1994	97 272	336 065	90.38%
1995–1999	35 771	371 836	100.00%
Total dated	371 836		
Undated	2 948		
Total	374 784		

Coverage

Up to June 1999, the recording scheme had collated 374,784 records from 2,445 ten kilometre squares; the great majority from Great Britain (2,361 ten kilometre squares), the remainder being from Ireland (79 squares), and the Channel Islands (five squares). The collated records cover all British species. There are 2,862 ten kilometre squares in Great Britain's National Grid which contain some land, so the scheme has received at least one record from 82.5%. Figure 1 shows all ten kilometre squares in Great Britain from which at least one record has been received, and Figure 2 shows the number of species recorded from each square. These maps, especially Figure 2, give a good general impression of the coverage that has been achieved so far. Coverage is patchy with some local recording schemes having surveyed their areas intensively – notably in Surrey, but also Essex, Somerset, Dorset, Oxfordshire, south-west Wales, the Sorby Naturalists' area, Rotherham, the Coventry area and the territory of the North West Hoverfly Recording Group. Some other areas remain poorly covered, especially the Welsh borders, Wiltshire and the areas around the Wash (which appears to be genuinely very poor for hoverflies). Coverage in Scotland is much better than is shown here, especially in the east, due to the activities of the Scottish Hoverfly Recording Scheme run by Ken Watt, but not all of these records were available to the National Recording Scheme for this Atlas. Although records from Northern Ireland have been collated at the Centre for Environmental Data and Recording (CEDaR) in Belfast, these have not been incorporated into the scheme as yet and very few records from the Irish Republic are available to us. Consequently, this atlas does not attempt to cover Ireland.

The records submitted to the scheme are overwhelmingly (76.2%) from dates after the publication of Stubbs and Falk (1983), with half

from 1987 onwards, and a rather small proportion (7.6%) from before 1970 (Table 1). Whilst there were undoubtedly far fewer active recorders in the past, older records are under-represented because there has been no concerted attempt to obtain records from the literature and museum collections. A few collections have been re-examined and records submitted to the scheme (notably the Diver collection of specimens from Studland, Dorset in the 1930s, the British Entomological & Natural History Society collection, Exeter Museum and Doncaster Museum), but the only other substantial source of older records is the data collated by Steven Falk in preparing the National Review of Diptera for the Nature Conservancy Council in the late 1980s (Falk 1991a). These records concentrate on the rarer species including both literature records and information from some major collections such as those of the Natural History Museum, Royal Scottish Museum, Cambridge University Museum of Zoology and the Hope Department, Oxford.

Figure 1. All ten kilometre squares in Great Britain from which at least one record has been received

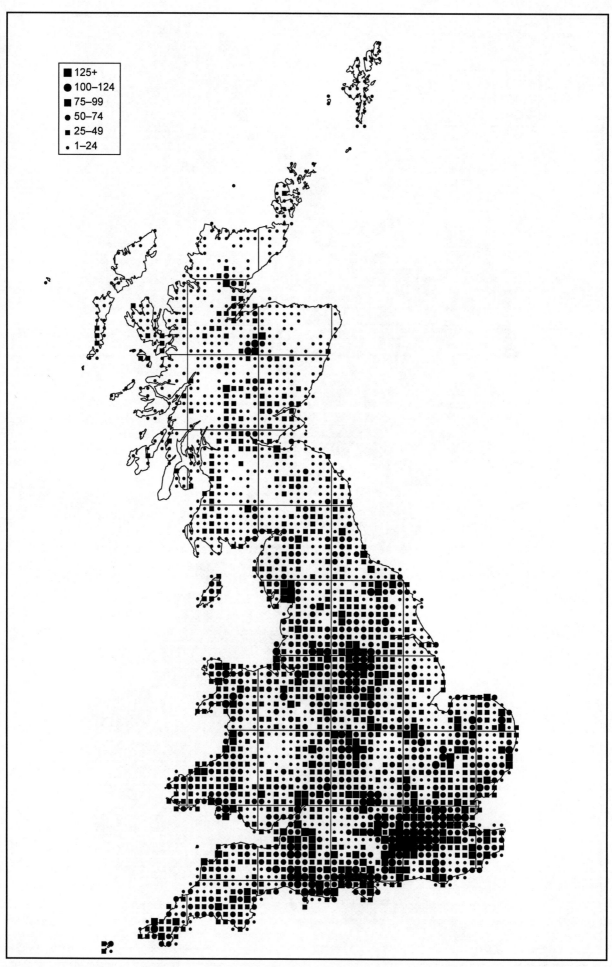

Figure 2. The number of species recorded from each square

STATUS OF HOVERFLIES IN BRITAIN

Species recorded from Ireland but not Britain

Paragus constrictus Simic, 1986

This species was separated from *P. tibialis* (Fallén) relatively recently and has proved to be widespread on limestone pavement in the Burren, County Clare (Speight & Chandler 1995). A record from the area of the Burren mentioned under *P. tibialis* in Stubbs and Falk (1983) proved to be this species. It is quite possible that it may occur on limestone pavement in Great Britain and any specimens of *P. tibialis* in collections from this habitat should be re-examined.

Cheilosia ahenea von Roser, 1840 (*C. laskai* Speight, 1978 in Stubbs and Falk (1983))

In Europe this appears to be a species of montane pastures, but it is only known in the British Isles from calcareous grasslands on limestone pavement and machair of western Ireland, with 16 records between 1979 and 1985 from counties Clare, Donegal, Fermanagh, Sligo and Mayo (Speight 1987). It most closely resembles *C. pubera* (Zetterstedt) and has been found by sweeping low-growing vegetation, or occasionally visiting flowers of *Antennaria, Hieracium, Ranunculus* and *Taraxacum*, mainly in May, but extending into June. It should be looked out for on limestone pavement in north-west England and Wales and could conceivably occur on machair in the Western Isles.

Cheilosia psilophthalma Becker, 1894

This hoverfly has only recently been adequately distinguished from the closely similar *C. praecox* (Zetterstedt) by Claussen and Kassebeer (1993). Martin Speight has re-examined Irish material which had previously been determined as *C. praecox* and found that all the specimens he examined were *C. psilophthalma*, but British specimens to which he had access were true *C. praecox* (Speight 1996a). Little is known as yet about *C. psilophthalma* except that it occurs in various scrub woodland situations and has an early flight period (Irish records: 21 April - 24 May). Speight (1996a) gives a key to *C. mutabilis* (Fallén), *C. praecox* and *C. psilophthalma* and Claussen and Kassebeer (1993) give illustrations of the male terminalia of these species and *C. latigens* Claussen & Kassebeer (which is part of the same species complex, but has only been found so far in the Pyrenees), but separation from *C. praecox* is very difficult and any suspected specimens of *C. psilophthalma* should be referred for expert examination.

Species believed to have become established, or to have increased

Two species of 'bulb fly', *Merodon equestris* (Fabricius) and *Eumerus tuberculatus* Rondani are believed to have been accidentally imported through the international trade in bulbs. *M. equestris* arrived in the latter part of the last century and was reported first from the garden of Verrall's brother in 1867 (Verrall 1901). *E. tuberculatus* arrived somewhat later and was added to the British list by Collin (1918). The recording scheme holds one pre-1920 record, a museum specimen taken in Surrey in 1905. Both of these genera are rich in species in southern and eastern Europe, especially around the eastern Mediterranean, and it is not inconceivable that more species of either genus could arrive by the same route (see, for example, Speight (1988a)).

Rather more species are thought to have become established, or to have spread, during this century in conifer plantations. *Xylota coeruleiventris* Zetterstedt appears to be unique amongst hoverflies in being recorded historically only from native Caledonian pine forest, but to have spread widely in planted conifers in recent years. It has now reached parts of southern and central England. *Eriozona syrphoides* (Fallén) is one of the most spectacular additions to our fauna and was first recognised from a 1968 specimen, although an earlier (1957) specimen was subsequently located. It is now being recorded quite frequently in conifer plantations in the north and west. *Dasysyrphus friuliensis* (van der Goot), first recorded in 1982 and possibly *Sphegina sibirica* Stackelberg discovered in 1991, may show a similar pattern of spread in the future. *Eriozona erratica* (Linnaeus) is another species associated with conifers which has been recorded more frequently in recent years.

Another spectacular migrant/vagrant that has become resident is *Volucella zonaria*. This was considered to be a very rare vagrant to the south coast at the start of the century, but became established in the London area in the 1940s. It is now frequent in and around London, especially in suburban gardens, and seems to be becoming more widely established along the south coast and may be moving northwards through Hertfordshire.

Species believed to be migrants, partial migrants or vagrants

Several hoverflies, especially members of the genera *Episyrphus, Eupeodes, Syrphus, Scaeva* and *Helophilus,* are believed to migrate regularly over large distances in Europe. Torp (1984) gives a table of species believed to be migratory in Denmark.

Migratory behaviour in these insects is not like that of birds in which the same individual travels north to breed in summer and then travels south for the winter. In the case of insect migrants, individuals travelling north in spring lay eggs which produce one or more new generations during the summer or early autumn, and it is their progeny which travel southwards. The arrival of such migrants in Britain depends upon weather patterns which bring them in our direction and, consequently, their abundance varies greatly from year to year. Many of these species are permanently resident, although their numbers may be reinforced in some years by the arrival of migrants, whilst others (eg *Scaeva pyrastri* (Linnaeus), *Helophilus trivittatus* (Fabricius)) may rely entirely on immigration and have no permanent breeding population. Some others (eg *Eristalis tenax* (Linnaeus), *Sphaerophoria scripta* (Linnaeus)) which are not noted as long-distance travellers, may be partial migrants (or at least very mobile) within the British Isles. For example, breeding populations of *S. scripta* do not appear to be permanently established in Ireland although adults are recorded regularly (Speight 1996b).

Spectacular arrivals of *Episyrphus balteatus* (De Geer), *Eupeodes corollae* (Fabricius) and *Scaeva pyrastri* have been described from the south and east coasts when great numbers are present in coastal localities and many are washed up dead on the tide-line. The Scottish Hoverfly Recording Scheme has arranged for water-traps to be operated on oil rigs in the North Sea and has obtained interesting information on the occurrence of hoverflies well away from land.

Other species such as *Eupeodes lundbecki* (Soot-Ryen), *Helophilus affinis* Wahlberg and *Scaeva albomaculata* (Macquart) are probably vagrants which reach Britain only occasionally and have been found mainly in localities such as Fair Isle, North Norfolk and parts of the south coast which are also noted for the occurrence of vagrant birds. It is possible that the very poorly known *Helophilus groenlandicus* (Fabricius) also belongs in this category (as a vagrant from the Arctic). The status of several species such as *Eupeodes lapponicus* (Zetterstedt), *Didea alneti* (Fallén) and *Xanthandrus comtus* (Harris) is less clear. Their sporadic occurrence and lack of any clear association of records with what is presumed to be their breeding habitats has led to suggestions that they may be migrants or vagrants which become locally established for a time. *Scaeva mecogramma* (Bigot) presents an interesting case: this Mediterranean species has been recorded only once in Britain in August 1905, from Arniston, near Edinburgh, which seems an unlikely place for a vagrant to turn up; it has been suggested that it may have been an accidental import (Stubbs & Falk 1983).

Species believed to be extinct in Britain

Myolepta potens (Harris, 1780)
Levy and Levy (1998) give an account of the history of this species, on which the following is based. It was discovered in 1945 by John Cowley, a Somerset naturalist, at two woodland sites near Shapwick in the Somerset Levels. J E Collin established their identity (Collin 1950) and located three older specimens in collections which had previously been identified as *M. dubia* (Fabricius) (with no data, but one is thought to date from 1828). Cowley found several more specimens in 1946, 1947 and 1949 sometimes in the company of ECM d'Assis-Fonseca who also found a single male in Blaise Wood near Bristol in 1949. Collin (1950) reports another specimen collected by Dr E E Lowe from Coombe Dingle (part of the Blaise Castle Estate) in 1945. In April 1961 J C Hartley found six larvae in a rot-hole at Ashton Court (near Blaise Castle). He preserved one larva and reared adults from the other five. The species has not been found again since 1961 despite searches by a number of eminent dipterists. The original locality at Loxley Wood has been largely coniferised and is thought to be unsuitable, but apparently suitable habitat remains in the Blaise Castle area.

Species which have declined significantly

Blera fallax (Linnaeus, 1758)
Records are confined to the Speyside area of the Central Highlands of Scotland, but some of the older literature describes it as 'numerous' around the turn of the century. Very few adults have been found in recent decades and almost exclusively from around Loch Garten in the Abernethy Forest. In 1996 the Malloch Society located the breeding site when a puparium was found in a rotten pine stump (Rotheray & Stuke 1998), so a more systematic search for larvae became possible. Subsequent searches have located two small populations, with only about 20 occupied stumps in total, in pine plantations near human habitation. Searches in native pinewood in Abernethy and Rothiemurchus have so far proved unsuccessful. The larvae in a given stump are of very mixed sizes, suggesting a larval period of several years and that the number of adults emerging in any one year may be very small. This is now thought to be the most threatened of the rare Scottish saproxylic hoverflies.

Callicera spinolae Rondani, 1944
This fly was discovered in 1924 at Thorndon, Suffolk and has been recorded from less than ten localities, all in East Anglia. It appears to be rare throughout its known European range: northern France south to the Pyrenees, central Spain and the Mediterranean, Germany, Italy, Roumania and Tajikistan (Speight 1998). It has only been found at two localities in the last two decades, both in Cambridgeshire, and it

appears to have become extinct at one of these by 1983. At the other it was reduced to breeding in only two trees, one of which blew down in the winter of 1994/95. English Nature commissioned a survey of the known localities, and also potential sites in East Anglia, under the Species Recovery Programme. In 1997, Graham Rotheray visited 18 sites in Norfolk, Suffolk and Cambridgeshire and searched about 170 rot-holes for larvae, but without success. In September 1998, about 60 rot-holes at 18 sites were searched, again without success, but two observations, both of single adults at ivy flowers, were made at a site in Suffolk.

Chrysotoxum octomaculatum Curtis, 1837

A rare species associated with extensive heathlands mainly in the New Forest, Dorset and Surrey (although generally found at the edges of heaths, rather than the main blocks of heathland habitat). Most of the very few recent records are from the vicinity of Thursley and Hankley Commons. A recent survey commissioned by English Nature, under the Biodiversity Action Plan, failed to rediscover the species at Studland, which had been one of its best localities. An association of larvae with ants is suspected and further work is needed to elucidate this.

Doros profuges Harris, 1780.

This is another species suspected to be associated in some way with ants, and which seems to have been recorded more frequently in the past. A 19th century observation suggests that the larvae may be associated with ants living in wood, where they probably feed on ant-attended aphids. A recent observation by R Hawkins suggested oviposition on the trunk of an isolated ash tree surrounded by scrub on chalk downland (Stubbs 1996), but Morris (1998) quotes Hawkins as stating that oviposition was not proven in the field. Speight (1988b) described the puparium and suggests (Speight 1998) that *Lasius fuliginosus* (Latreille) is the most likely host species. Most records are associated with well-drained, basic soils and most frequently, but not exclusively, come from unimproved chalk or limestone grassland. Adults are typically found sunning themselves on leaves, or visiting flowers such as *Rubus*, on the edges of scrub. However, adults seem to be very elusive and Speight (1998) suggests they may be primarily arboreal. Whilst the majority of records come from south-east England, there are a wide scatter elsewhere. There are a number of old records from around Morecambe Bay, and it was recently rediscovered at two localities in this area (Gorman and Sumner quoted in Stubbs, 1996). It was also taken on the coast of Mull (Ravenscroft quoted in Stubbs, 1996).

Eristalis cryptarum (Fabricius, 1794)

This is a species of south-west England which occurred mainly in the New Forest, the Dorset heaths, Dartmoor and Cornwall. Most of the older records come from the New Forest (probably because this is where the dipterists traditionally looked), but it has not been found there since the early 1950s. There were a number of records from Dorset, especially in the 1930s, but recent extensive searches for the Dorset Hoverfly Atlas (Levy, Levy & Dean 1992) failed to rediscover it. There is a long history of records from Dartmoor, but the last one that could be authenticated was made in 1973, despite a number of searches in the late 1970s and 1980s. Consequently it was feared extinct. Then, in 1993, we investigated historic localities on Dartmoor and rediscovered a population at one of them (Levy & Levy 1994). Subsequent searches revealed populations in two adjoining ten kilometre squares. In 1998 Gordon Ramel surveyed sites in this area and, despite it being a disappointing season, found the species at seven localities. These typically included somewhat acid (pH 6.33–6.59) boggy pools with plants such as *Sphagnum, Menyanthes, Narthecium* and *Caltha*.

Hammerschmidtia ferruginea (Fallén, 1817)

This hoverfly was discovered by Col. Yerbury on Speyside, Scotland, late in the last century and this area has always been its stronghold, although records are scattered somewhat more widely in the Scottish Highlands. Although some accounts from the turn of the century suggest it was quite frequent, modern dipterists have found it rarely and in small numbers. Recent work by the Malloch Society showed that the larva feeds under the bark of recently fallen aspen *Populus tremula* and located it in eleven ten kilometre squares. Mature stands of aspen are a scarce habitat, and the hoverfly is therefore considered very vulnerable. Action is needed to protect existing breeding sites and to establish sympathetic management of aspen groves in the Highlands. There is concern that plans to reintroduce the European beaver *Castor fiber* Linnaeus in the Scottish Highlands potentially pose a threat to this species. The most important aspen stands are all close to watersides in the proposed reintroduction areas and aspen is the beaver's preferred foodplant.

Declining species associated with dead wood

There are a number of threatened hoverflies, including members of the genera *Brachyopa, Caliprobola, Callicera, Myolepta, Mallota* and *Pocota,* whose larvae are associated with ancient trees. For example, *Brachyopa* breed in sap runs, *Callicera, Myolepta, Mallota* and *Pocota* in rot holes. This is a vulnerable and declining habitat because many sites that once supported old trees have been cleared for agriculture and forestry and, where they do remain, individual ancient trees are often removed by landowners and foresters for reasons of tidiness and safety. However, recent studies targeted on the larvae rather than the elusive adults have shown that some (eg *Callicera rufa, Pocota personata*) are not as restricted as was thought and may be able to survive in areas with few, isolated breeding trees. The provision of artificial breeding sites has also proved feasible for *Callicera* (MacGowan 1994). Whilst there is no room for complacency, this certainly suggests that more work on larval biology and surveys targeting larvae would be appropriate.

Declining ant associated species

Together with *Chrysotoxum octomaculatum* and *Doros profuges*, discussed above, several other species, including *Chrysotoxum elegans* Loew and *Microdon devius* (Linnaeus) appear to have been recorded less frequently in recent decades than in the past and are considered threatened. The larvae of *M. devius* live in nests of the ant *Lasius flavus* (Fabricius) on chalk downland and so, over and above the general reduction in chalk grassland, it is possible that loss of open areas to scrub may be important. *C. elegans* is poorly known and, although its larvae are suspected to be associated with ants, there is no definite information. The relationship between hoverfly larvae and social Hymenoptera is a fascinating subject and better information is required so that more systematic searches can be made to establish the status of such species more firmly.

Rarity and threat

Several attempts have been made to assess the rarity of, and threat to, British hoverfly species. The British Insect Red Data Book (Shirt 1987) listed 56 species, although detailed accounts are given for only the most threatened species. The introduction to this work gives a detailed description of the meaning of the categories and the criteria used to assess species. They are based on the criteria developed by the International Union for the Conservation of Nature (IUCN) for Red Data Lists. Falk (1991a), in the National Review of Diptera, re-assessed the IUCN categories into which the species fell and also considered another tier of species - those recorded from 16 to 100 of the ten kilometre squares of the National Grid (termed 'Notable' or, more recently, 'Nationally scarce'). Falk (1991a) includes detailed accounts for all species listed. Table 2 summarises the statuses assigned to species listed in these works.

Subsequent to these publications, IUCN has developed a new system, with different categories and more stringent, quantitative criteria, which was published in 1994. The considerable increase in knowledge of the biology, status and distribution of hoverflies resulting from this recording scheme and other recent work, and the adoption by the Joint Nature Conservation Committee of the new IUCN criteria for future British Red Lists, would make a re-assessment of statuses timely, but this is not the place to undertake the task.

Biodiversity Action Plans

The Biodiversity Steering Group Report (UK Biodiversity Steering Group 1995) took a rather different approach in trying to identify species which require conservation action as a high priority. The report contained three lists:

- The 'long lists' included 1,252 species (including 14 hoverflies) which met a set of criteria (though by no means all species meeting the criteria are included).
- A 'short list' of 116 species (including two hoverflies) was drawn from the 'long list' which were considered the highest priority and the report includes action plans for these species.
- A 'middle list' included around 300 more species (including two more hoverflies) for which it was intended to draw up action plans.

The criteria used to select species for the 'long list' were as follows:
- Species considered to be threatened with extinction at International or European level (essentially species listed in IUCN World Red Lists or on various International Conventions and Directives).
- Species for which Britain has particular responsibility; where Britain supports 25% or more of the total population at some period during their life. This includes any endemic species.
- Species which have declined by 25% or more in Britain during the last 25 years.
- Very localised species (those occurring in 15 or fewer ten kilometre squares in Britain).
- Species protected by various pieces of domestic or international legislation.

The species selected for the 'short list' were those qualifying under category 1 or where Britain supported 75% of the total population, or those showing a 75% or more decline. Table 2 shows the species included in the short, middle and long lists.

Following the publication of the Steering Group Report in 1995, there has been much activity. The UK Biodiversity Group agreed to revise the structure and terminology of the lists to ensure clarity, and to publish a revised list of species for which action plans are being prepared. This publication (UK Biodiversity Group 1998) defines two categories:

- **Species of Conservation Concern**. All species which meet the published 'long list' criteria (shown above).

- **Priority Species**. From within the list of Species of Conservation Concern, all species which qualify under the published 'short' and 'middle list' criteria are classified as Priority Species. Species which qualify under one of the following criteria should be considered as Priority Species:
  - Species which are globally threatened
  - Species which are rapidly declining in the UK, ie by more than 50% in the last 25 years.

Annex 3 of the report lists 389 Priority Species, including seven species of hoverfly which are listed in Table 2. All Priority Species should be the subject of targeted action and are in the process of having action plans written.

Habitat-indicator statuses

Another type of assessment attempts to identify 'indicator species' – those whose presence reveals something about the nature of the site they inhabit. This concept has been applied most frequently to woodland species and some invertebrates have been identified as 'habitat continuity indicators'. These are species which tend to occur in sites with historical continuity of cover by mature deciduous woodland. They are frequently associated in some way with ancient or over-mature trees and appear to have poor dispersal ability. Therefore, in our highly fragmented countryside, in which sites that support these conditions are scarce and often isolated, it is argued that, if such a species is lost through inappropriate management (eg clear-felling), even if this is only for a relatively short period, it is unlikely that the site could be re-colonised. Consequently, the presence of such species is evidence that their habitats have been continuously present in the area over a long time span. Stubbs (1982) selected 'primary woodland indicators' and placed them in three categories: H1 – Strong, H2 – Good and H3 – Weak.

Speight (1989b) identified species across a broad range of insect groups which he considered 'useful in identifying forests of international importance to nature conservation'. This list includes 10 species of hoverfly which occur in Great Britain. There have been attempts to identify indicators for habitats other than woodland, but these are less well developed as yet. For example, Whiteley (1995) gives a provisional list of wetland indicator species for the Sheffield area and Morris (1998) gives lists of species associated with chalk, heathlands, wetlands and woodlands in Surrey.

Table 2. Species which have been assigned threat, rarity or habitat indicator status. Where the name currently in use differs from the name used in the original source, the latter name is shown in parenthesis.

Species	Shirt (1987)	Falk (1991a)	DoE (1995)	UK BG (1998)	Stubbs (1982)	Speight (1989b)
Anasimyia interpuncta	Vulnerable	Rare				
Anasimyia lunulata		Notable				
Blera fallax	Endangered	Endangered	Long		H1	
Brachyopa bicolor	Vulnerable	Rare			H1	
Brachyopa insensilis		Notable			H3	
Brachyopa pilosa	Rare	Notable			H1	
Brachyopa scutellaris					H2	
Brachypalpoides lentus					H1	
Brachypalpus laphriformis	Rare	Notable			H1	
Caliprobola speciosa	Endangered	Endangered			H1	
Callicera aurata (aenea)	Vulnerable	Rare			H3	
Callicera rufa	Endangered	Rare			H2	
Callicera spinolae	Endangered	Endangered	Short		H3	
Chalcosyrphus eunotus	Vulnerable	Vulnerable			H1	
Chalcosyrphus nemorum					H2	
Chamaesyrphus caledonicus	Endangered	Endangered				
Chamaesyrphus scaevoides	Rare	Rare				
Cheilosia barbata		Notable			H3	
Cheilosia carbonaria	Rare	Notable			H1	
Cheilosia chrysocoma		Rare			H2	
Cheilosia cynocephala	Rare	Notable				
Cheilosia lasiopa (honesta)					H2	
Cheilosia mutabilis	Rare	Notable				
Cheilosia nebulosa	Rare	Rare				
Cheilosia nigripes	Rare	Rare				
Cheilosia pubera	Rare	Notable				
Cheilosia sahlbergi	Rare	Vulnerable				
Cheilosia semifasciata		Rare			H1	
Cheilosia soror		Notable				
Cheilosia species B	Rare	Endangered				
Cheilosia velutina	Rare	Notable				
Chrysotoxum elegans	Rare	Rare				
Chrysotoxum octomaculatum	Vulnerable	Vulnerable	Short			
Chrysotoxum vernale	Endangered	Endangered				
Criorhina asilica		Notable			H2	
Criorhina berberina					H2	
Criorhina floccosa					H3	
Criorhina ranunculi		Notable			H2	
Didea alneti	Endangered	Endangered	Long			
Didea fasciata		Notable			H1	
Didea intermedia		Notable				
Doros profuges (conopseus)	Vulnerable	Vulnerable	Long			
Epistrophe diaphana		Notable				
Epistrophe grossulariae					H3	
Epistrophe nitidicollis					H2	
Eriozona erratica (Megasyrphus annulipes)		Notable				
Eristalis cryptarum	Vulnerable	Vulnerable	Long			
Eristalis rupium		Notable				
Eumerus ornatus		Notable	Long		H1	
Eumerus sabulonum	Rare	Notable				
Eupeodes lapponicus (Metasyrphus)		Notable	Middle			
Eupeodes latilunulatus (Metasyrphus)		Notable				
Eupeodes nielseni (Metasyrphus)		Notable			H3	
Eupeodes nitens (Metasyrphus)		Notable			H1	
Ferdinandea cuprea					H2	
Ferdinandea ruficornis	Vulnerable	Notable			H2	
Hammerschmidtia ferruginea	Endangered	Endangered	Long		H1	
Helophilus groenlandicus	Rare	Vulnerable				
Heringia brevidens (Neocnemodon)		Notable				
Heringia latitarsis (Neocnemodon)		Notable				
Heringia pubescens (Neocnemodon)		Notable				

continued...

Species	Shirt (1987)	Falk (1991a)	DoE (1995)	UK BG (1998)	Stubbs (1982)	Speight (1989b)
Heringia verrucula (*Neocnemodon*)		Notable				
Lejops vittatus	Vulnerable	Vulnerable	Long			
Mallota cimbiciformis	Vulnerable	Notable			H2	
Melangyna barbifrons		Notable				
Melangyna ericarum		Rare				
Melanogaster aerosa (*Chrysogaster macquarti*)	Rare	Notable				
Melanostoma dubium		Notable				
Melanostoma species A		Notable				
Meligramma euchromum (*Epistrophe euchroma*)	Rare	Rare			H2	
Meligramma guttatum (*Melangyna guttata*)	Rare	Notable			H2	
Meligramma trianguliferum (*Melangyna triangulifera*)		Notable			H3	
Microdon analis (eggeri)	Rare	Notable			H2	
Microdon devius	Vulnerable	Vulnerable	Long			
Microdon mutabilis	Rare	Notable				
Myolepta dubia (luteola)	Rare	Notable			H2	
Myolepta potens	Endangered	Endangered	Middle		H2	
Neoascia geniculata		Notable				
Neoascia interrupta		Notable				
Neoascia obliqua	Rare	Notable				
Orthonevra brevicornis	Rare	Notable				
Orthonevra geniculata	Rare	Notable				
Paragus albifrons	Rare	Vulnerable				
Paragus tibialis		Notable				
Parasyrphus nigritarsis	Endangered	Endangered	Long			
Parhelophilus consimilis	Vulnerable	Vulnerable				
Pelecocera tricincta	Rare	Rare				
Pipiza lugubris		Notable				
Pipiza luteitarsis					H3	
Pipizella maculipennis	Rare	Rare				
Pipizella virens		Notable				
Platycheirus discimanus		Notable			H2	
Platycheirus immarginatus		Notable				
Platycheirus melanopsis	Rare	Rare				
Platycheirus perpallidus	Rare	Notable				
Platycheirus podagratus		Notable				
Platycheirus sticticus		Notable				
Platycheirus tarsalis					H3	
Pocota personata	Vulnerable	Vulnerable	Long		H1	
Portevinia maculata					H2	
Psilota anthracina	Vulnerable	Vulnerable			H2	
Rhingia rostrata	Vulnerable	Rare			H2	
Riponnensia splendida (*Lejogaster*)		Notable				
Sphaerophoria loewi	Vulnerable	Vulnerable				
Sphaerophoria virgata		Notable				
Sphegina clunipes					H2	
Sphegina elegans (*kimakowiczii*)					H2	
Sphegina verecunda		Notable			H1	
Triglyphus primus		Notable				
Volucella inanis		Notable				
Volucella inflata		Notable			H1	
Volucella zonaria		Notable				
Xanthandrus comtus	Vulnerable	Notable				
Xylota abiens		Notable			H2	
Xylota coeruleiventris		Notable				
Xylota florum		Notable			H2	
Xylota sylvarum					H3	
Xylota tarda		Notable			H2	
Xylota xanthocnema		Notable			H2	

NOTES ON THE DISTRIBUTION MAPS AND SPECIES ACCOUNTS

The maps

The maps show the squares of the National Grid from which records have been received in Great Britain. Ireland is not mapped. The date class of the most recent record from each square is indicated using one of three symbols:

- from 1980 onwards
- from 1960 to 1979
- before 1960 or undated

Most of the species maps show the conventional ten kilometre squares of the distribution. However, for three species, *Blera fallax*, *Callicera spinolae* and *Hammerschmidtia ferruginea*, the maps have been plotted using 50 kilometre squares. This reduced accuracy has been used at the request of the recorders to disguise the exact localities of these species, which are considered to be especially vulnerable to collectors.

Whilst we have attempted to check doubtful or inconsistent records, there are many which have yet to be followed up and which are omitted from the maps where we feel uncertain about their accuracy.

Nomenclature

The nomenclature used in this atlas follows Chandler (1998) with one additional species, *Platycheirus splendens* Rotheray, 1998, which was described after the checklist was published. Alternative names for species, which appear in major works such as Coe (1953), Kloet and Hincks (1976), Stubbs and Falk (1983), Rotheray (1994), Stubbs (1996) and notes published in *Hoverfly Newsletter* and *Dipterists Digest* have been listed at the head of species accounts and are included in the index. Stubbs (1995) gives a chronological list of the additions to the British hoverfly fauna from Verrall (1901) to 1990, which can be helpful in interpreting older records.

Plant nomenclature follows Stace (1997).

Species accounts

Information about the biology of species is synthesised from a number of sources. Larval information comes mainly from Rotheray (1994) and Speight (1998), supplemented by Smith (1989). Other comments are based on Stubbs and Falk (1983), Stubbs (1996) and Speight (1998) with some extra information from Coe (1953) and our own experience. These major sources are not

referred to every time unless there is some specific point of emphasis or disagreement. Other information has been culled from the *Hoverfly Newsletter, Dipterists Digest* and other more recent literature, and references are quoted at the relevant point for such information.

The paragraph on distribution summarises general patterns of distribution and comments on issues of abundance, localisation, habitat preferences etc, which are not evident from the map. Records which do not appear on the map may occasionally be referred to, either because full details were not available at the time of writing, or because some vague localities (eg 'West Suffolk') in older literature cannot be mapped at this scale.

Phenology histograms

The phenology histograms for each species show the number of records in fortnightly intervals from 24 February to 16 November. Records which are known to relate to larvae, pupae or reared adults have been excluded from the histograms; the remainder have been assumed to relate to adults observed in the field. For some species it is likely that unusual dates relate to larval and pupal records where life-stage information has not been reported to the scheme. Figure 3 shows the total number of records received in each period to illustrate the seasonal coverage of recording. Figure 4 shows how many species have been recorded in each period and indicates that peak diversity occurs from the end of May to June, but that the main season extends from about mid-May to early September without great variation in the number of active species.

All the phenology histograms show the number of records on the vertical axis, but the scale on this axis varies greatly depending on the total number of records for each species. However, all are scaled so that the longest bar is roughly the same height, to facilitate comparisons of seasonal pattern between species.

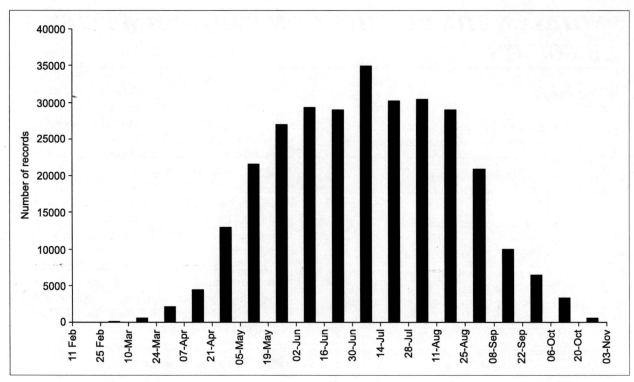

Figure 3. Total number of records received in each fortnightly period

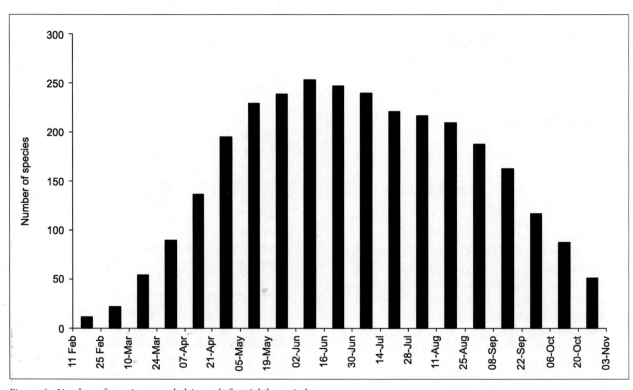

Figure 4. Number of species recorded in each fortnightly period

MAPS AND SPECIES ACCOUNTS

Anasimyia contracta Claussen & Torp, 1980

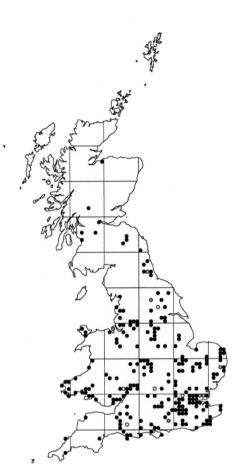

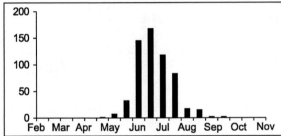

Biology
Larvae are of the 'long-tailed' type, living in ponds and ditches where decaying vegetation is abundant, especially in fen. Adults are rarely found far from the margins of breeding sites. This species seems to be very closely associated with *Typha*; the larvae have been found between submerged leaf sheaths, whilst adults have been recorded feeding on the pollen in Germany (Imhof 1979) and are often found sitting on the leaves of the plant. Adults are also found at *Iris pseudacorus*, but possibly not feeding.

Distribution
Separated from *A. transfuga* relatively recently (Stubbs 1981), and earlier records are confused with that species. Recent records have shown that this is the more frequent of the pair, the recording scheme having received approximately twice as many records as for *A. transfuga*. It is widespread in southern Britain, extending northwards as far as Nairn in Scotland, though tending to be more frequent in the eastern lowlands.

Anasimyia interpuncta (Harris, 1776)

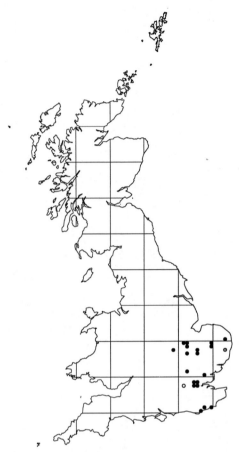

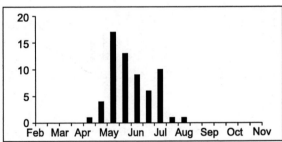

Biology
Larvae of this genus are of the 'long-tailed' type, but have not yet been described for this species. Adults are found in fens and river margins where decaying vegetation, especially *Glyceria*, is abundant, although the species has been recorded at localities dominated by *Phragmites*. They have been found at Woodwalton and Wicken Fens around paths adjacent to areas flooded in winter where they will visit flowers, especially *Caltha*.

Distribution
A scarce species with a limited distribution in the fens of East Anglia, the Norfolk Broads, the Thames marshes and the marshes of East Sussex. It is mainly an early flying species, so it is perhaps overlooked, but recent records from the Norfolk Broads show that there is at least a partial second generation in July and August.

Anasimyia lineata (Fabricius, 1787)

Helophilus lineatus Fabricius in Coe (1953)

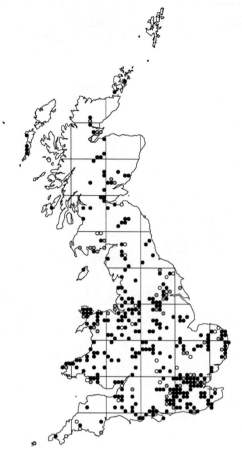

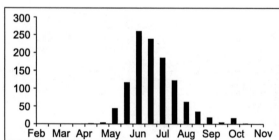

Biology

Larvae are of the 'long-tailed' type, living in eutrophic wetlands of all sorts in rotting plant debris just below the surface. Typical sites support emergent plants such as *Typha*, *Glyceria* and *Sparganium* and can be very small (eg *Typha* filled roadside ditch). Adults are most frequently found among marginal vegetation, often resting on leaves, but also at the flowers of *Ranunculus*, *Caltha*, etc.

Distribution

A frequent and widely distributed species in the British lowlands, which can be abundant at some localities.

Anasimyia lunulata (Meigen, 1822)

Helophilus lunulatus Meigen in Coe (1953)

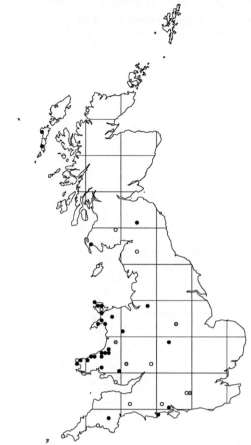

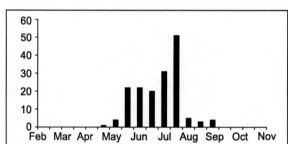

Biology

Larvae are of the 'long-tailed' type and live principally in more acid localities than is typical for other members of the genus including valley bogs and cut-over bogs where vegetation is regenerating. It is possible that sites with some base influence are preferred and this might account for the restricted distribution of this species. Adults are rarely found far from the water's edge and often perch on floating leaves. Visits *Caltha*, *Menyanthes*, and white umbels.

Distribution

Most recent records are from west Wales where it can be abundant at some sites, although there is a scattering elsewhere, including South Uist, Cheshire, Dorset and the New Forest. There are old records from eastern Britain including East Anglia, but some of these may stem from confusion with *A. interpuncta* which was not added to the British list until 1981 (Stubbs 1981).

Anasimyia transfuga (Linnaeus, 1758)

Helophilus transfuga Linnaeus in Coe (1953)

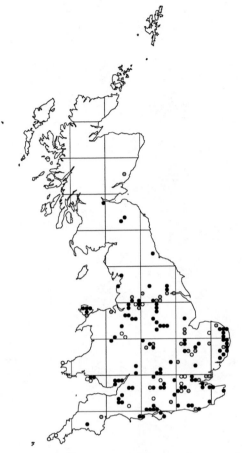

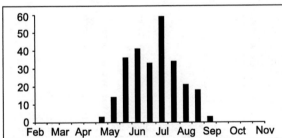

Biology
Due to the confusion with *A. contracta*, it is not certain to which species larval descriptions under this name in earlier literature apply. Found in wetland margins where decaying vegetation is abundant, and tall emergent vegetation such as *Glyceria, Scirpus* or *Sparganium* also occurs. This species will tolerate smaller and more shaded water bodies than those typically favoured by other members of the genus, occurring for example in ditches beside woodland rides.

Distribution
Much the least common of the three widespread *Anasimyia* species, occurring most often in the southern lowlands of England north to Scotland. It is scarce in the south-west, Wales and northern Britain. It appears to be genuinely scarcer than *A. contracta*, from which it was separated by Stubbs (1981), and with which confusion may have occurred in the past.

Arctophila superbiens (Müller, 1776)

Arctophila fulva (Harris) in Stubbs and Falk (1983),
A. mussitans (Fabricius, 1775)

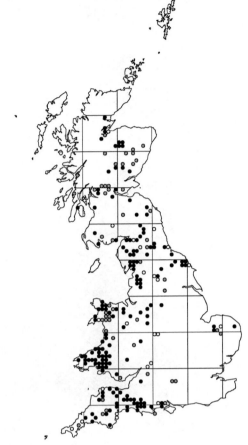

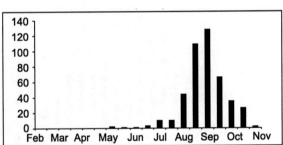

Biology
The larvae remain undescribed, but are thought to be aquatic or semi-aquatic. Stubbs and Falk (1983) report an observation of a female ovipositing in a water-filled hoofprint in a shaded muddy path beside a stream. Found near springs, wet flushes or streams, usually near the edge of woodland or carr. Adults visit purple flowers, especially *Succisa,* white umbels and yellow composites.

Distribution
A northern and western species which is locally abundant in suitable localities, these tending to be sheltered, and on neutral to acid soils. In the area of East Anglia where it occurs, this species is part of a fauna which includes northern elements in several taxa.

Baccha elongata (Fabricius, 1775)

Baccha obscuripennis Meigen, 1822 has been considered a distinct species in previous British literature, but not here

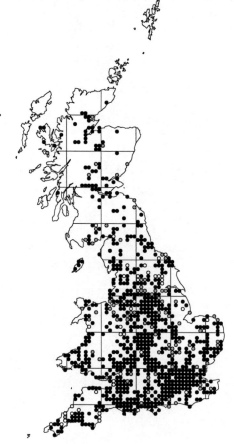

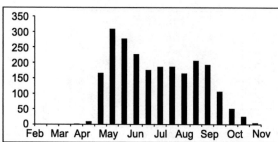

Biology

The larvae are aphidophagous, preying on a variety of ground-layer species in shaded situations, eg *Uromelan jaceae* on *Centaurea scabiosa*, *Brachycaudina napelli* on *Aconitum*, and the bramble aphid *Sitobion fragariae* on *Rubus*. It overwinters as a larva. Adults are found in shady places such as woodland rides and edges, hedgerows and mature gardens, and may be seen hovering low amongst ground-layer plants.

Distribution

Widely recorded throughout Britain, but like most woodland species, scarce or absent from poorly-wooded areas such as the East Anglian fens and the Scottish islands. There is considerable uncertainty about the status of *B. obscuripennis* which has often been regarded as a distinct species. Most records submitted to the scheme are attributed to 'Baccha sp.', but analysis of those where separation has been attempted do not suggest any differences in range, flight period or habitat preference.

Blera fallax (Linnaeus, 1758)

Cynorrhina fallax Linnaeus in Coe (1953)

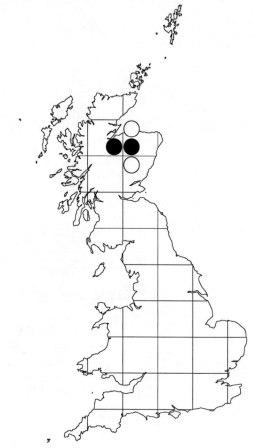

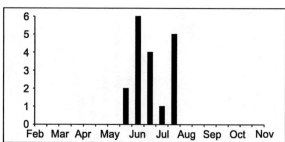

Biology

Larvae are associated with *Pinus sylvestris* in Scotland. A puparium has been found in a rot-hole in a pine stump (Rotheray & Stuke 1998). Larvae have subsequently been found in wet, heart-rot cavities in pine stumps. A single cavity may contain larvae of very mixed size, suggesting a larval period spanning several years. The adults are found in *Pinus* forest, and have been observed sunning themselves on trunks and flying about the base of large, live, native *Pinus* trees.

Distribution

A very rare species of the Caledonian pine forest, with the few recent records confined to Speyside. Old records, whilst still confined to the Speyside area of central Scotland, are more widespread, and some accounts around the turn of the century describe the species as 'numerous'. Records of this species have been mapped by 50 kilometre squares.

Brachyopa bicolor (Fallén, 1817)

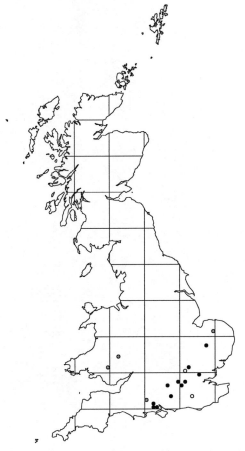

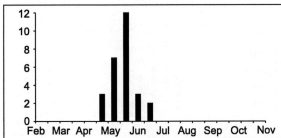

Biology

The larvae occur in runs or other accumulations of sap, usually under the bark of *Fagus*, but also *Aesculus* and *Quercus*. Adults are usually found sitting on sun-lit tree trunks or vegetation near the larval habitat, and have also been taken at burrows of the goat moth *Cossus cossus* (Linnaeus) (Perry quoted in Stubbs, 1996). Males will hover close to sap-runs. Does not seem to visit flowers.

Distribution

A rare southern species which has been found most frequently in the New Forest and the Windsor area. Old records require caution, as this was the only member of its genus recognised as British prior to 1939, and the additional species were not covered by a widely available key until that by Coe (1953). Consequently, older records could refer to any *Brachyopa* species, and must be treated as such unless a specimen still exists and can be checked.

Brachyopa insensilis Collin, 1939

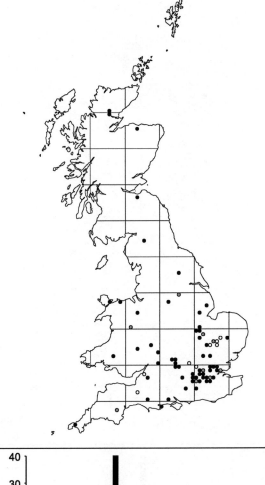

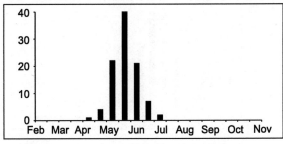

Biology

The larvae of this species occur in runs or accumulations of sap under the bark of trees. Although traditionally associated with *Ulmus*, in recent years it has been found on a wide range of broad-leaved tree species including *Fraxinus, Fagus, Tilia,* and particularly *Aesculus,* often in urban and suburban situations. Adults are usually found sitting on tree trunks or vegetation near the larval habitat, and can often be seen hovering in small groups immediately in front of a sap run. Stirring up a sap run (presumably releasing odours) often results in the rapid arrival of adults (but should not be done on a regular basis as it can kill young larvae).

Distribution

Since the realisation that both adults and larvae can easily be found at sap runs on *Aesculus,* this species has been recorded much more frequently and over a much wider area, although most records of adults are still from the south and east of Britain. Rotheray (1994, 1996) considers it the commonest species of the genus based on larval records, and it will probably be found in any urban location where *Aesculus* is present.

Brachyopa pilosa Collin, 1939

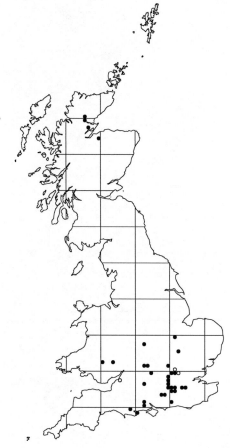

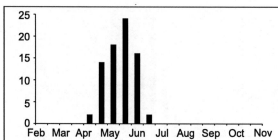

Biology

The larvae inhabit runs or other accumulations of sap under the bark of *Populus tremula* in Scotland (Rotheray 1996), but usually of *Fagus, Betula* or occasionally *Quercus* in southern England. Adults have been found in association with *Populus alba/canescens* in the south-east (Morris 1998). They are usually found sitting on tree trunks or vegetation near the larval habitat, but have also been taken at the flowers of *Prunus padus* in Sutherland (Entwistle quoted in Stubbs (1996)).

Distribution

This species is uncommon, with a markedly disjunct distribution. It is scarce but widespread in southern England with records north to Northamptonshire. In Surrey and the Windsor area (where it is rather more frequent than in other southern localities) it may have temporarily benefited from the large number of trees felled by the 1987 storm. In Scotland it has only been found in the Moray and Cromarty Firth areas (Rotheray 1996).

Brachyopa scutellaris Robineau-Desvoidy, 1843

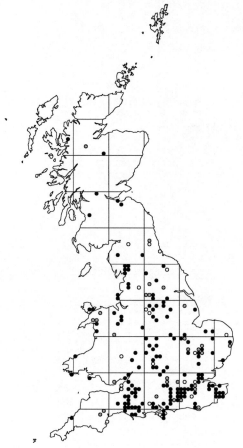

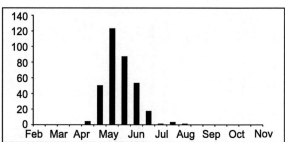

Biology

The larvae of this species occur in runs or accumulations of sap under bark near the base of trees, a variety of host species being used, including *Fraxinus, Populus tremula, Taxus* and *Ulmus*. Adults are usually found sitting on sun-lit vegetation near the larval habitat, or hovering, sometimes in large numbers, around *Quercus* and *Betula* trees. Of the *Brachyopa* species, this is the most likely to be swept from vegetation which is not obviously near a sap run (perhaps only because basal sap runs are more difficult to find). This can be one of the commonest woodland hoverflies on hot spring days in south-east England (eg Wealden woods), but its emergence period appears to be quite short (Morris 1998).

Distribution

Widespread, but slightly more frequent in the south and east. This is the commonest species in the genus based on adult records (Rotheray 1996).

Brachypalpoides lentus (Meigen, 1822)

Xylota lenta Meigen in Coe (1953), *Xylotomima lenta* (Meigen, 1822) in Kloet and Hincks (1976)

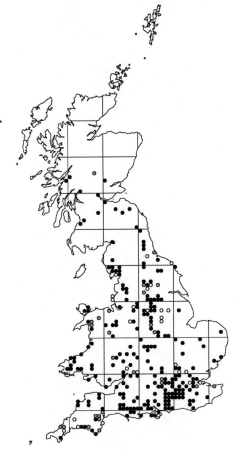

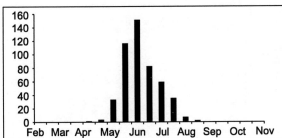

Biology
The larvae of this species occur in the decaying heartwood of *Fagus*, particularly in live trees with exposed decay at ground level. Adults are often seen flying around the base of, or basking on *Fagus* trunks and stumps. They have occasionally been found at *Crataegus* flowers, and have also been recorded visiting flowers of *Ranunculus*. There are several records of specimens found indoors on windows in wooded districts.

Distribution
This species is proving to be more frequent and widespread than previously believed and, whilst it is recorded most frequently from well-wooded areas of southern Britain, it is widespread north to central Scotland.

Brachypalpus laphriformis (Fallén, 1816)

Brachypalpus bimaculatus (Macquart, 1829) in Coe (1953) and Kloet and Hincks (1976)

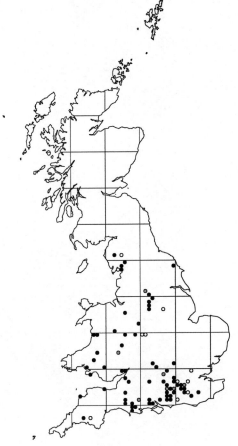

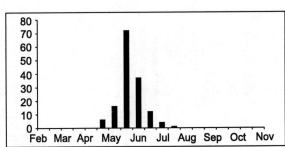

Biology
The larvae are found in rot-holes in large broad-leaved trees, usually *Fagus*, but also *Fraxinus* and *Quercus*. Males are usually found sunning themselves on trunks or flying around fallen trees in clearings. Females are more elusive, but can be found investigating trees suitable for breeding. In flight, they closely resemble solitary bees of the genus *Osmia* and may therefore have been overlooked. Occasionally found at the flowers of trees and shrubs such as *Prunus*.

Distribution
A scarce species of well-wooded areas in southern Britain. Whilst probably most frequent in 'classic' dead-wood localities, especially the New Forest, there have also been recent records from south-west England and south Wales. Its distribution extends north to the Lake District.

Caliprobola speciosa (Rossi, 1790)

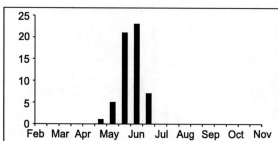

Biology

The larvae inhabit the decaying heartwood of *Fagus*, particularly large old stumps, where they may occur deep in the roots. Adults are usually found resting on, or flying around suitable stumps, and may be attracted to heart rot when this is exposed or disturbed. They can also be found visiting flowers, especially *Crataegus*, at some distance from breeding sites. Speight (1998) reports that they can be found away from forests, feeding on flowers along large rivers with gallery forest. He suggests that they are using these riverine 'corridors' to move between forests.

Distribution

Recent records of this rare species are almost confined to the New Forest and the Windsor area, and it is not uncommon at the latter site. There is an undated record (quoted in Coe (1953)) from the remnants of Needwood Forest near Burton on Trent, and a sighting at Fairmile Common, Surrey in 1995.

Callicera aurata (Rossi, 1790)

Callicera aenea (Fabricius, 1777) in Coe (1953), Kloet and Hincks (1976) and Stubbs and Falk (1983); see Speight (1991)

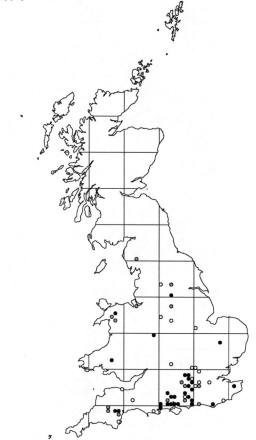

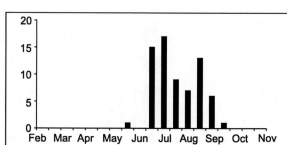

Biology

The larvae usually inhabit water-filled rot-holes in *Fagus*, although other tree species can be used; there is, for example, a recent record from a rot-hole in *Betula*. This species may frequent trees in urban situations, as well as in woodland. Recent experiments in the New Forest have shown that artificial 'hoverfly nest-boxes' (plastic bottles containing water and sawdust with a side opening) are successful in supporting larvae. Adults are elusive, and may be mainly arboreal, but can be found visiting *Crataegus* flowers. They have also been recorded at *Rosa canina, Rubus, Cotoneaster, Prunus lusitanica,* and white umbels.

Distribution

A rare species occurring mainly in southern forests. The majority of records come from the New Forest, although there are scattered records north to the Lake District. Like other members of the genus, the adults of this species are very difficult to find, and it is probably easier to record by searching for larvae.

Callicera rufa Schummel, 1842

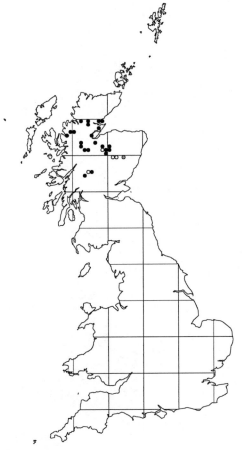

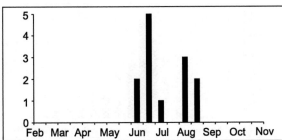

Biology
The larvae occur in rot-holes in *Pinus* filled with saturated debris, and have recently also been found in a similar situation in *Larix* (MacGowan 1994). Adults are hardly ever seen, but when found are usually sitting on pine trunks or stumps or hovering nearby. Experiments have shown that rot-holes created artificially by cutting into pine trunks with a chain-saw are utilised readily and can be occupied within two years.

Distribution
This species, found only in the Caledonian pine forest of Scotland, was considered an extreme rarity until a survey was carried out by the Malloch Society, who, by searching for larvae rather than adults, succeeded in finding the species in most of the remaining forest areas which they examined (Rotheray & MacGowan 1990).

Callicera spinolae Rondani, 1944

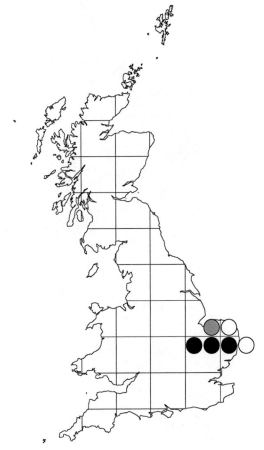

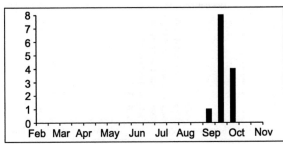

Biology
The larvae inhabit water-filled rot-holes in large, old *Fagus*, and have also been reared from *Populus* in continental Europe. Adults are seldom found, but several records refer to individuals feeding on *Hedera* flowers in the autumn.

Distribution
This extremely rare species has always been confined to East Anglia, and there are recent records only from two Cambridgeshire sites. It was extinct at one of these by 1983 and, at the other, was reduced to breeding in two trees, one of which blew down in the winter of 1994/95. English Nature has commissioned a survey of all historic localities, and other potential sites in East Anglia, under the Biodiversity Action Plan. No specimens were found in the 18 sites visited in 1997, but two observations of a single adult were made at one site in Suffolk in 1998. Survey work is ongoing. Records of this species have been mapped by 50 kilometre squares.

Chalcosyrphus eunotus (Loew, 1873)

Brachypalpus eunotus Loew, 1873 in Coe (1953) and Kloet and Hincks (1976)

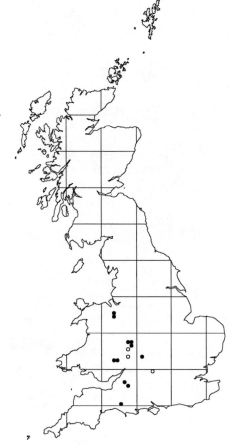

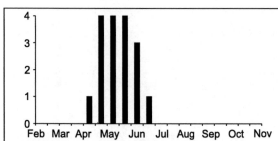

Biology

The larvae are found in sap-runs and other accumulations of sap under bark. This species has been bred from an artificial rot-hole on the Continent. It may be especially associated with dead wood lying in water, as adults are nearly always found in association with small streams and have been seen sitting on partially submerged logs in streams. Males appear to patrol small to very small streams, frequently resting on logs and projecting stones (Speight 1998). In the field, it is extremely similar in appearance to *Brachypalpus laphriformis*.

Distribution

A rare species with recent records from woodlands in Dorset, Gloucestershire and the Welsh borders, including a locality near Wrexham, and another on the River Monnow in Wales. It is possibly under-recorded because of its early flight period.

Chalcosyrphus nemorum (Fabricius, 1805)

Xylota nemorum Fabricius in Coe (1953), *Xylotomima nemorum* (Fabricius, 1805) in Kloet and Hincks (1976)

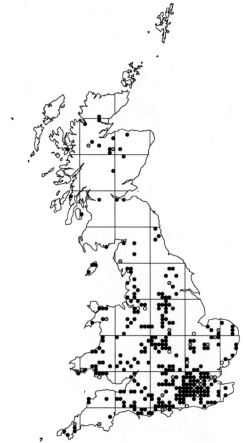

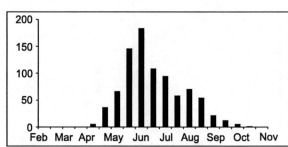

Biology

The larvae are found in sap-runs and other accumulations of sap under the bark of water-sodden fallen trees or branches or in wet rot-holes. This species is generally found in wet, wooded situations, but adults can also occur on sunny vegetation at the edges of woods and along rides. They may be regular visitors to *Ranunculus* and other yellow flowers.

Distribution

Although widespread in Britain, this species is very local everywhere and never seems to be found in abundance. It is more frequent in the south than elsewhere.

Chamaesyrphus caledonicus Collin, 1940

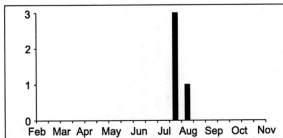

Biology
The larva of this species remains undescribed. Adults have been found by sweeping heathy vegetation under *Pinus*, including dunes planted with pines, in Scotland.

Distribution
This little known and extremely rare hoverfly was discovered in Britain by Dr D Sharp at 'Boat-o'-Garten' in July 1903, but was identified as *C. lusitanicus*, a species known otherwise only from Spain and Portugal. In August 1935, C J Wainwright and J E Collin caught 'a few specimens at Culbin Sandhills' and Collin was able to compare them with cotypes of *C. lusitanicus*, concluding that they belonged to a new species which he described as *C. caledonicus* (Collin 1940). Recently, it has been taken by I Perry in Rothiemurchus in July 1988 and again at Culbin Sands (under *Pinus* growing on the dunes) by A Wass in July 1991. The only other record available is a specimen in the British Museum collection taken in July 1917 by J J F X King from 'Rannoch'.

Chamaesyrphus scaevoides (Fallén, 1817)

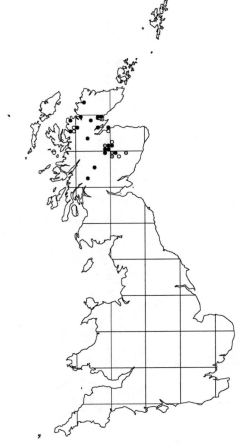

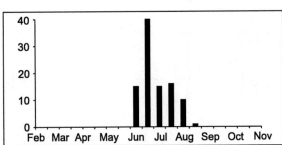

Biology
The larva of this species remains undescribed. Adults have been found in a variety of locations within Caledonian pine forest, often visiting *Potentilla erecta* flowers among heathy vegetation and along ride margins, where they are most frequently caught by sweeping.

Distribution
This is a common species in the native pine woods of central and north-western Scotland. It has also been found in conifer plantations in the same geographic area and may be more widely distributed than previously thought.

Cheilosia albipila Meigen, 1838

Cheilosia albitarsis (Meigen, 1822)

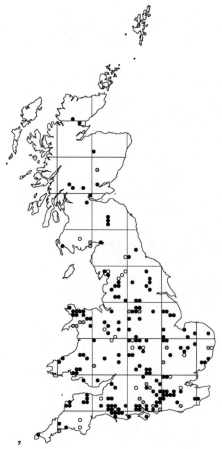

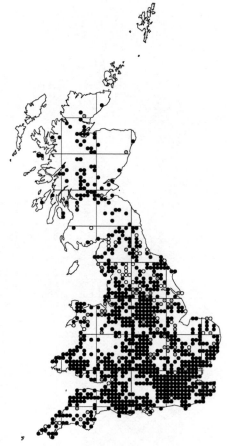

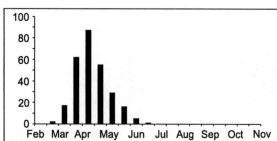

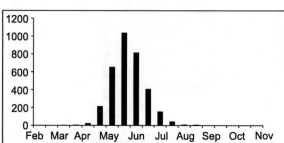

Biology

The larvae are stem-miners usually in *Cirsium palustre* and *Carduus*. Overwinters as a puparium. Adults are usually found visiting early spring-flowering shrubs such as *Salix* and *Crataegus*, in the vicinity of wet grassy places where the larval food-plant occurs, often in woodland or scrub. The edges of damp, grassy tracks or rides in woods are typical localities, where males can be found hovering near flowering shrubs.

Distribution

This species is widespread throughout Britain, and probably under-recorded, because of its very early flight period. Searching for larvae in thistle stems is probably the best way to establish its presence at a site.

Biology

The larvae have been found in the rootstocks of large *Ranunculus repens* plants in late summer. Adults can be found in damp meadows, marshy places and grassy woodland rides, where they are most frequently seen at flowers of *Ranunculus repens* and *R. bulbosus* (rarely *R. acris*), but other white and yellow flowers are also visited. According to Speight (1998) this is an 'anthropogenic species, favoured by present-day farming practices.'

Distribution

A widespread and often abundant species throughout Britain.

Cheilosia antiqua (Meigen, 1822)

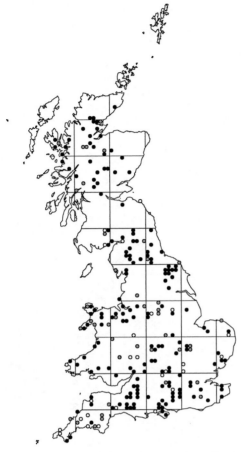

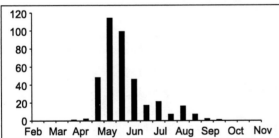

Biology
The larvae feed in the rootstocks of *Primula*, where they hollow out cavities in the thickened stem bases, often killing the plants. Found in woodland clearings and tracksides and unimproved pastures where the foodplants grow. Adults are generally found along woodland rides or edges, and along old hedges, where they fly low amongst the vegetation.

Distribution
Records are thinly scattered from throughout Britain. Some records for *C. antiqua* may actually refer to *Melanogaster hirtella*, male specimens of which are frequently mistaken for this species.

Cheilosia barbata Loew, 1857

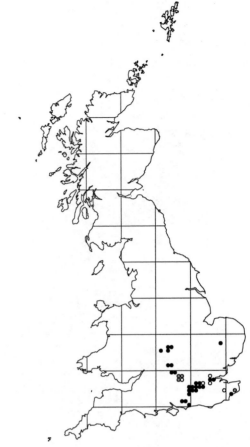

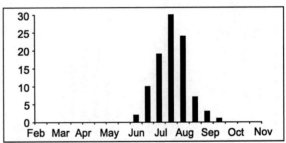

Biology
The larva of this species remains unknown. Adults are found on chalk downs or in woodlands on clay, or occasionally on sandy soils, as in Surrey where they visit a wide range of white and yellow flowers including most white umbels.

Distribution
Mainly recorded from southern downland extending from Kent, through Surrey and Sussex to Hampshire, and in woodlands on the clay through Oxfordshire to Warwickshire.

Cheilosia bergenstammi Becker, 1894

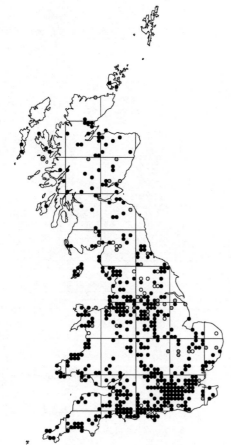

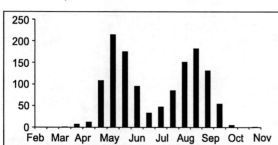

Biology

The larvae mine the stems and roots of *Senecio jacobaea* and may cause plants to wilt. It is also likely that other *Senecio* species are utilised. Adults are often found on or near the larval foodplant in open areas in woodland (including conifer plantations), rough grassland and waste ground, including derelict urban and industrial sites.

Distribution

Rather local throughout Britain, this species is most frequent in drier locations, such as occur on chalk and sandy soils.

Cheilosia carbonaria Egger, 1860

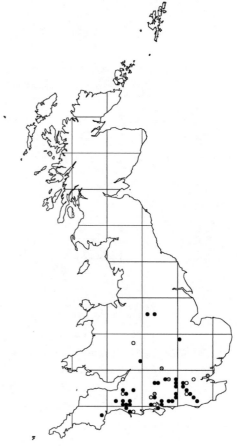

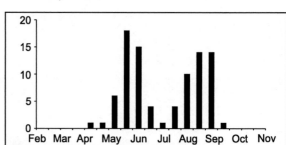

Biology

The larva of this species remains unknown. Adults are most frequently found along woodland rides and edges, usually on well-drained and calcareous soils. They fly low along tracksides, woodland edges and large hedgerows and visit a range of white umbels and yellow composites.

Distribution

An uncommon species found mainly in well-wooded areas of central-southern England from Sussex to Devon, but with a few isolated records from as far north as Derbyshire. Although Stubbs (1982) lists this as a 'good' primary woodland indicator, it has proved not to be confined to ancient woodlands.

Cheilosia chrysocoma (Meigen, 1822)

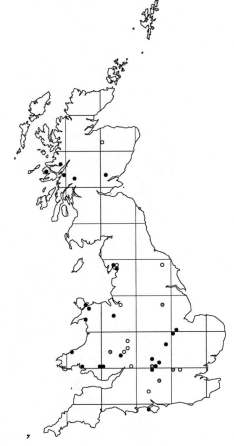

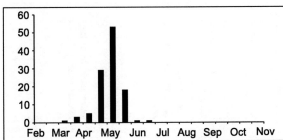

Biology
The larva of this species remains unknown, but egg laying has been observed on *Angelica sylvestris* in Europe (Doczkal 1996). Adults are typically found sitting on paths, or occasionally at flowers such as *Salix* catkins, in woodland rides, glades or edges, often, but not exclusively, on calcareous soils and usually with marshy conditions nearby.

Distribution
Records are thinly scattered north to central Scotland, including north-west England and Wales, with a group of recent records in Berkshire and Oxfordshire.

Cheilosia cynocephala Loew, 1840

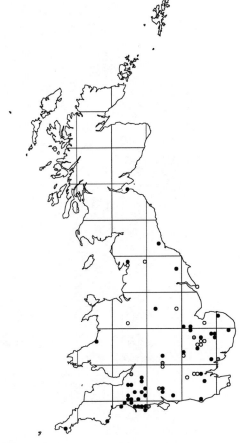

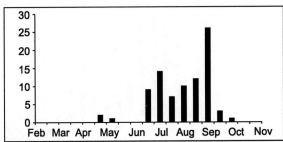

Biology
The larvae mine the stems of *Carduus nutans*. Usually found in unimproved calcareous grassland where the larval foodplant occurs, often near rivers, streams or flushes. Adults fly low amongst the vegetation and visit a range of flowers including white umbels and yellow composites.

Distribution
The distribution of this species mainly follows the chalk and limestone (on which its larval foodplant occurs) from East Anglia to the Mendips. Records are somewhat concentrated towards the south-west (Dorset, Somerset and Wiltshire), with few records from the chalk of south-east England, despite this being a relatively well-recorded area. There are thinly scattered records from Wales and northern England, and one locality in Scotland, near Edinburgh.

Cheilosia fraterna (Meigen, 1830)

Includes *Cheilosia* species C *sensu* Stubbs and Falk (1983)

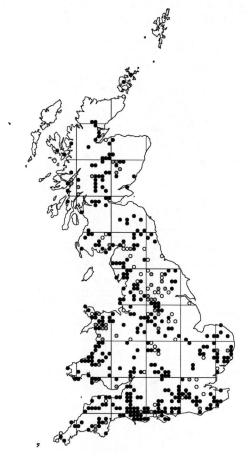

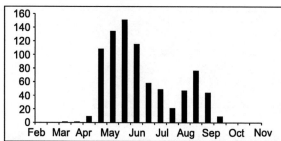

Biology
The larvae mine the stems and basal rosettes of *Cirsium palustre*. Adults are often seen visiting flowers such as *Ranunculus* in situations where the larval food-plant occurs, such as marshes and damp meadows. According to Speight (1998) this is a woodland species found in clearings, often along streams or rivers.

Distribution
Although widely distributed and frequent, this species seems to be more abundant in the north and west. The specimen described as 'Cheilosia species C' by Stubbs and Falk (1983), seems to be a particularly small individual from the second generation of this species (Falk quoted in Stubbs (1996)).

Cheilosia griseiventris Loew, 1857

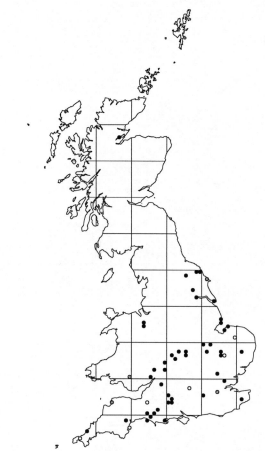

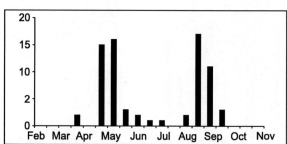

Biology
Separated from *C. latifrons* (= *intonsa*) by Stubbs and Falk (1983); the available British voucher specimens are distinctly different from that species, with longer bodies and darker wings. Not considered as distinct from *C. latifrons* by most European workers. The larvae are unknown, but thought to be associated with yellow composites such as *Hypochoeris*. Adults have been found in a variety of locations including sites on chalk, sand and clay soils.

Distribution
Almost all records lie south of a line between the Severn and the Vale of Pickering, with more records from the west of this area.

Cheilosia grossa (Fallén, 1817)

Cheilosia corydon (Harris)

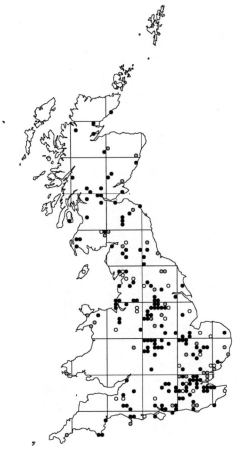

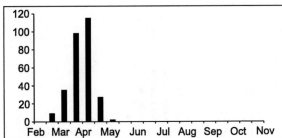

Biology
The larvae mine the stems and roots of a wide range of thistles (*Cirsium* and *Carduus* spp.), especially *Cirsium palustre*, which tend to become stunted and multi-stemmed. Females have been observed to oviposit on small, young, flowering spikes growing from the centre of the rosette (G E Rotheray, pers. comm.). Adults are found visiting flowers such as *Salix* catkins in the early spring, usually in sheltered situations such as woodland rides or edges. Males typically hover at considerable height.

Distribution
Adult records are scarce, probably because this very early-flying species is often missed by collectors, but also because individuals tend to fly high and out of reach, hovering or visiting flowers near the tops of bushes. It is much easier to record by searching for larvae in thistle stems, and records gathered using this method have shown that it is not uncommon throughout most of Britain, although records are scarce in Wales and south-west England.

Cheilosia illustrata (Harris, 1780)

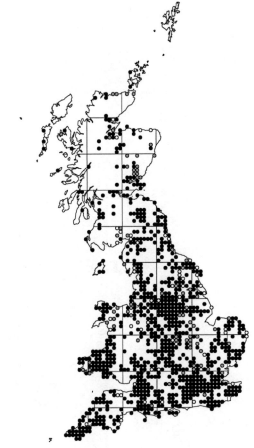

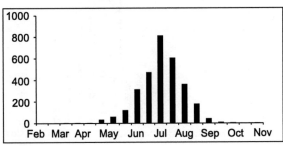

Biology
The larvae have been found in the large rootstocks of *Heracleum sphondylium* (G E Rotheray, pers. comm.). Adults are most commonly found at flowers of *Heracleum* and other white umbels along glades, tracksides, hedges, etc and are a typical component of the mid-summer fauna of hogweed flowers.

Distribution
A very common species throughout Britain wherever white umbellifers such as *Heracleum* and *Angelica* grow.

Cheilosia impressa Loew, 1840

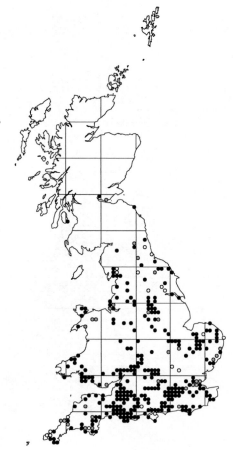

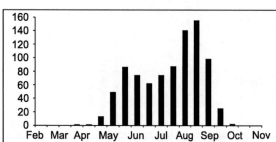

Biology
The larva of this species remains unknown. Adults are found in damp situations such as carr woodland and wooded river-banks, where they visit white umbels, especially *Oenanthe crocata*, and a range of other flowers including yellow composites and *Ranunculus*. Males hover at moderate height in sheltered situations in clearings and glades.

Distribution
A frequent species in southern England south of a line from the Wash to the Severn, becoming increasingly scarce further north and extending as far as Stirling.

Cheilosia lasiopa Kowarz, 1885

Cheilosia honesta Rondani in Stubbs and Falk (1983)

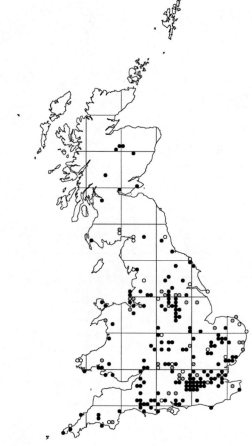

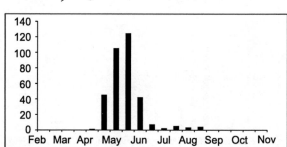

Biology
The larva of this species remains unknown. Adults are often found visiting flowers such as *Anthriscus sylvestris* in wooded localities, both broad-leaved and coniferous. Usually found in sheltered situations such as clearings and tracksides and often settles on sun-lit foliage.

Distribution
Not uncommon in southern Britain north to about Merseyside and southern Yorkshire. Elsewhere there are very few, widely scattered records north to Aberdeenshire. There appear to be many more records from the east of its range.

Cheilosia latifrons (Zetterstedt, 1838)

Cheilosia intonsa Loew in Stubbs and Falk (1983)

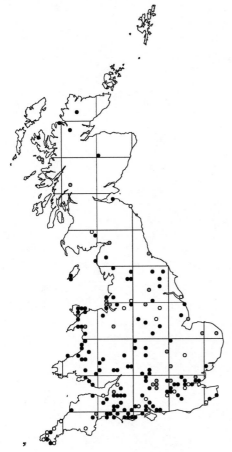

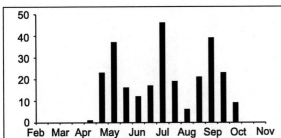

Biology

The larva of this species remains unknown, but it is thought that they may be associated with *Leontodon autumnalis*. Adults are found in dry grassland, including coastal grassland and dunes, where they fly low amongst the vegetation. According to Speight (1998) they visit yellow composites, *Ranunculus*, and wind-pollinated flowers such as *Plantago* and *Luzula*.

Distribution

Cheilosia latifrons has a widespread, but scattered distribution throughout Britain, although confusion with the recently-separated *C. griseiventris* may cast doubt over the validity of some records. There are few records north of Yorkshire, in East Anglia or the East Midlands, but many from the London area, including the Thames marshes.

Cheilosia longula (Zetterstedt, 1838)

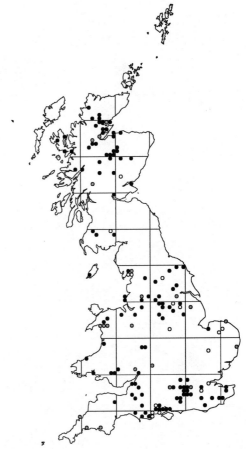

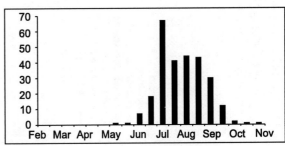

Biology

The larvae inhabit large fungal fruiting bodies including *Boletus*, *Suillus* and *Leccinum*. The occupied fruiting body eventually loses its shape and becomes a brown smudge on the ground. Adults are usually found along woodland (broad-leaved and coniferous) edges and rides, or in glades where they can often be found on sun-lit vegetation. A range of flowers including white umbels and yellow composites are visited.

Distribution

This species is widely distributed throughout Britain. It is frequent in both the north and south of England, where it occurs in acidic, sandy locations, especially heathland, but there are comparatively few records from similarly well-recorded parts of the English Midlands.

Cheilosia mutabilis (Fallén, 1817)

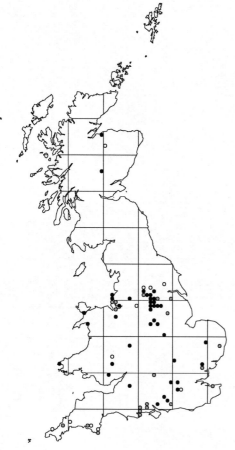

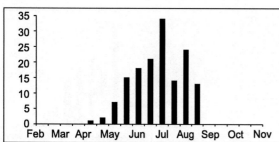

Biology
The larvae have been found in the roots of *Carduus acanthoides*. Adults are recorded from a variety of habitats including marsh and fen, scrub, woodland, acid heath and dunes. Speight (1998) lists 'well-drained sites often susceptible to short-duration winter flooding' amongst its preferences and notes that in the north of its range (Denmark, Sweden and northern Germany) it is primarily coastal.

Distribution
Older records indicate a wide distribution north to Central Scotland, but there is a marked concentration of recent records in Cheshire, South Lancashire and South Yorkshire, and a number of records from large dune systems in Wales and north-west England.

Cheilosia nebulosa Verrall, 1871

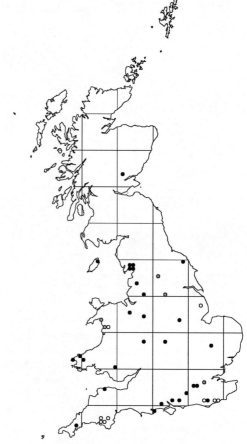

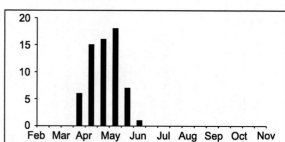

Biology
The larva of this species remains unknown. Adults are found visiting flowers such as *Salix* catkins along woodland rides and edges, often near carr or marshes. Males hover high up beside flowering *Salix* or *Crataegus* bushes.

Distribution
Very scarce but widely scattered north to central Scotland.

Cheilosia nigripes (Meigen, 1822)

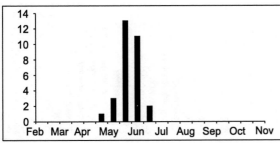

Biology

The larva of this species remains unknown. Adults are usually found on flowers in woodland rides and edges on calcareous soils. Males can sometimes also be found in large numbers basking on sunlit leaves.

Distribution

This is a common species within its very restricted range on the chalk downs of south-east England, especially in Surrey, Sussex and Hampshire. There are also a few records, both old and recent, from the limestone in Gloucestershire and Somerset.

Cheilosia pagana (Meigen, 1822)

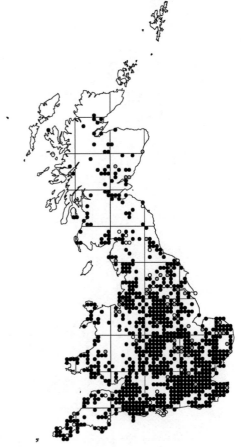

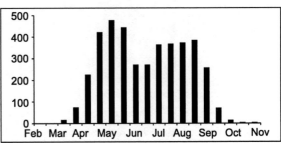

Biology

The larvae inhabit semi-liquid, decaying tissue in the roots of plants. For example, there is a rearing record from decaying roots of *Anthriscus sylvestris* (Stubbs 1980). Adults are usually found on flowers, often white umbels such as *Anthriscus* and *Heracleum*, in clearings and rides in woods, on waste ground, roadsides, hedgerows, rough field-edges, etc.

Distribution

Widespread and common throughout Britain.

Cheilosia praecox (Zetterstedt, 1843)

Cheilosia globulipes Becker was considered as a doubtfully distinct species by Stubbs and Falk (1983) but is here considered synonymous

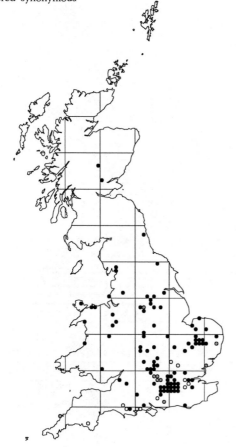

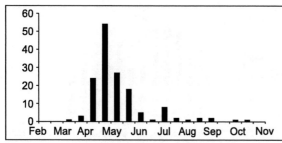

Biology
The larva has been recorded from a mine in the basal rosette of *Hieracium pilosella*. Adults are usually seen visiting flowers such as *Salix* catkins, early in the spring in woodland edges (broad-leaved and coniferous), scrub and damp grassland. Males tend to hover in sheltered, sunny locations whilst females can be found hovering over short turf with *Hypochoeris*, *Leontodon* and *Hieracium*.

Distribution
Although generally scarce, this species is widespread in Wales and England north to the Humber, and there are a small number of recent records from as far north as Scotland. It is possibly missed by some recorders because of its early flight period.

Cheilosia proxima (Zetterstedt, 1843)

Includes *Cheilosia* species D & E *sensu* Stubbs and Falk (1983)

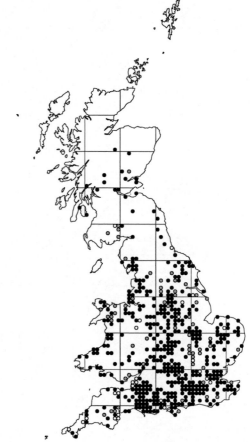

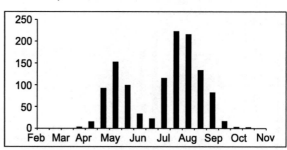

Biology
The larvae inhabit the roots of *Cirsium* spp, especially *Cirsium palustre*. Adults are frequently found visiting white umbels such as *Heracleum* and flowering bushes such as *Crataegus* and *Prunus spinosa*, along woodland rides and edges (broad-leaved and coniferous), scrub and hedgerows. Males tend to hover quite high up near trees and bushes and both sexes frequently settle on sun-lit foliage at some height above the ground.

Distribution
A widespread and common species north to Yorkshire and Cumbria, becoming scarcer further north, although records extend into northern Scotland. The segregation into species D and E by Stubbs and Falk (1983) has been found, on further investigation, to represent the spring and summer generations of a single species.

Cheilosia pubera (Zetterstedt, 1838)

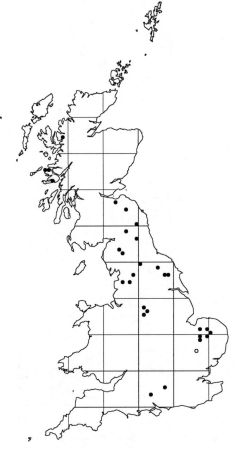

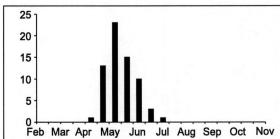

Biology
The larva of this species remains unknown. Adults have been found at *Caltha* flowers, and sunning on leaves at scrub edges, in wet pasture, fen edges and lake shores. They fly low over the vegetation in grassy, open areas often along streams or other wet edges.

Distribution
Although recorded from southern England, recent records range from the northern half of East Anglia north to the west coast of Scotland and the Hebrides, with most coming from northern England.

Cheilosia sahlbergi Becker, 1894

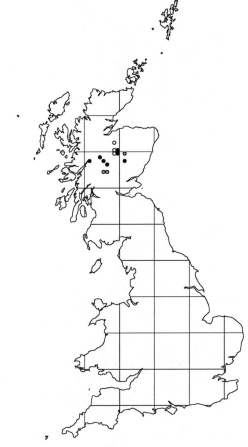

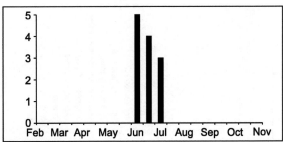

Biology
The larvae have been found in association with *Polygonum viviparum*, where they seemed to be grazing externally on the roots (G E Rotheray, pers. comm.). Adults are found at high altitude (700 m upwards) and have been recorded visiting the flowers of *Potentilla erecta* and *Saxifraga* spp. usually near water. They fly low and rapidly over the vegetation often perching on sun-lit stones and rocks in sheltered spots.

Distribution
There are many records from the Ben Lawers area of central Scotland. The species has a rather restricted high-altitude habitat within which it is probably widespread.

Cheilosia scutellata (Fallén, 1817)

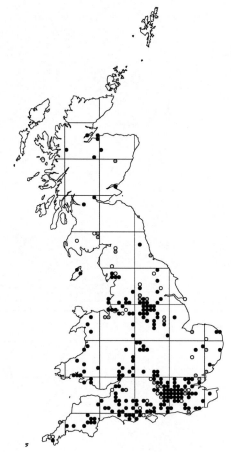

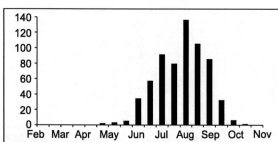

Biology
The larvae inhabit large fungal fruiting bodies, including *Boletus*, *Polyporus*, etc. The occupied fruiting body loses its shape and becomes a brown smudge on the ground. Adults are usually found in woodland (broad-leaved and coniferous) and may be common on the flowers of white umbels such as *Heracleum* and *Pastinaca*. They are often to be found resting on foliage of bushes and tall herbs in dappled sunlight along glades and tracksides.

Distribution
Frequent in well-wooded areas in southern Britain but scarce north of the Humber, with a few widely scattered records extending as far as the Inverness area.

Cheilosia semifasciata Becker, 1894

Cheilosia fasciata Schiner & Egger in Coe (1953)

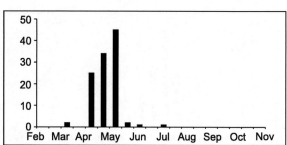

Biology
The larvae form 'blotch mines' on the leaves of *Sedum telephium* in southern England and *Umbilicus rupestris* in the south-west and Wales. Adults are rarely found far from stands of the larval foodplant. The early flight period may lead to the adults being overlooked, and its presence is probably better established by searching for larval mines (illustrated in Rotheray (1994)). Even these may be difficult to find, as larger larvae completely consume the contents of a leaf causing it to drop, and then move to another.

Distribution
This is a rare species with few recent records. In southern England, where its food-plant is scarce, it is confined to a few scattered localities. In North Wales its food-plant is widespread, but recent observations suggest that many patches, even those close to known colonies, are unused. At one strong colony it was noted that the plants remained green and fleshy in late June, whilst at many other localities in the same area they had turned brown and withered. It is possible that the larvae require a plant to be growing in a situation where its leaves remain suitable for larval feeding longer than usual (A P Fowles, pers. comm.).

Cheilosia soror (Zetterstedt, 1843)

Cheilosia ruffipes (Preyssler)

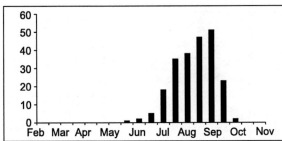

Biology
The larvae are believed to inhabit fungi, and this species is reported to have been bred from truffles. Adults are strongly associated with chalk and limestone, where they have been found feeding on the flowers of white umbels, especially *Heracleum* and *Pastinaca*, in grassy rides and glades. According to Speight (1998) they are found in 'clearings, tracksides, hedgerows, usually in partial shade'.

Distribution
Records are widely scattered from chalk and limestone areas, mainly in eastern England, as far north as Morecambe Bay. Recent records from London suburbs suggest that it may be more widely distributed, possibly influenced by the calcareous content of concrete and rubble in urban areas.

Cheilosia uviformis (Becker, 1894)

Cheilosia argentifrons Hellén, 1914

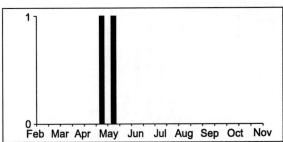

Biology
The larvae remain undescribed. Speight (1987) concludes that this species is associated with broad-leaved woodland, and in most cases with areas that are seasonally flooded. Males hover 7–10 m above the ground, and females have been found sitting inconspicuously on tussocks of dead grass. Adults visit spring-flowering shrubs such as *Salix* and *Crataegus*.

Distribution
This species was added to the British list only relatively recently by Speight (1986) as *C. argentifrons*. Originally found in Ireland in 1985, it has subsequently been found in Scotland (not mapped), Yorkshire and Derbyshire (Speight 1986; Whiteley 1988; Stubbs 1996). There are too few records as yet to allow any further interpretation of its status and distribution.

Cheilosia variabilis (Panzer, 1798)

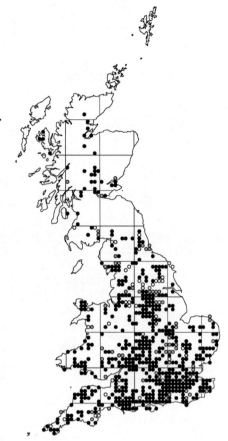

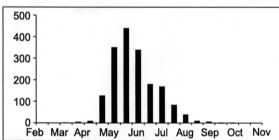

Biology

The larvae have been found in the roots of *Scrophularia nodosa* and *S. auriculata*. Adults are usually found in damp woodland rides or similar lush, wooded locations, and have been seen visiting the flowers of *Scrophularia*. The males, which are distinctive because of their large size, elongate form and long, dark wings, are commonly found basking on sunlit leaves.

Distribution

Widespread and common throughout Britain.

Cheilosia velutina Loew, 1840

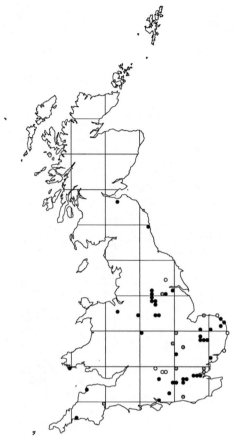

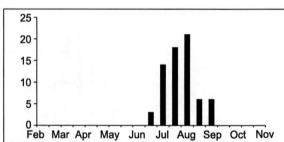

Biology

The larval host is given as *Scrophularia nodosa* by Brischke (1880) and Speight (1998) quotes an American reference, according to which it mines the stems of *Cirsium palustre*. This is a very poorly-understood species whose habitat requirements are difficult to define. It is most frequently found in mid- to late summer amongst a profusion of its close relative, *C. proxima*, at the flowers of white umbels such as *Pastinaca*.

Distribution

This species remains poorly known with very few confirmed records, mainly on the eastern side of Britain, including a recent one from near Edinburgh. It is perhaps most likely to be found where there is a profusion of *C. proxima*; checking a large number of specimens of this common species is essential if *C. velutina* is to be recorded.

Cheilosia vernalis (Fallén, 1817)

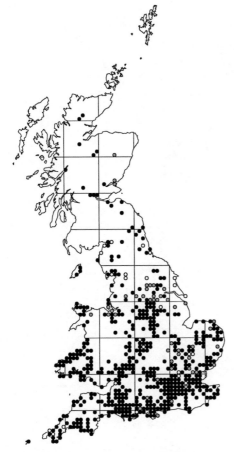

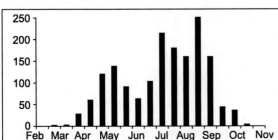

Biology
The larvae are thought to tunnel in the stems of *Achillea, Matricaria, Tragopogon* and *Sonchus.* Adults are usually found on low-growing Asteraceae or white umbels in open, flowery situations such as dry grassland, heathland margins, road verges and waste ground. Also in grassy clearings in woodland and in dunes.

Distribution
Widespread and frequent in southern Britain. Less frequent in the north, with some records extending to northern Scotland.

Cheilosia vicina (Zetterstedt, 1849)

Cheilosia nasutula Becker in Stubbs and Falk (1983)

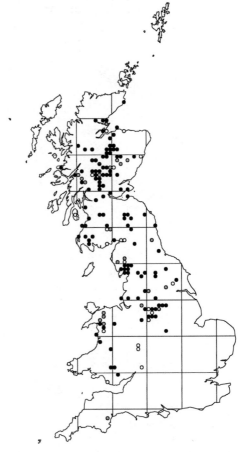

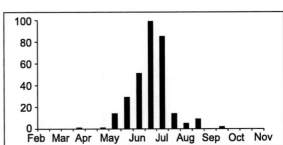

Biology
The larva of this species remains unknown. Adults are most often found visiting flowers in either open or wooded situations (broad-leaved or coniferous), or (especially males) basking on sunlit leaves.

Distribution
This species has a markedly northern distribution. It is frequent from north Wales and the Pennines northwards, and is one of the commoner *Cheilosia* species in Scotland. There are a few records from southern England, but confusion with *C. antiqua* is possible.

41

Cheilosia vulpina (Meigen, 1822)

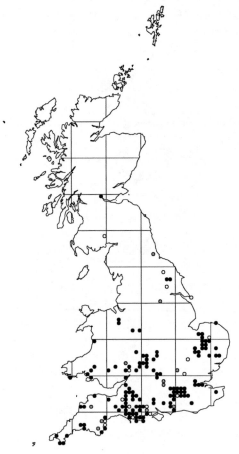

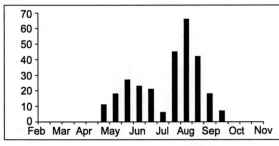

Biology
The larvae have been found in decaying tissue in the roots of cultivated globe artichoke *Cynara scolymus* in France. Adults are usually found visiting flowers of white umbels such as *Heracleum* in open woodland (broad-leaved or coniferous) and unimproved grassland, usually on well drained soils.

Distribution
Reasonably frequent in southern Britain, with scattered records north to southern Scotland.

Cheilosia species A *sensu* Stubbs and Falk (1983)

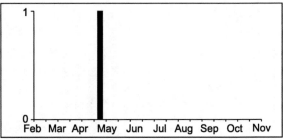

Biology
Unknown.

Distribution
A single male in the Verrall Collection was taken at Wooditton Wood, Cambridgeshire in 1912. The locality has subsequently been coniferised.

Cheilosia species B *sensu* Stubbs and Falk (1983)

Chrysogaster cemiteriorum (Linnaeus, 1758)

Chrysogaster chalybeata Meigen in Stubbs and Falk (1983)

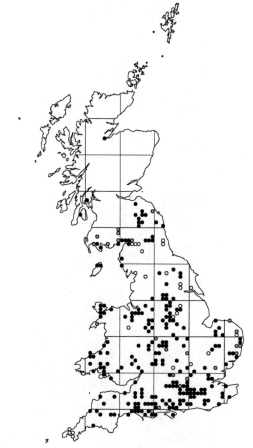

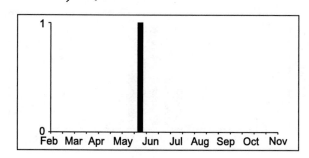

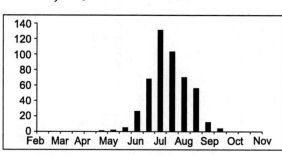

Biology

Unknown.

Distribution

A single specimen was taken by I MacGowan on the banks of the River Dee at Ballater, central Scotland in 1981.

Biology

Larvae unknown, but probably aquatic in common with other *Chrysogaster* species. Adults are usually found in wet meadows, fens and valley-bogs where they visit flowers, especially white umbels, but they can also be frequent in damp woodlands where they should be sought amongst *C. solstitialis*.

Distribution

A widespread but local species, found most frequently in the west. It is rather scarce in south-east England, although it is present throughout the weald of Sussex.

Chrysogaster solstitialis (Fallén, 1817)

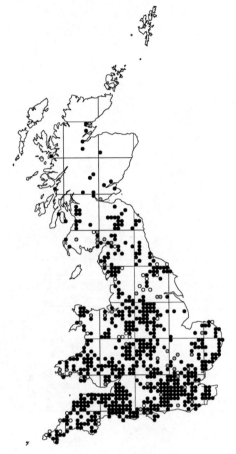

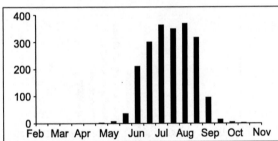

Biology

The larvae inhabit organically-rich mud at the edge of seepages, brooks and small water bodies in woodland and scrub. They live beneath fallen leaves or other debris in very shallow water. Adults are usually seen on the flowers of white umbels such as *Heracleum*, *Angelica*, *Oenanthe* and *Torilis*, especially in damp shady locations.

Distribution

Widespread and very common, except in urban environments.

Chrysogaster virescens Loew, 1854

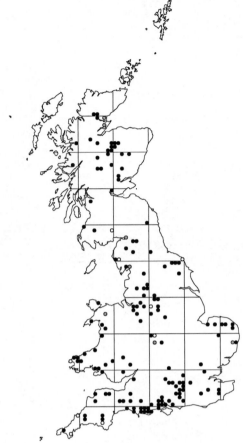

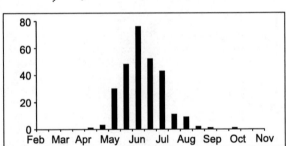

Biology

Larvae unknown, but probably aquatic in common with other *Chrysogaster* species. Associated with boggy, acidic locations with carr, wooded stream-sides or damp scrub. Adults are frequently found at flowers, including those of *Sarothamnus scoparia*, white umbellifers, *Filipendula* and *Ranunculus*.

Distribution

Although widely distributed, this species appears to occur mainly in the north and west, and is locally frequent in the Scottish Highlands. In the south-east it seems to be confined to acid heathland locations.

Chrysotoxum arcuatum (Linnaeus, 1758)

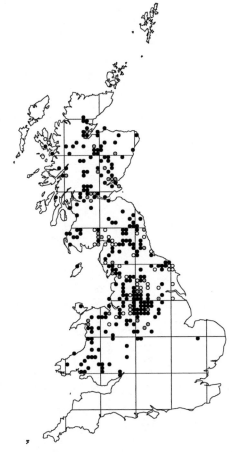

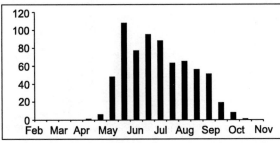

Biology

The larvae have been found feeding on root aphids associated with the nests of ants. They are not easy to find, and the best time to search for them is at night (G E Rotheray, pers. comm.). Occurs widely in upland and moorland locations, in unimproved grassland with scrub, and in grassy openings in woodland. Adults fly low among ground vegetation and visit a wide range of flowers in sheltered situations.

Distribution

A predominantly northern and western species, locally frequent north of a line from the Severn to the Humber, although there is a recent record from the Breckland of Norfolk.

Chrysotoxum bicinctum (Linnaeus, 1758)

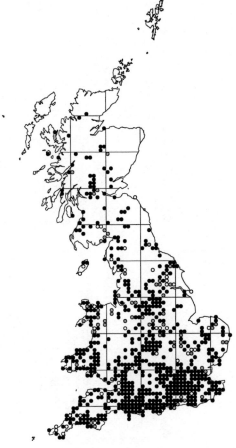

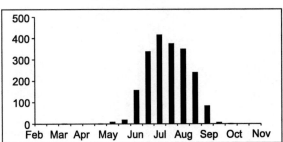

Biology

Larvae of species in this genus are thought to be associated with ants, perhaps feeding on ant-attended root aphids, although a larva of this species has been reared in the laboratory on pea aphids. Adults are usually found in grassy places, often on the edges of woodland or scrub or along hedgerows where they visit a wide range of flowers.

Distribution

Widely distributed throughout Britain but usually encountered in small numbers.

Chrysotoxum cautum (Harris, 1776)

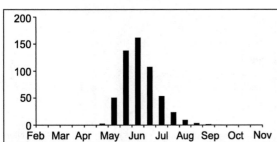

Biology
The larva of this species remains unknown, but is thought to be associated with ants, perhaps feeding on ant-attended root aphids. Adults are usually found in well drained grassy places, often near shelter such as woodland edge or hedgerows where they visit a wide range of flowers. Seen in flight, they have a striking resemblance to a social wasp.

Distribution
This species occurs south and east of a line from the Severn to the Humber (an almost complete reversal of the range of *C. arcuatum*), except for scattered localities along the coast of Wales and the coast of north-west England. It is locally abundant, especially in central-southern England.

Chrysotoxum elegans Loew, 1841

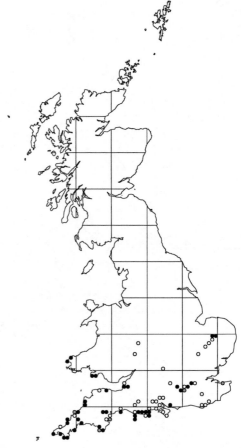

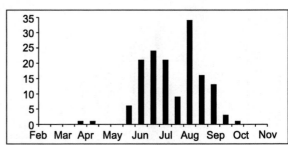

Biology
The larva has been described from a fully grown specimen found beneath a stone in grassland. Found in a variety of well drained, grassy situations ranging from woodland edge and scrubby downland in south-east England, to open cliff-tops in the south-west. Adults fly low and fast over low vegetation and visit flowers, including white umbels, *Pastinaca sativa* and *Ranunculus*.

Distribution
Very scarce, but widely distributed in southern England, this species becomes more frequent towards the south-west where it is often, but not exclusively, associated with coastal habitats.

Chrysotoxum festivum (Linnaeus, 1758)

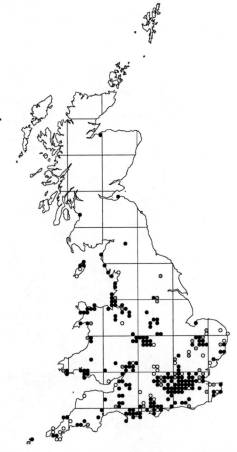

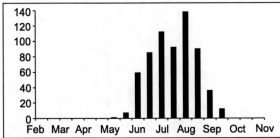

Biology

The larva and puparium have been described by Speight (1976) who found a mature larva with ants (*Lasius niger*) under a stone in a scrubby pasture. Normally found in grassy places near the shelter of woodland edge, scrub or hedgerows. Adults fly fast and males hover at 2–4 m. Visits a wide range of flowers.

Distribution

Widespread in southern Britain, although usually encountered in small numbers; scarce and largely coastal in the north.

Chrysotoxum octomaculatum Curtis, 1837

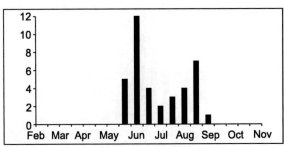

Biology

The larva remains unknown, but is thought to be associated with ants. Usually found near the edges of extensive dry heathland where it is fast-flying and elusive. Speight (1998) reports that females fly fast and low over bare ground and short vegetation whilst males hover at a height of 3–5 m around trees and bushes, settling at 2 m or above.

Distribution

Older records are problematic, since *C. verralli* was not distinguished from this species until 1940. There are very few recent records, all from Dorset, Hampshire and Surrey. Only Thursley and Hankley Commons seem to have produced reasonably regular records in the last two decades, other records being scattered singletons. Although it was recorded fairly regularly at Studland in the past, a recent survey commissioned by English Nature failed to find it, and its status in Britain must now give cause for serious concern.

Chrysotoxum vernale Loew, 1841

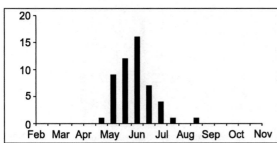

Biology

The larva remains unknown, but is thought to be associated with ants. There are insufficient records to develop a clear picture of this species' habitat requirements.

Distribution

Very scarce. Records are mostly old, and come from Hampshire, Dorset, Devon and Cornwall.

Chrysotoxum verralli Collin, 1940

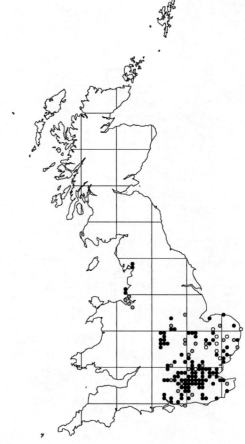

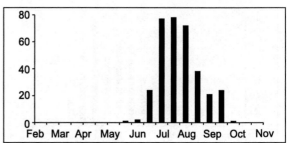

Biology

This species has been reared from larvae found in a nest of the ant *Lasius niger* (Linnaeus). Pupae have been found under a stone, and females have been seen ovipositing close to the entrances of ant nests. Found on well drained soils usually near the shelter of trees or hedgerows. Typical situations include grassy places in scrub, woodland rides and glades or on the fringes of heathland. Adults are often seen resting on vegetation, and occasionally visit flowers such as *Rubus* and *Rosa*.

Distribution

Mainly southern England, but extending through the Midlands in a broad band to Merseyside and South Lancashire. Whilst very local, it can be abundant where it occurs.

Criorhina asilica (Fallén, 1816)

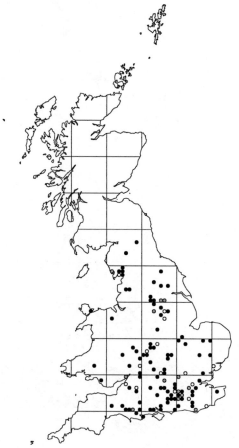

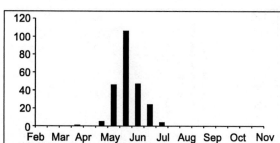

Biology

Larva undescribed, but has been reared from heartwood debris in a cavity in *Fagus*. Adults, which are convincing hive-bee mimics, are usually found in or near woodland with overmature trees and can often be seen visiting flowers, especially *Crataegus*, or sitting or flying around the base of stumps and dead or dying trees. Males patrol flowering trees and shrubs at some height.

Distribution

Widespread but scarce. More frequent in well-wooded districts of southern Britain, but extending northwards to the Tyne Valley.

Criorhina berberina (Fabricius, 1805)

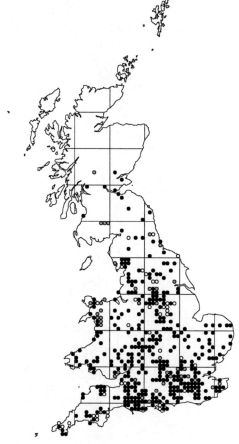

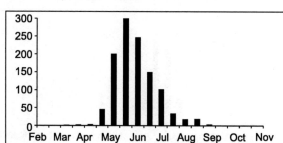

Biology

Larvae have been found in rotten wood in cavities in the trunks of *Betula* and rotten roots of *Fagus*, but are probably associated with rotting wood in a range of broad-leaved species. Adults are usually found in woodland with overmature trees and are often seen visiting flowers or settled on sunlit foliage. Males patrol flowers and flowering shrubs. Females can be found flying around the bases of stumps and dead or dying trees.

Distribution

The commonest member of the genus, occurring most frequently in well-wooded areas in central and southern Britain, but extending northwards into Scotland.

Criorhina floccosa (Meigen, 1822)

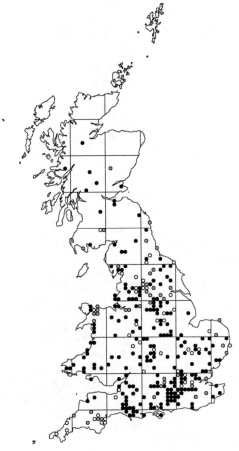

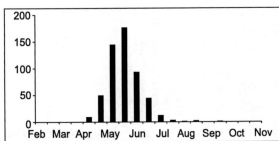

Biology
Larvae have been found in wet, decaying wood debris in cavities in *Ulmus* and *Acer* and also in wet decaying roots of a *Fagus* stump. Adults are usually seen visiting flowers, especially *Crataegus*, in woodland rides and glades, but also in hedgerows and other places where old trees and stumps are present. Adults frequently bask on sunlit *Acer pseudoplatanus* leaves.

Distribution
Widespread, but scarce. Most frequent in well-wooded areas of southern Britain, but extending northwards to the Inverness area.

Criorhina ranunculi (Panzer, 1804)

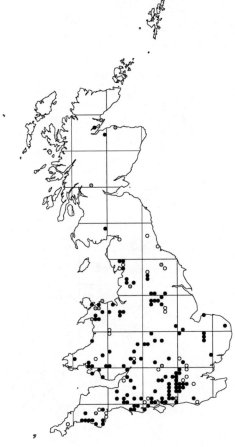

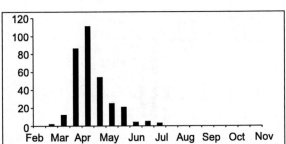

Biology
Larvae have been found in a rotting *Fagus* stump. According to Speight (1989b) it 'almost certainly occurs in trunk-base, fungus-infected, wet-rot cavities' in a range of broad-leaved trees. Whilst large, old broad-leaved trees in woodland are probably the normal breeding habitat, females have been seen inspecting the bases of birch trees in heathland. Adults fly early in the spring and are usually seen visiting the blossom of early-flowering shrubs such as *Prunus spinosa,* and occasionally *Crataegus*, or basking on sunlit foliage. Males fly with a characteristic high-pitched whine.

Distribution
Both the early flight period and the tendency to stay high up when visiting flowering shrubs may lead to this species being under-recorded. Whilst the bulk of records are from southern Britain, there are scattered records throughout the north including northern Scotland and around the Moray Firth. Recent observations suggest that it is locally abundant in some localities in north-west England.

Dasysyrphus albostriatus (Fallén, 1817)

Syrphus albostriatus Fallén in Coe (1953)

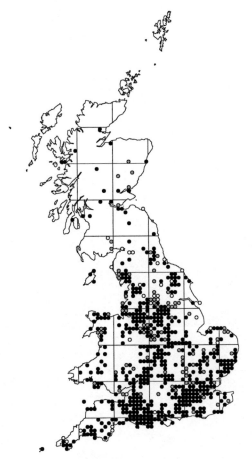

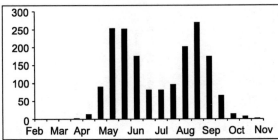

Biology
The larvae of this species are aphidophagous and arboreal, occurring on both coniferous and broad-leaved trees. They feed nocturnally, resting near the aphid colony by day on twigs and branches, where they are superbly camouflaged by their bold colour patterns and 'frilly edges'. Adults are usually found near trees in situations such as woodland rides and edges, hedgerows and gardens where they can be found visiting flowers, such as white umbels and yellow composites, or settled on sun-lit vegetation.

Distribution
Widespread throughout Britain, but scarce in the extreme north of Scotland.

Dasysyrphus friuliensis (van der Goot, 1960)

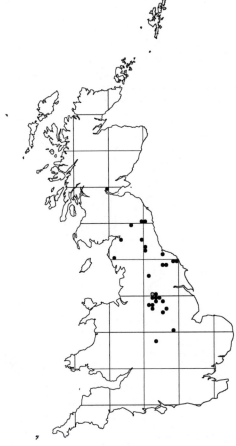

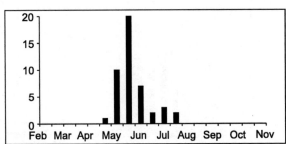

Biology
The larvae are aphid-feeding and overwinter in leaf litter on the forest floor. Adults have most often been found in rides, or near the edges of coniferous plantations where they visit flowers such as white umbels and *Ranunculus*. On the continent, it is considered to be associated with *Picea* forests and plantations.

Distribution
This species was first recorded in Britain in 1979 from Yorkshire, and has subsequently been found in north and central England, and at least one locality in Wales. It is thought to be a recent colonist of conifer plantations, and is likely to be found more widely in future.

Dasysyrphus hilaris (Zetterstedt, 1843)

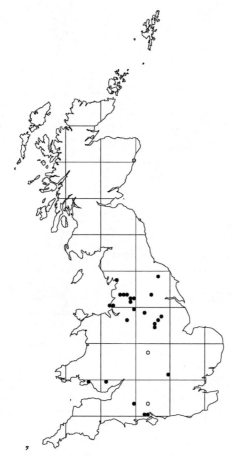

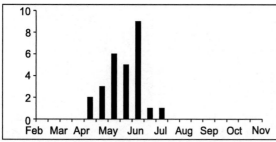

Biology
The taxonomic status of this species is unclear. Although it may be a pale-faced variety of *D. venustus* (see discussion in Stubbs and Falk (1983)), a male specimen has recently been found in Scotland by Philip Entwistle which has genitalia distinct from either *D. venustus* or *D. friuliensis*, and its specific status may therefore be justified (Entwistle 1995; Stubbs 1996).

Distribution
Specimens attributed to this taxon have been found at widely scattered localities from southern England to the Scottish Highlands.

Dasysyrphus pinastri (De Geer, 1776)

Syrphus lunulatus Meigen in Coe (1953), *Dasysyrphus lunulatus* (Meigen) in Stubbs and Falk (1983)

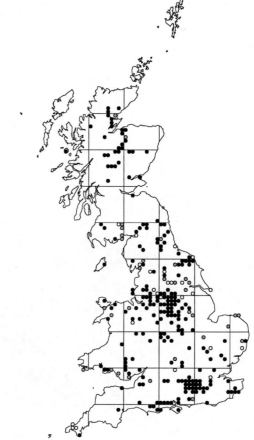

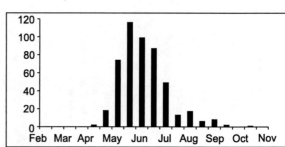

Biology
The larvae are aphidophagous and arboreal, occurring on both coniferous and broad-leaved trees. Usually found near trees in localities such as woodland rides and edges and around mature hedgerows, most frequently in or near coniferous forest and plantations. Adults visit a wide range of flowers.

Distribution
Widespread throughout Britain, but more abundant in the northern half of the country.

Dasysyrphus tricinctus (Fallén, 1817)

Syrphus tricinctus Fallén in Coe (1953)

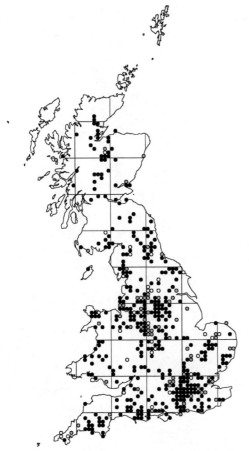

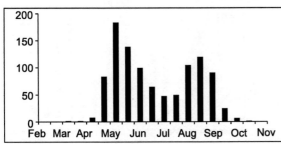

Biology
The larvae (illustrated in Rotheray (1994)) occur on both coniferous and broad-leaved trees and have been observed feeding on sawfly larvae and lepidopterous caterpillars, but Rotheray (1994) reports that it is a frequent predator of aphids on *Acer pseudoplatanus*. Adults are usually found in or near woodland along rides, edges and tracksides where they visit a range of flowers.

Distribution
Widespread throughout Britain to northern Scotland. It is often common in both broad-leaved and coniferous woodlands, and in south-east England it tends also to be associated with heathland.

Dasysyrphus venustus (Meigen, 1822)

Syrphus venustus Meigen in Coe (1953)

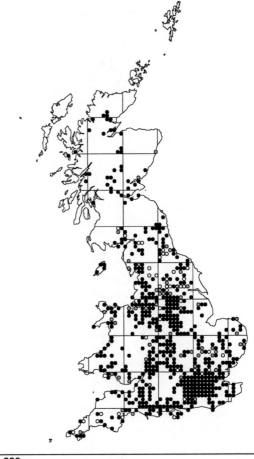

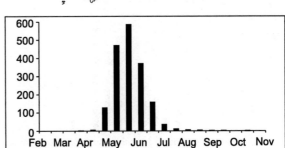

Biology
The larvae are aphidophagous and arboreal, occurring on both coniferous and broad-leaved trees. They feed nocturnally and rest near the aphid colony by day on twigs and branches where they are superbly camouflaged by their bold colour patterns and 'frilly edges' (see photograph in Rotheray (1994)). Adults are usually found near trees in situations such as woodland rides and edges, hedgerows and gardens. A wide range of flowers are visited.

Distribution
Widespread throughout Britain to northern Scotland, but more frequent in southern Britain and scarce in the northern part of its range.

Didea alneti (Fallén, 1817)

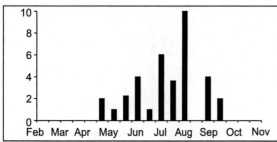

Biology
The larvae are aphidophagous and usually associated with conifers, although they have also been found feeding on arboreal aphids on broad-leaved trees, such as those on *Salix* and *Lachnus* sp. on *Quercus*. Adults occur in or near woodland, including conifer plantations where they are primarily arboreal, but will descend to visit flowers.

Distribution
This species has an unusual distribution, with several widely separated areas producing a number of records over a period of a few years (eg Forest of Dean in the 1890s, Sutton Park around the turn of the century, Speyside area in 1930s) followed by apparent local extinction. This pattern suggests an occasional migrant or vagrant (or accidental import?) that sometimes establishes temporary populations. The only recent records come from Slaley Forest, a large conifer plantation in southern Northumberland, where it was found twice in 1989.

Didea fasciata Macquart, 1834

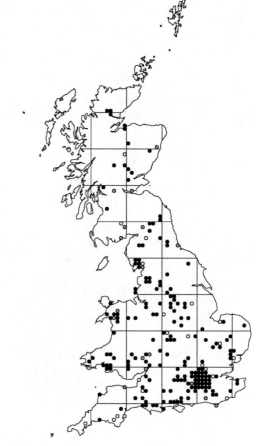

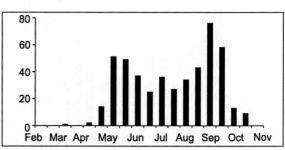

Biology
The larvae are aphidophagous and arboreal on both coniferous and broad-leaved trees. Adults are generally found in or near woodland, including conifer plantations and scrub, where the males aggressively defend sunlit patches. Typical localities include rides, clearings and tracks through trees.

Distribution
Widespread throughout Britain. Whilst listed by Stubbs (1982) as a 'good' primary woodland indicator, records submitted to the recording scheme suggest that it occurs in woodland of all types, including conifer plantations, secondary woodland and scrub.

Didea intermedia Loew, 1854

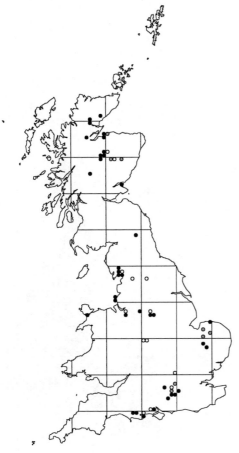

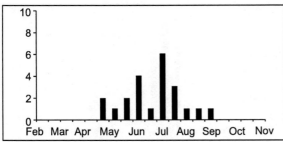

Biology
Larvae are strongly associated with *Pinus* and have been found feeding on aphids on *Pinus nigra*. Adults are almost always associated with coniferous forest, including conifers planted on sand dunes. A few records from broad-leaved woodland in southern Britain are suspect, and may well be misidentifications of *D. fasciata*.

Distribution
A northern species, with most records from Scotland and northern England. It also occurs on coniferised heathlands in Norfolk, Suffolk, Surrey, Hampshire and Dorset. According to Coe (1953) there are old but reliable records from the New Forest.

Doros profuges Harris, 1780

Doros conopseus (Fabricius) in Stubbs and Falk (1983)

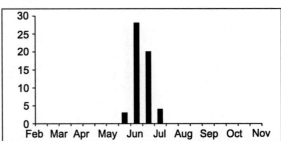

Biology
A 19th century observation suggests that larvae may be associated with ants living in wood, probably feeding on ant-attended aphids. Adults have most frequently been seen at the edge of scrub or woodland around *Rubus*, either visiting the flowers or resting on vegetation. They have also been recorded sitting on a rotten tree trunk, around sap-runs and on reeds. On chalk downland in Surrey, oviposition was observed low down on the trunk of a young *Fraxinus* (Hawkins quoted in Stubbs (1996)) although this was not proven (Morris 1998). Adults appear to be very elusive and may be primarily arboreal; recent records include several specimens in Malaise traps at sites where the species has not otherwise been recorded.

Distribution
This species is strongly associated with soils on a basic substrate. Although older records are more widespread, most recent records come from on or near the chalk of southern England, although there are some from the southern Lake District, and from Mull (not mapped). There is a long series of records from Leigh and Benfleet in Essex from the 19th Century to the 1960s.

Epistrophe diaphana (Zetterstedt, 1843)

Syrphus diaphanus Zetterstedt in Coe (1953)

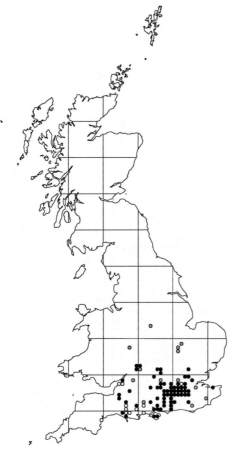

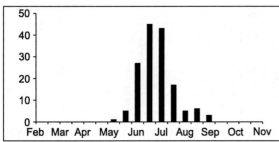

Biology
The larva of this species is undescribed, but other members of the genus are aphidophagous, and mainly associated with trees, but also shrubs and tall herbs. Females have been observed ovipositing on *Heracleum* (Dobson 1997). Adults usually occur at woodland edges or in scrubby habitats where they can be found visiting flowers or resting on sunlit vegetation. Males hover at 2–4 m in open patches. Adults visit white umbels and sometimes other flowers.

Distribution
A scarce species, with most records coming from the southern counties of England.

Epistrophe eligans (Harris, 1780)

Syrphus eligans Harris (*bifasciatus* Fabricius) in Coe (1953)

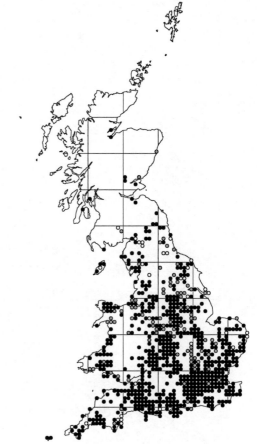

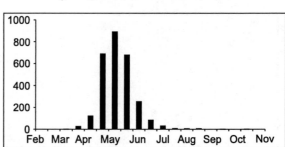

Biology
The larva is aphidophagous, and mainly arboreal, but also found on shrubs and sometimes *Rubus*. Adults are characteristically found in the spring, hovering around, and visiting the flowers of trees and bushes, particularly *Prunus spinosa* and *Crataegus*. Males hover singly, or in small groups, beneath the branches of mature trees. Woodland edges, scrub, orchards, mature hedgerows and larger gardens with well established trees are likely localities.

Distribution
A characteristic early spring species throughout England and Wales, becoming scarcer in the extreme north of England and with only a few records from the southern half of Scotland.

Epistrophe grossulariae (Meigen, 1822)

Syrphus grossulariae Meigen in Coe (1953)

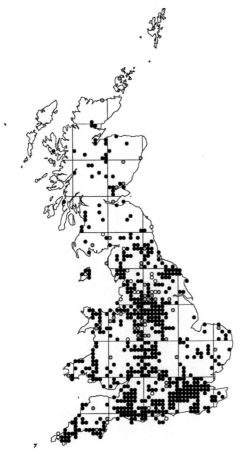

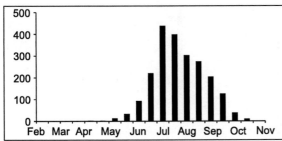

Biology
The larvae are frequently found feeding on aphids on *Acer pseudoplatanus*, but may also prey on other arboreal aphid species. A species of broad-leaved woodland. Adults are usually found visiting flowers, especially white umbels and *Succisa pratensis* along woodland rides and edges, scrub and around mature hedgerows. Males hover in clearings, over tracks, etc.

Distribution
Widespread throughout Britain, but less frequent in eastern England. Although this species remains on the wing until October, early specimens may be overlooked amongst the many black and yellow species active in spring.

Epistrophe melanostoma (Zetterstedt, 1843)

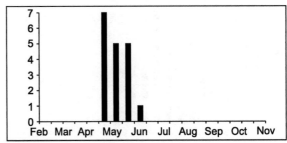

Biology
The larva of this species remains undescribed, but other members of the genus are aphidophagous, associated mainly with trees, shrubs and tall herbs. Adults have been found where grassland, woodland and scrub occur together, and in woodland clearings where they visit flowers. Adults fly extremely rapidly (Speight 1988a).

Distribution
Recently added to the British list. This species was first caught in Surrey in 1986 (Beuk 1990), and seems to be spreading. The occurrence of the species in Britain was predicted by Speight (1988a), and separation from other British members of the genus is dealt with by Speight (1988a) and Stubbs (1996).

Epistrophe nitidicollis (Meigen, 1822)

Syrphus nitidicollis Meigen in Coe (1953)

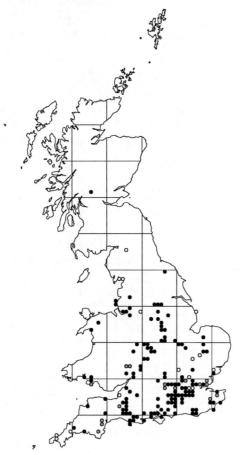

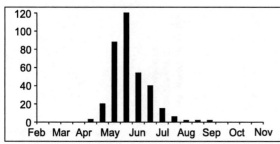

Biology

Larvae feed on arboreal aphids and have been found on a variety of trees and shrubs including *Malus*, *Prunus* and *Sambucus*. Adults are found in woodland rides and glades where they are usually seen basking on sunlit foliage, but will visit flowers including white umbels, *Ranunculus* and *Rubus*.

Distribution

Local in the southern half of Britain north to the Midlands, but with a recent record from the southern edge of the Scottish Highlands.

Epistrophe ochrostoma (Zetterstedt, 1849)

Biology

The larva of this species remains undescribed, but other members of the genus are aphidophagous and mainly associated with trees, but also shrubs and tall herbs. In continental Europe adults are found in woodland clearings, perhaps including those in conifer forests, often flying rather high (Speight 1988a).

Distribution

This species was recently added to the British list on the basis of a single specimen found by David Heaver on a partly wooded slope on the south side of the Menai Strait in North Wales (Heaver 1990). The occurrence of this species in Britain was predicted by Speight (1988a) and separation from other British members of the genus is dealt with by Speight (1988a) and Stubbs (1996).

Episyrphus balteatus (De Geer, 1776)

Syrphus balteatus De Geer in Coe (1953)

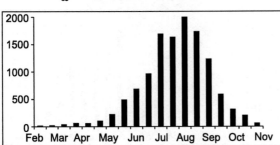

Biology
The larvae prey on a wide range of aphids on trees, shrubs and herbs, including cereal crops and cabbages (especially in gardens), but appear to prefer aphid colonies low down. Adults are usually seen visiting flowers or basking on foliage. They are very frequent in gardens, parks, waste ground and urban areas, sometimes in large numbers.

Distribution
This species migrates north from southern Europe in the spring, breeding along the way. Migrants typically arrive in Britain in late June and July when aphid numbers are building up. Hoverfly larvae can reach high densities in cereal crops, resulting in vast numbers of emerging adults in late summer. In the autumn these migrate southwards and the adults overwinter. It normally has a single generation in Britain, but some adults overwinter here and unseasonal records can occur if the weather is mild. This is one of the most abundant and widespread hoverflies, and the species for which the recording scheme has received most records, although numbers vary considerably from year to year depending on conditions for migration and on aphid numbers.

Eriozona erratica (Linnaeus, 1758)

Syrphus annulipes Zetterstedt in Coe (1953), *Megasyrphus annulipes* (Zetterstedt) in Stubbs and Falk (1983), *Didea annulipes* (Zetterstedt) in Rotheray (1994)

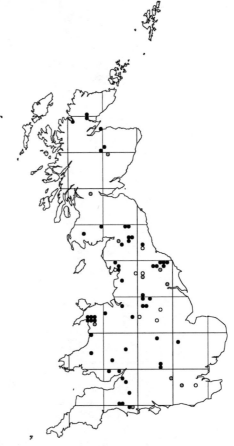

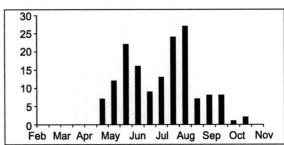

Biology
The larvae are aphidophagous, and usually associated with conifers (*Abies*, *Picea* and *Pinus*), although they are also known to feed on other arboreal aphids such as those on *Salix*. Adults are often associated with open rides and glades in conifer plantations, where they visit a wide range of flowers. They are easily confused with *Syrphus* in the field, but the thorax is quite noticeably blacker and shiny, and in life the markings are orange rather than yellow.

Distribution
This widespread species was formerly regarded as very scarce, but it has been recorded more frequently in recent years, possibly because recorders have paid more attention to rides in conifer plantations. It is also possible that its populations undergo large fluctuations, resulting in large numbers of records being received following occasional good years. For example, 40% of all records submitted to the recording scheme date from 1992 and 1993.

Eriozona syrphoides (Fallén, 1817)

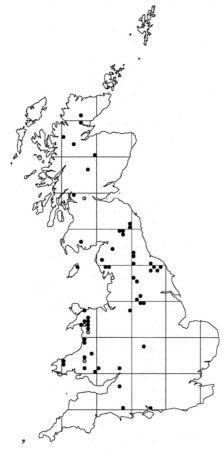

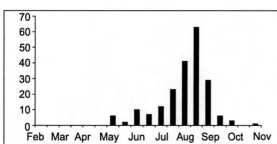

Biology

The larvae are aphidophagous, and usually associated with mature conifers (*Abies, Picea*). In the former Czechoslovakia, they have been found feeding on the aphid *Cinara pineae* in established (40 year old) *Picea* plantations. Adults are usually found visiting flowers along rides or edges in conifer plantations, but they have also been found in broad-leaved woodland. Males hover in dappled sunshine beneath the canopy.

Distribution

This species was first reported from Snowdonia in 1968, but an earlier specimen (from Lancaster in 1957) was subsequently located. Recent records are widely scattered throughout northern and western Britain. The species is probably spreading in conifer plantations and likely to be found more widely in future. There is a rather anomalous record of a specimen found dead on a pavement in the centre of Coventry in 1982 (Palmer 1985); it is possible that this was a road casualty carried by a vehicle from a more typical habitat.

Eristalinus aeneus (Scopoli, 1763)

Eristalis aeneus Scopoli in Coe (1953)

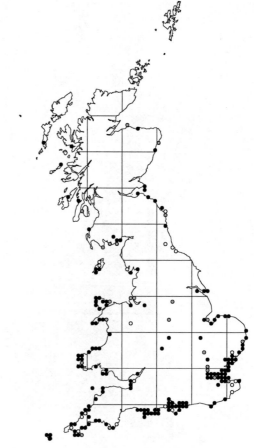

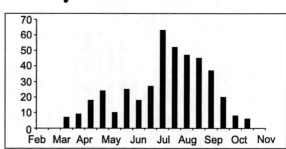

Biology

This is a coastal species in Britain. The larvae are of the 'long-tailed', aquatic type, and live in brackish pools and rock-pools where decaying seaweed accumulates. Adults are often found basking on bare areas or rocks on paths and banks, or visiting flowers such as *Senecio*, rarely more than a few tens of metres from the high-tide mark. It overwinters as an adult.

Distribution

This species occurs widely around the coast of Britain on both rocky shores and in saltmarsh. It can be abundant at some localities. Although almost entirely coastal in the northern part of its range, it occurs inland further south in Europe and is distinctly anthropogenic, breeding in sewage farms or in association with animal dung (Speight 1998).

Eristalinus sepulchralis (Linnaeus, 1758)

Eristalis sepulchralis Linnaeus in Coe (1953)

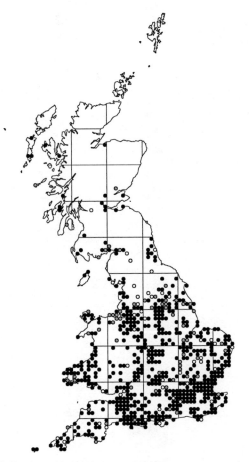

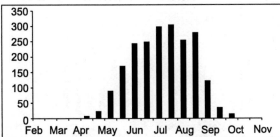

Biology
The larvae of this species are of the 'long-tailed', aquatic type, occurring in rotting vegetation around ponds and marshes especially when enriched with animal dung, etc. They can also breed in polluted conditions, such as the run-off from dung heaps and silage clamps. Adults can often be seen settled on bare mud, or swept from long vegetation near breeding places, and may be found visiting a wide range of flowers. Adults overwinter.

Distribution
Widely distributed and often abundant in wetlands in southern Britain, but especially abundant in lowland and coastal wetlands (eg coastal grazing marshes). It is more restricted in the north, becoming a mainly coastal species in Scotland.

Eristalis abusivus Collin, 1931

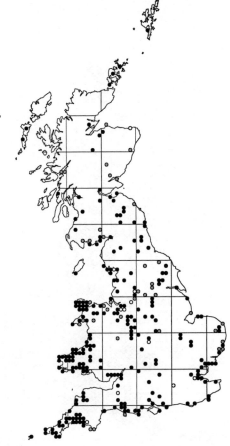

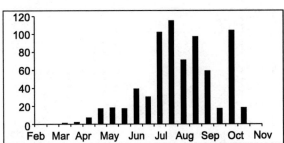

Biology
The larvae are of the 'long-tailed', aquatic type, and are associated with wet, decaying organic matter such as that around ponds. It has been found at the edge of a pond on moorland (Smith 1989). Adults are usually seen visiting flowers around the edges of scrub, hedges and tall vegetation near the larval habitat.

Distribution
Widely distributed throughout Britain, but more frequent near the coast, this may be the most abundant *Eristalis* in some coastal wetlands. It may easily be overlooked amongst other small eristalines, and care with identification is required.

Eristalis arbustorum (Linnaeus, 1758)

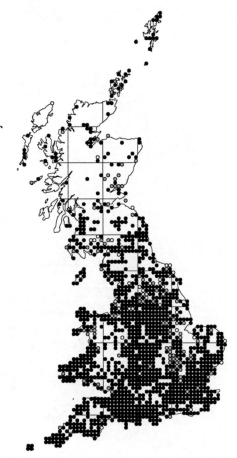

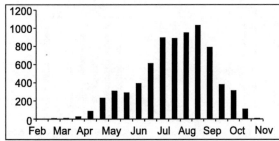

Biology
The larvae are of the 'long-tailed', aquatic type, and are associated with shallow standing water including wet, decaying organic matter around ponds and ditches, farmyard manure heaps and silage runoff. Adults are usually found visiting flowers in open situations such as woodland rides, hedgerows, meadows, road verges and urban wastelands. It is a frequent visitor to gardens.

Distribution
Regarded as a pronounced migrant and quite strongly anthropogenic, so it is one of the commonest hoverflies in parks, gardens and farmland as well as all sorts of wetland situations. Found throughout Britain.

Eristalis cryptarum (Fabricius, 1794)

Eoseristalis cryptarum (Fabricius, 1794) in Levy and Levy (1994)

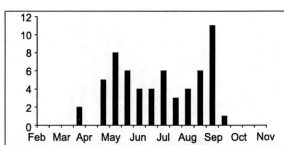

Biology
The larva remains unknown, but is likely to be of the 'long-tailed', aquatic type and appears to be associated with sheltered and somewhat acid pools supporting plants such as *Sphagnum, Menyanthes, Narthecium* and *Caltha*. Adults can be found visiting flowers nearby including *Ranunculus, Caltha, Menyanthes* and *Cardamine*. Has a very long flight period and is probably multi-brooded.

Distribution
A south-western species with many old records from Dartmoor and the New Forest, mostly dating from the last century up to about 1950; also from Dorset, especially Studland, in the 1930s, and Cornwall in 1910. Records became increasingly scarce through the 1960s, and there is only a single record from the early 1970s, from Dartmoor. Two Dipterists' summer field meetings in Devon in the late 1970s and 1980s failed to find it and the species was feared extinct. Then in 1993 it was re-discovered at one of its old localities on Dartmoor and it has subsequently been found at seven localities in the immediate vicinity.

Eristalis horticola (De Geer, 1776)

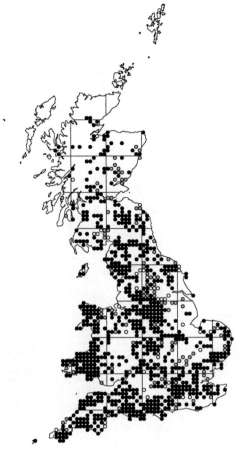

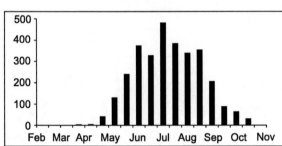

Biology

The larvae are of the 'long-tailed', aquatic type, and are found in most types of wetland, but especially the margins of ponds and wooded streams. Adults are usually found visiting flowers, especially white umbels, often in the vicinity of trees or scrub. They sometimes visit garden flowers.

Distribution

Widespread and frequent throughout Britain. It is probably present in all districts, but appears to be more abundant in northern England and Scotland. Care is needed in separation from some other *Eristalis* species, especially *E. interruptus* and *E. rupium*.

Eristalis interruptus (Poda, 1761)

Eristalis nemorum (Linnaeus) in Stubbs and Falk (1983)

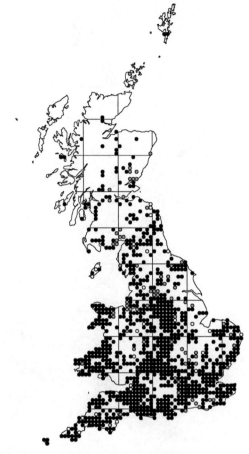

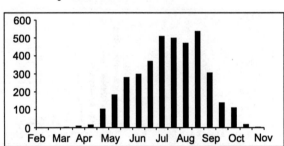

Biology

The larvae of are of the 'long-tailed', aquatic type and are found in shallow water and semi-aquatic situations at the margins of streams and pools, often where there is nutrient enrichment (cow-dung, etc). Adults are usually seen visiting flowers, especially white umbels, often in the vicinity of trees or scrub. Males make themselves conspicuous because of their fast and noisy flight. This species has a very characteristic courtship in which the male hovers above a female which is visiting a flower (see photograph in Stubbs and Falk (1983)).

Distribution

An abundant flower-visiting species, found throughout Britain.

Eristalis intricarius (Linnaeus, 1758)

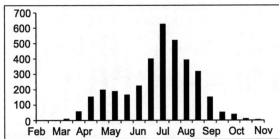

Biology

The larvae are of the 'long-tailed', aquatic type and occur in semi-liquid organic matter such as organically enriched mud and waterlogged peat besides ponds and drains, but also in slurry pits and cow-dung. Adults are usually found visiting flowers, especially flowering shrubs, white umbels, *Senecio* and *Cirsium*, often in the vicinity of trees or scrub. Males can be seen hovering at some height above tracks and in woodland rides. This is a good bumblebee mimic, occurring in three colour forms.

Distribution

Widespread and common throughout Britain, possibly more local in the north.

Eristalis pertinax (Scopoli, 1763)

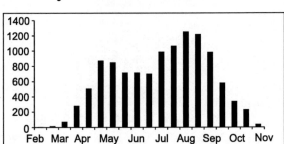

Biology

The larvae are of the 'long-tailed', aquatic type and occur in a wide range of situations where wet, decaying vegetable matter accumulates, including wet manure heaps in farmyards. Adults are usually found visiting flowers such as flowering shrubs, white umbels, yellow composites and *Rubus*, and are frequent visitors to gardens. Males often hover near flowering shrubs.

Distribution

One of the commonest species throughout Britain. Has a very long flight season and is one of the most abundant early spring species as well as one of the most abundant on ivy flowers at the end of the season.

Eristalis rupium Fabricius, 1805

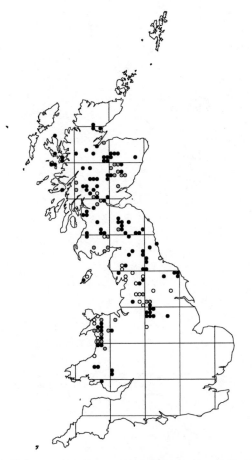

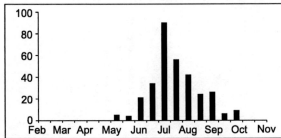

Biology
The larvae are of the 'long-tailed' type and are apparently aquatic in clean-water situations, such as spring-fed permanent streams. Adults are usually found in fairly open situations such as wet meadows and streamsides with abundant flowers, often in the uplands (to about 300 m). They can sometimes be found in glades in conifer plantations where flowers are abundant.

Distribution
This is a northern and western species which can be very local, even in apparently suitable areas. Care is needed in identification as it is easily confused with *E. interruptus* and *E. horticola*.

Eristalis similis (Fallén, 1817)

Eristalis pratorum (Meigen, 1822) in Falk (1990) and Stubbs (1996)

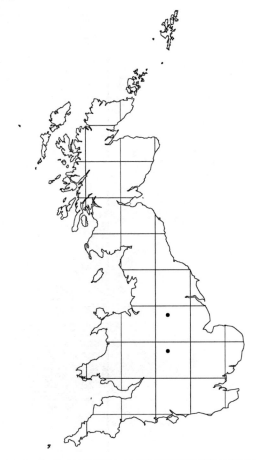

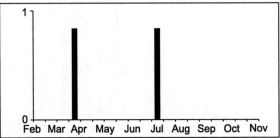

Biology
The larva of this species remains undescribed, but other members of this genus are of the 'long-tailed', aquatic type. Single adults have been found on two occasions in a woodland ride and a damp area in a conifer plantation. In continental Europe it is associated with mature to over-mature broad-leaved forest and Mediterranean evergreen forests. Adult males hover at 2–4 m over woodland tracks, and both sexes can be found sitting on sunny trunks or visiting flowers (Speight 1988a).

Distribution
Falk (1990) added this species to the British list on the basis of a single specimen found in Warwickshire in March 1990. He illustrates the specimen and gives characters to separate it from other British members of the genus. A second specimen was found by Austin Brackenbury in Derbyshire in July 1997. The occurrence of this species in Britain was predicted by Speight (1988a) who comments on the difficulty of distinguishing it from *E. pertinax*. It appears to have become more frequent in recent years in nearby parts of continental Europe (Speight 1998).

Eristalis tenax (Linnaeus, 1758)

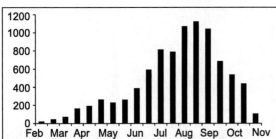

Biology

The larvae are of the 'long-tailed', semi-aquatic type, living in organically enriched ooze such as the mud fringing eutrophicated and/or polluted water bodies, the run-off from farmyard manure heaps, silage and slurry pits, and even exudates from putrefying corpses. When mature, larvae leave to look for somewhere dry, often a little above ground, to pupate. In doing so they may travel tens of metres from the larval habitat and turn up in unusual places. Adults disperse widely and visit a wide range of flowers. Can be abundant in gardens. Adults overwinter (not infrequently in houses), and occasional individuals can be seen during warm spells throughout the winter.

Distribution

Widespread and very common. Markedly anthropogenic, a pronounced migrant and with a very long flight period.

Eumerus ornatus Meigen, 1822

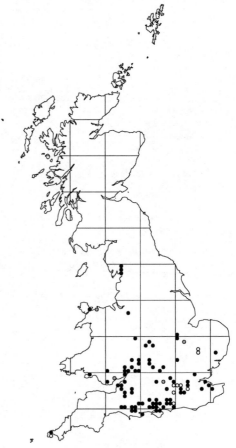

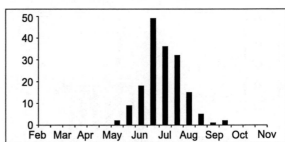

Biology

The larva of this species is undescribed, but other members of this genus usually live in plant bulbs or roots. Adults are normally found in broad-leaved woodland where they can be found resting on bare patches on paths and banks, flying low over, or sunning on, short vegetation. Males are distinctly territorial and defend sunlit patches. Occasionally visits flowers such as *Geranium robertianum*.

Distribution

A local species in well-wooded areas of southern Britain, with scattered records north to the Lake District. Recent records suggest that this species is less scarce than was thought, and may often be overlooked because of its habit of flying close to the ground.

Eumerus sabulonum (Fallén, 1817)

Eumerus strigatus (Fallén, 1817)

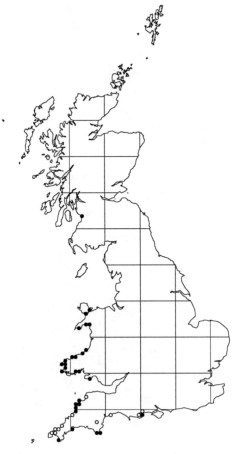

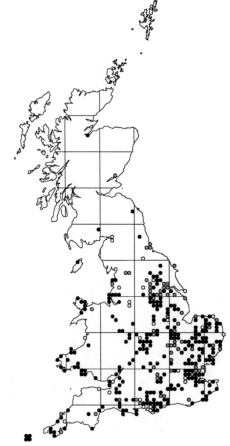

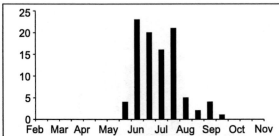

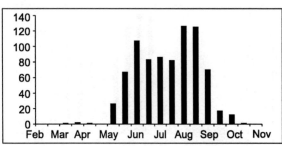

Biology

The larvae remain unknown, but are thought to tunnel in bulbs or roots. Circumstantial evidence suggests *Jasione montana* is among possible host species. Adults have been found resting in the sun on bare ground and sandy banks, or flying low over short vegetation, when they resemble small solitary bees. Most localities are coastal, and range from steep grassland slopes with bare ground to sand dunes. Occasionally visits flowers.

Distribution

A coastal species whose range extends from Hampshire and Dorset westwards and northwards to Anglesey, and which has been recently discovered in Ayrshire. Adults are difficult to locate or catch, so the species is probably under-recorded. The recent increase in records has resulted from the a better understanding of this species' requirements, gained during the Dipterists' summer field meeting in Devon in 1989.

Biology

The larvae tunnel in the bulbs of *Narcissus* and rhizomes of *Iris*, as well as a range of other cultivated and wild species, usually when there is some damage and rot is present. There is a possibility that *Pastinaca sativa* is a wild host (A E Stubbs pers . comm.). Adults are usually found flying low among vegetation or resting on dead stems and bare soil. They occur in gardens, but are more frequent in wetland habitats; they were, for example, much more abundant than *E. tuberculatus* in material from water traps in the East Anglian fens.

Distribution

Widespread throughout lowland Britain, but less frequently recorded than *E. tuberculatus*.

Eumerus tuberculatus Rondani, 1857

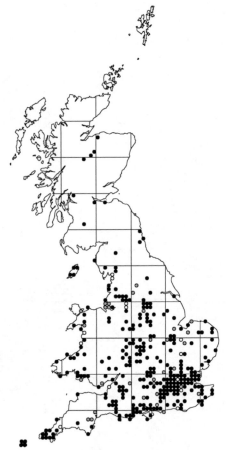

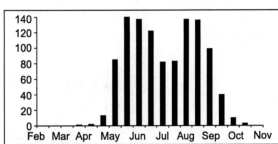

Biology
The larvae tunnel in damaged bulbs of *Narcissus* and many other cultivated and wild species. Adults are usually found low in vegetation or resting on dead stems or bare patches of soil. They are abundant in gardens.

Distribution
The commonest member of the genus, frequent in gardens, where it is known to gardeners as the 'lesser bulb fly' and sometimes regarded as a pest. Speight (1985) concludes that this species is not established in Ireland, and points out that it was not recorded in Britain until the beginning of this century, suggesting that it may have been introduced from southern or central Europe via imported bulbs. *E. tuberculatus* was added to the British list by Collin (1918) and the recording scheme holds only one pre-1920 record, a museum specimen taken in Surrey in 1905.

Eupeodes corollae (Fabricius, 1794)

Syrphus corollae Fabricius (*consisto* Harris) in Coe (1953), *Metasyrphus corollae* (Fabricius) in Stubbs and Falk (1983)

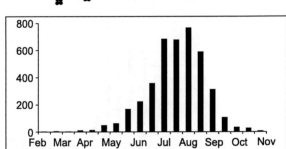

Biology
The larva feeds on aphids on various low growing plants, especially Fabaceae. Adults are highly mobile and may be found at flowers in all sorts of fairly open situations from woodland clearings to arable farmland and urban areas. Visits a wide range of flowers and commonly occurs in parks and gardens. This species overwinters as a puparium and has a very long flight period.

Distribution
One of the commonest flower-visiting species throughout Britain, and believed to be boosted in abundance, at least in some years, by migration from the continent.

Eupeodes lapponicus (Zetterstedt, 1838)

Syrphus lapponicus Zetterstedt in Coe (1953), *Metasyrphus lapponicus* (Zetterstedt) in Stubbs and Falk (1983)

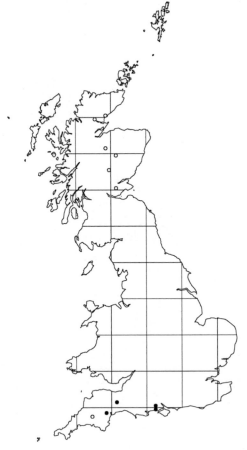

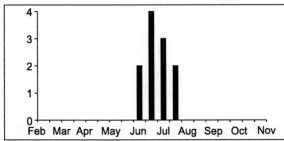

Biology

The larvae have been found feeding at some height in conifers (*Picea*), but also feeding on aphids on *Euonymus* and *Quercus*. Although little is known of adult requirements, an association with coniferous woodland is suspected. Some, but not all British records are from areas of native pinewood, but it has also been found recently visiting flowers along rides in a conifer plantation (Levy & Levy 1998). There is some evidence that it overwinters as an adult, but over-wintering larvae and puparia have also been found in forest floor litter. The overall picture is, therefore, confusing and the status and requirements of *E. lapponicus* are unclear.

Distribution

A very rare species with old records from the Scottish Highlands, but with the very few recent records from south-west England. It is considered to be a highly migratory species in continental Europe.

Eupeodes latifasciatus (Macquart, 1829)

Syrphus latifasciatus Macquart in Coe (1953), *Metasyrphus latifasciatus* (Macquart) in Stubbs and Falk (1983)

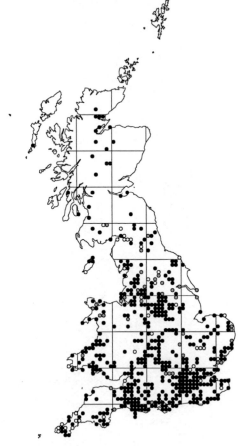

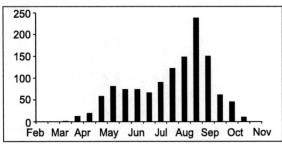

Biology

Larvae have been found feeding on root aphids. In laboratory culture they will feed on a wide range of aphids associated with low growing herbs and shrubs. Generally found in wetland situations, with a preference for wet meadows with *Juncus* or other lush vegetation. Adults visit a range of white and yellow flowers of low growing species, often in the vicinity of water.

Distribution

Widely distributed but scarce, with the number of records varying greatly from year to year. This suggests that it may be a migrant, or at least boosted in abundance in some years by immigration.

Eupeodes latilunulatus (Collin, 1931)

Syrphus latilunulatus Collin in Coe (1953), *Metasyrphus latilunulatus* (Collin) in Stubbs and Falk (1983)

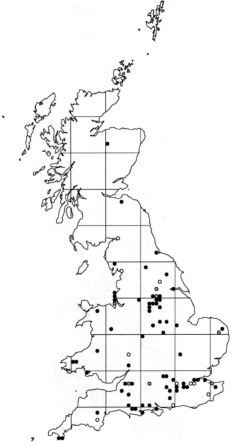

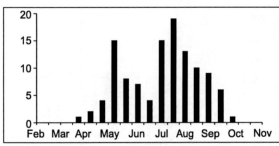

Biology

The larvae are aphidophagous and have been found on *Cirsium arvense*. Adult requirements are little known, but most records refer to conifer woods, with acid heathlands and wetlands also mentioned. It has been found visiting yellow composites, *Euphorbia*, *Narthecium*, *Salix*, *Sorbus* and *Stellaria* and has also been recorded from a garden Malaise trap.

Distribution

Records are few and widely scattered; misidentifications are a problem, and it may be overlooked amongst large numbers of similar black and yellow hoverflies. There is a possibility that this could be a rare migrant/vagrant. Large-scale movements apparently occur out of Scandinavia in August/September.

Eupeodes lundbecki (Soot-Ryen, 1946)

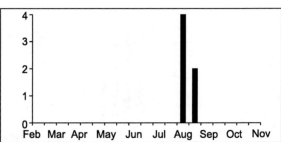

Biology

The larva is unknown. This is a common species on the Continent, where adults are found in mixed woodland, conifer plantations, gardens, etc, and visit a variety of flowers, especially white umbels, *Cirsium* and *Carduus* and often settle on sun-lit vegetation. According to Speight (1998) in flight it is very reminiscent of *Scaeva*.

Distribution

Added to the British list by Watt and Robertson (1990) from specimens at Aberdeen in 1976, Fair Isle in 1982 and Tynron, Dumfries in 1984, and recorded in several years from Stiffkey, Norfolk by Ivan Perry. It is regarded as migratory in continental Europe and large-scale movements apparently occur out of Scandinavia in August/September. Occurrences on the east coast are consistent with this being a migrant/vagrant from northern Europe.

Eupeodes luniger (Meigen, 1822)

Syrphus luniger Meigen in Coe (1953), *Metasyrphus luniger* (Meigen) in Stubbs and Falk (1983)

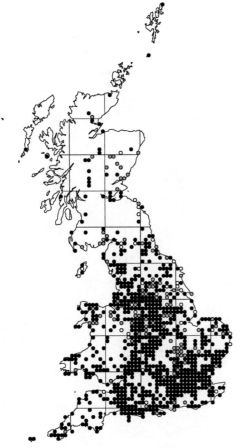

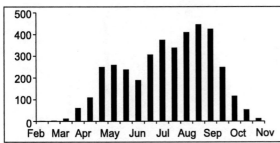

Biology
Larvae are aphidophagous on a variety of low growing plants. The adults are very mobile and likely to be found visiting flowers in almost any fairly open situation from clearings in woods, to farmland and urban parks, gardens and waste ground. They are frequent visitors to gardens. Males hover at some height beside bushes and in shafts of sunshine in woodland.

Distribution
Like *E. corollae*, this is a very widespread and common species. Of the two, this is the more frequent species earlier in the year. It can be commoner than *E. corollae*, especially in south-east England. It is highly migratory and numbers are probably augmented in some years by immigrants from southern Europe.

Eupeodes nielseni Dusek & Laska, 1976

Metasyrphus nielseni Dusek & Laska in Stubbs and Falk (1983)

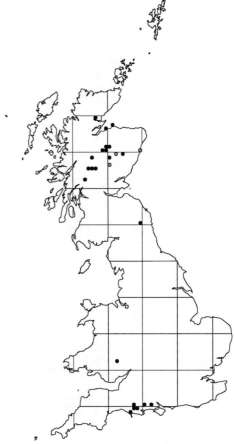

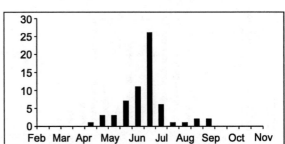

Biology
The larvae are aphidophagous and associated with conifers. *E. nielseni* is a little-known species, described in 1976. Adults have been found mainly at the edges of mature *Pinus* forest, where they visit flowers such as *Potentilla erecta*, *Sorbus* and *Salix repens*, but have also been found in partially-coniferised woodland. According to Speight (1998) they are largely arboreal.

Distribution
There are very few records; the majority are from the Scottish Highlands but there are a few from scattered localities in southern England. It is possible that this species is spreading in conifer plantations in the south, and will be found more widely in future.

Eupeodes nitens (Zetterstedt, 1843)

Syrphus nitens Zetterstedt in Coe (1953), *Metasyrphus nitens* (Zetterstedt) in Stubbs and Falk (1983)

Eupeodes species A *sensu* Stubbs (1983)

Metasyrphus species A in Stubbs and Falk (1983)

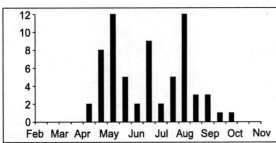

Biology
The larvae are undescribed, but it has been reared from a larva collected off *Cirsium* in alpine grassland (Goeldlin quoted in Speight (1998)). Adults are usually found in mature broad-leaved woodland where they visit flowers, especially white umbels and yellow composites, in glades and rides. According to Speight (1998) they are largely arboreal.

Distribution
A scarce species with records widely scattered throughout Britain, but concentrated in the forest belt of central-southern England, and the woods of Herefordshire and Worcestershire, such as Wyre Forest.

Biology
Recorded from the edges of *Picea* plantations, and also from partially-coniferised broad-leaved woodland where *Picea* is present.

Distribution
This taxon was first recognised in 1947 from South Devon. The very few British specimens have been taken at widely scattered localities in England and Wales, and it has also been found in southern Scandinavia and the Alps. It has possibly only recently colonised British conifer plantations.

Ferdinandea cuprea (Scopoli, 1763)

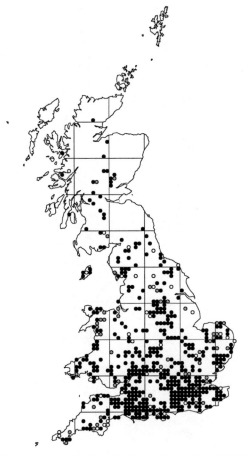

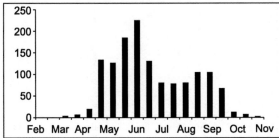

Biology
The larvae, which when present are often numerous, are usually found in sap-runs on broad-leaved trees, but have also been found in a variety of other situations where semi-liquid rotting material is present including the decaying roots of cultivated globe artichoke *Cynara scolymus* in France. They are adapted to manoeuvre into small spaces such as below bark, and remain hidden deep within the sap. The pupae usually occur under loose bark near a sap-run. Adults are often found sunning themselves on tree trunks or posts, and sometimes visiting flowers such as *Ranunculus*. They usually occur in or near woodland, but can also be associated with trees in hedgerows, parks and other situations.

Distribution
Widespread throughout Britain but never common, occurring most frequently in areas with plenty of broad-leaved woodland.

Ferdinandea ruficornis (Fabricius, 1775)

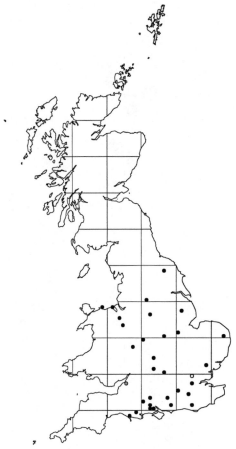

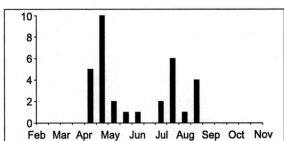

Biology
The larvae remain undescribed but are thought to be associated with sap-runs. The species has been reared from a burrow of the goat moth *Cossus cossus* (Linnaeus) on *Populus* and puparia have been found at the base of *Populus* attacked by *Cossus* larvae. Believed to be associated with broad-leaved woodland with overmature trees. Adults are seldom found and may be largely arboreal, but have been found sunning on tree trunks and visiting *Heracleum* umbels.

Distribution
A scarce species, with recent records being dominated by specimens from Malaise traps, some of these operating well away from substantial areas of woodland. It is possible that adults are overlooked, perhaps by staying high in the canopy. Stubbs and Falk (1983), however, suggest genuine scarcity due to a close association with burrows of the goat moth, which is itself a scarce insect (see map in *British Wildlife* 4(5), 323).

Hammerschmidtia ferruginea (Fallén, 1817)

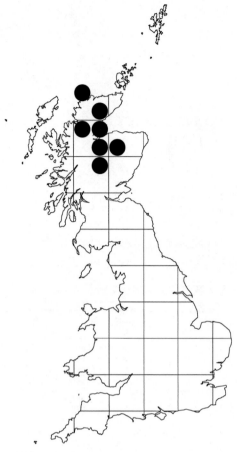

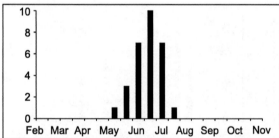

Biology

The larvae inhabit sap-runs or (more often) accumulations of decaying sap under the bark of recently dead, mature *Populus tremula*. Adults are usually found near the larval habitat, either sitting on trunks and stumps or visiting flowers nearby such as *Salix* and *Rosa*. They have been found visiting the flowers of *Prunus padus* in Sutherland (Entwistle quoted in Stubbs, 1996).

Distribution

A very rare species, recorded mainly from Speyside. A recent survey by the Malloch Society found larvae in 11 localities where mature groves of *Populus tremula* occurred. Stands of mature aspen are a scarce habitat and this species is regarded as very vulnerable. Records of this species have been mapped by 50 kilometre squares.

Helophilus affinis Wahlberg, 1844

Biology

The larvae are undescribed. According to Speight (1998), it is associated with small water bodies in unimproved grassland, acid fen and the edges of raised bogs. Adults hover over small pools.

Distribution

This species was recently added to the British list by Stuke (1996), based on a single specimen in the Royal Museum of Scotland collected by A B Duncan in August 1982 on Fair Isle, and originally identified as *H. hybridus*. It has been rapidly extending its range southwards from Scandinavia and northern Europe in recent decades. It has been recorded regularly from Denmark (previously only isolated specimens), and for the first time in the Netherlands and north-west Germany since 1980 and recently in south-west Germany and Switzerland (Speight 1998). Speight (1988a) predicted its occurrence in Britain, and gives a key to separate it from the other British members of the genus.

Helophilus groenlandicus (Fabricius, 1780)

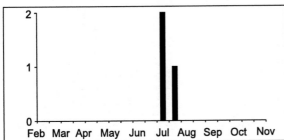

Biology
The larva is unknown. Adult habits are little known, but it is an insect of tundra bogs.

Distribution
This species is known only from a very few specimens from the north-west coast of Scotland and the Inner Hebrides, although there are as yet unconfirmed recent records from the Isle of Man (Thorpe quoted in Stubbs (1996)). This is a species with a northern Holarctic distribution, occurring in Norway, the Baltic countries, northern Russia, northern Siberia, Greenland and North America from Nova Scotia to Alaska and the mountainous parts of Canada and the USA (but not recorded from Iceland) (Speight 1998). Its status in Britain is not known. It is possibly established in remote areas of north-western Scotland where field recorders are few, or could be a vagrant from further north, although it is unusual for vagrants to be recorded mainly from the north-west.

Helophilus hybridus Loew, 1846

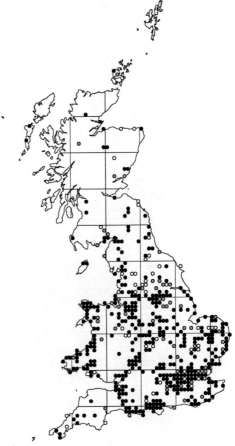

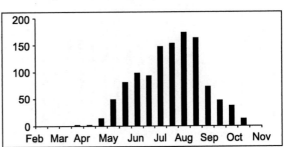

Biology
The larvae are of the 'long-tailed' aquatic type, associated with wet, decaying organic matter, particularly accumulations of decaying vegetation at the edges of ponds and ditches. They have been recorded from decaying rhizomes of *Typha*. Usually found in the richer types of wetland including fen, coastal marshes and wet woodland. Adults seem to stay close to water and are usually swept from, or found visiting flowers, in tall vegetation fringing wetlands.

Distribution
A widespread but local species which seems not to stray far from breeding habitat.

Helophilus pendulus (Linnaeus, 1758)

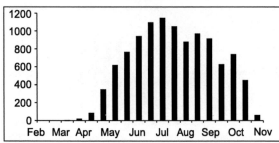

Biology

Larvae are of the 'long-tailed' aquatic type and can be found in almost any enriched, wet or semi-liquid medium ranging from waterlogged, rotting vegetation at the edges of ponds and ditches to water-filled tree hollows, water-butts, wet compost heaps, slurry pits and even in cow-dung. Adults appear to be very mobile and can be found almost anywhere, frequently well away from water, and visiting a wide range of flowers from ground vegetation to tree-flowers. They are frequent visitors to garden flowers.

Distribution

One of the most widespread and common British hoverflies. Speight (1998) describes it as 'anthropogenic and ubiquitous in some regions of Europe because of its ability to use a wide range of standing water and sub-aqueous habitats'.

Helophilus trivittatus (Fabricius, 1805)

Helophilus parallelus (Harris, 1776) in Kloet and Hincks (1976)

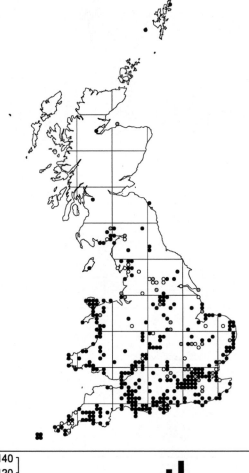

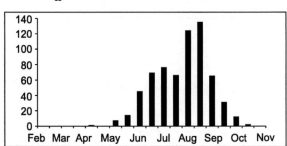

Biology

Larvae undescribed, but have been reared in captivity from eggs laid on an infusion of hay in water and from larvae found in semi-liquid mud mixed with animal dung. Speight (1998) describes it as a species of open wetlands including river-margins, seasonally flooded grassland and saltmarsh. Adults are found visiting a wide range of flowers, not infrequently well away from sites suitable for breeding.

Distribution

This is a very widespread but usually infrequent species, found only as single specimens. There is no obvious association with any particular habitat (some records coming from very dry habitats, quite unsuitable for breeding), but it is possibly more frequent near the coast. This pattern of occurrence suggests that it is very mobile and it is regarded as a migrant in continental Europe.

Heringia brevidens (Egger, 1865)

Neocnemodon brevidens (Egger) in Stubbs and Falk (1983)

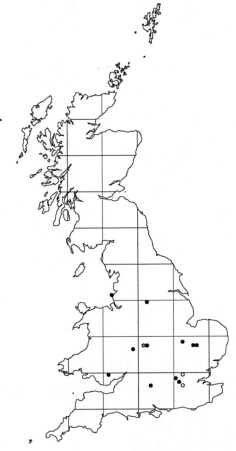

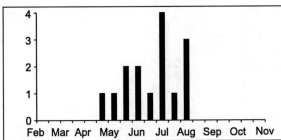

Biology

The larva is unknown. There is a possible association with poplar, including *Populus* and *Salix* fringing small ponds in woodland. Adults can be seen visiting flowers (eg *Caltha palustris*, *Rubus*), but they typically fly very close to the ground, making them very difficult to spot.

Distribution

This species was added to the British list in 1980, but specimens in collections date back to 1949. There are very few records, widely scattered in England and Wales.

Heringia heringi (Zetterstedt, 1843)

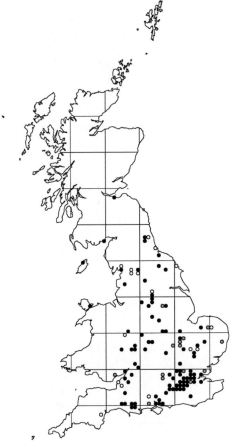

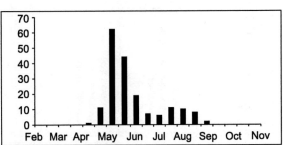

Biology

The larvae attack the gall-forming aphid *Schizoneura lanuginosa* on *Ulmus*, and have also been reared from aphid galls on *Populus* and *Salix*. This is a woodland species usually found resting on sunny vegetation in woodland rides, clearings and edges or in mature hedgerows. According to Speight (1998), adults prefer partially shaded situations and also visit flowers in partial shade. This species may have suffered a decline as a result of Dutch elm disease.

Distribution

A local species in southern England with scattered records further north and west to Lothian. Recent records suggest it is scarcer than was thought, but like most pipizines, it could be overlooked or ignored by many recorders.

Heringia latitarsis (Egger, 1865)

Cnemodon latitarsis Egger in Coe (1953), *Neocnemodon latitarsis* (Egger) in Stubbs and Falk (1983)

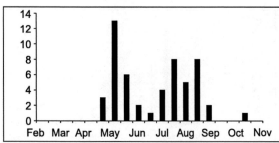

Biology

The larvae are aphidophagous and have been found attacking the woolly aphid *Dreyfusia picea* on *Abies*. It has also been found feeding on aphids on *Malus*, *Populus* and *Ulmus*. A species of mature coniferous and mixed woodlands. Adults can be found visiting flowers (eg *Anthriscus sylvestris*, *Prunus*, *Rubus*, *Rosa*) along woodland rides and edges and settled on sunlit leaves. Speight (1998) describes this species as largely arboreal, but descending to visit flowers.

Distribution

There are a few scattered records mainly in the southern half of Britain, including Wales, but one from Midlothian, Scotland.

Heringia pubescens Delucchi & Pschorn-Walcher, 1955

Neocnemodon pubescens Delucchi & Pschorn-Walcher in Stubbs and Falk (1983)

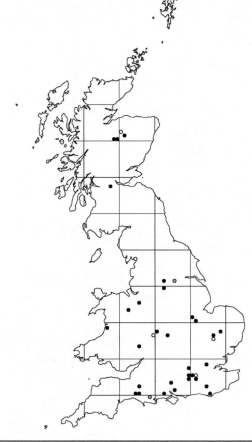

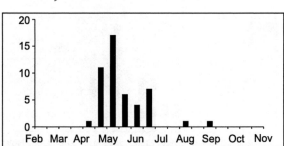

Biology

The larva is undescribed. The species is associated with a range of broad-leaved and mixed woodland and adults can be seen visiting flowers in woodland rides (for example, they were seen in abundance feeding on *Mercurialis perennis* pollen by Stubbs (1996)), but they typically fly very close to the ground, making them difficult to spot.

Distribution

There are few, scattered records, mostly from southern England, but also Wales, Yorkshire and the Scottish Highlands.

Heringia verrucula (Collin, 1931)

Cnemodon verrucula Collin in Coe (1953), *Neocnemodon verrucula* (Collin) in Stubbs and Falk (1983)

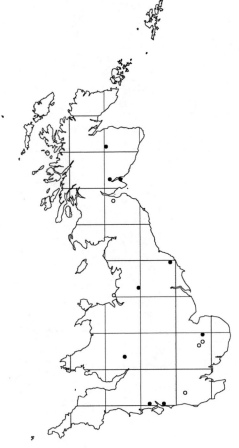

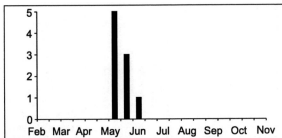

Biology
The larva is undescribed. Associated with a range of broad-leaved and mixed woodland. Adults fly rapidly amongst low vegetation along woodland rides and clearings. An early flying species which can be found visiting spring flowering shrubs such as *Salix*.

Distribution
Very few, widely scattered records north to the Scottish Highlands.

Heringia vitripennis (Meigen, 1822)

Cnemodon vitripennis Meigen in Coe (1953), *Neocnemodon vitripennis* (Meigen) in Stubbs and Falk (1983)

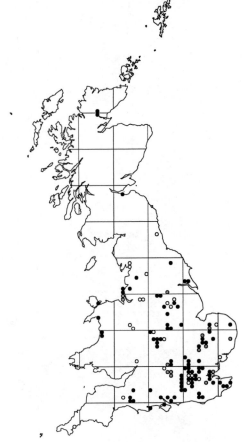

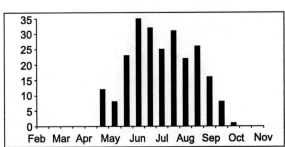

Biology
The larvae are predatory on adelgid bugs and have also been found attacking the woolly aphid *Dreyfusia picea* on *Abies,* and coccids on *Populus italica*. Associated with a range of woodland types including conifer plantations and even urban parks and mature gardens. Adults visit a range of low growing flowers, but also flowering shrubs. They have been caught in numbers in water traps set among *Rubus*.

Distribution
Though still infrequent, this is the least scarce member of the genus. Records are concentrated towards the south-east, but there are scattered records from Wales, northern England and Scotland. This species was separated from *H. pubescens* in 1955, before which, records of these two species were confused.

Lejogaster metallina (Fabricius, 1777)

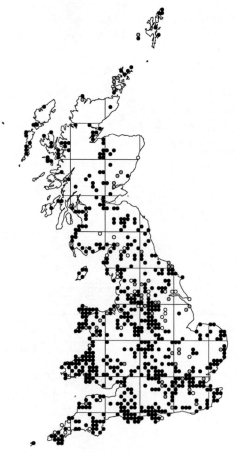

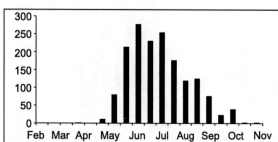

Biology
The larvae are aquatic and found amongst plant roots just below the water surface in slow flowing situations. Found in all types of open wetland habitats including wet meadows, marshes, fens and flushes (including mildly acidic conditions), especially where *Juncus* is abundant. Adults are frequently found visiting flowers, *Ranunculus* being especially favoured, usually close to breeding habitat.

Distribution
A widespread and frequent species in suitable localities throughout Britain.

Lejogaster tarsata (Megerle in Meigen, 1822)

Lejogaster splendida (Meigen) in Stubbs and Falk (1983)

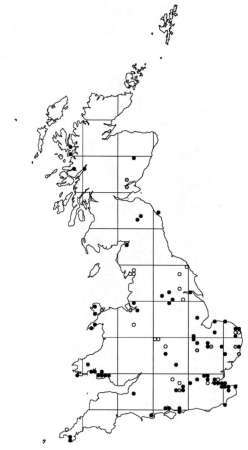

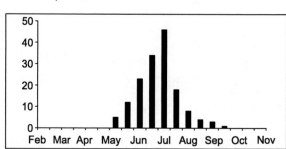

Biology
The larvae are aquatic and have been found amongst floating, decaying vegetation in a pond. Adults are most often found in or near coastal marshes, for example at the fringes of mildly brackish ditches, or in the transition zone between fresh and saline water in coastal flushes. They visit flowers, especially white umbels and *Ranunculus*.

Distribution
Although this is mainly a coastal species in Britain there are confirmed inland records, but confusion with *L. metallina* makes the distribution difficult to assess. It appears to be a scarce species generally, but can be abundant at some localities.

Lejops vittatus (Meigen, 1822)

Helophilus vittatus Meigen in Coe (1953)

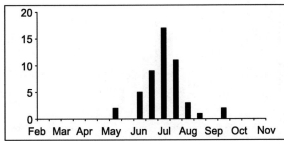

Biology

The larvae are aquatic. Speight (1998) quotes a German description of the development: eggs are apparently laid on stems and leaves of emergent plants. After hatching larvae remain at the water surface amongst floating plants until the last instar when they move into submerged organic ooze. In Britain, it is associated with stands of *Bolboschoenus maritimus* in grazing marsh ditches, from which adults can be swept. Adult females have been found feeding on the pollen of this plant (Stubbs 1996).

Distribution

A very local species of coastal grazing marshes, with most records from the Thames Marshes. There are also recent records from Norfolk (Halvergate Marshes), Kent (Romney Marsh), Sussex (Pevensey and Lewes Levels), Somerset (Somerset Levels and Bridgewater Bay) and Glamorgan (Gwent Levels). It is frequent where it occurs. Apparently not confined to coastal marshes elsewhere in Europe and there is a seemingly genuine inland record: an old, undated specimen in the Natural History Museum collection from Felden, Hertfordshire collected by A Piffard who lived and died in 1909.

Leucozona glaucia (Linnaeus, 1758)

Syrphus glaucius Linnaeus in Coe (1953)

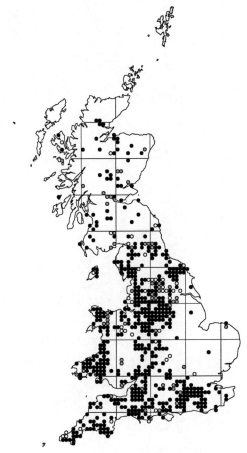

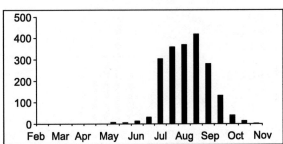

Biology

The larvae prey on ground layer aphids. A woodland species, typically found in clearings, rides, and tracksides, but also in tall vegetation along roadside hedgerows, scrub, etc. Adults are usually seen visiting flowers, especially white umbels such as *Heracleum* and *Angelica*,

Distribution

Widely distributed in well-wooded lowland areas throughout Britain, but possibly more of a northern and western species than *L. laternaria*. The gap in distribution in eastern England and East Anglia appears to be genuine, and not an artefact of recorder effort.

Leucozona laternaria (Müller, 1776)

Syrphus laternarius Mueller in Coe (1953)

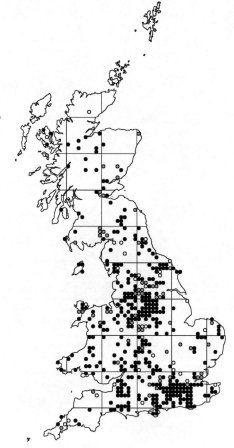

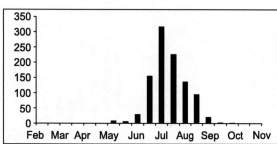

Biology
The larvae are associated with *Cavariella* aphids on white umbels. Its habits and requirements appear to be very similar to *L. glaucia* and the two are often found together on the same flowers.

Distribution
Like *L. glaucia*, this species is widely distributed in well-wooded lowland areas throughout Britain, and the two are often found together. Despite showing a similar gap in its distribution in eastern England, this is a more eastern species than *L. glaucia,* and is much less frequent in South Wales and the south-west peninsula than that species.

Leucozona lucorum (Linnaeus, 1758)

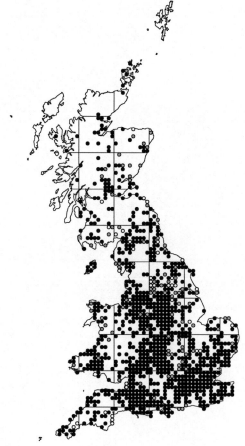

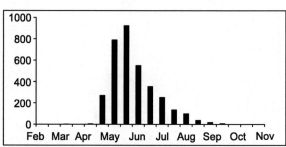

Biology
The larvae prey on ground layer aphids. Adults fly in dappled sunshine in situations such as woodland rides and edges, roadside verges and hedgerows, where they are often found in association with *Silene dioica* and *Stellaria holostea*.

Distribution
One of the characteristic hoverflies of early spring throughout lowland Britain, with an earlier flight period than the other *Leucozona* species. However, it can be found in small numbers throughout the summer suggesting a partial second brood.

Mallota cimbiciformis (Fallén, 1817)

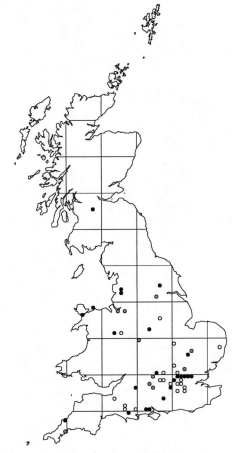

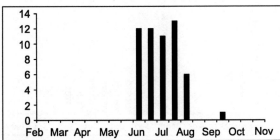

Biology
The larvae, which are of the 'long-tailed' type, are found in water-filled rot-holes in a wide range of broad-leaved trees, but often *Fagus* and *Castanea*. Holes of all sizes and positions on the tree are used, but there seems to be a preference for holes some metres above the ground with a narrow entrance. Several larvae may occur together in one hole. Adults are extremely convincing hive-bee mimics and elusive, but are sometimes found visiting flowers such as *Prunus lusitanica*, *Rubus* and *Rosa canina*.

Distribution
Scarce, but with records widely scattered over southern Britain north to a line between the Humber and the Mersey, and with recent records from North Yorkshire and the Clyde Valley (Barr 1996). There does not seem to be a strong association with woodland, and isolated large trees provide suitable breeding sites even in urban areas. Adults are probably under-recorded, and presence at a site may be better established by searching for larvae.

Melangyna arctica (Zetterstedt, 1838)

Syrphus arcticus Zetterstedt in Coe (1953)

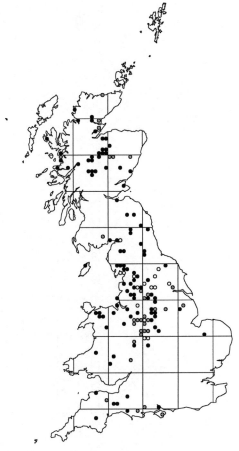

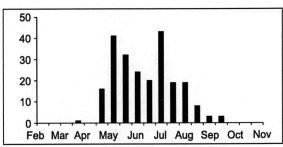

Biology
The larvae are aphidophagous, appearing to have a clear preference for *Pterocallis ulnii* on *Alnus*. Adults usually fly around foliage and flowers in trees, but can also be found visiting flowers at ground level. They usually occur in or near woodland, both coniferous and broad-leaved.

Distribution
This is mainly a northern species with most records from Scotland and northern England. There are scattered records throughout Britain except for the East Midlands and extreme south-east England.

Melangyna barbifrons (Fallén, 1817)

Syrphus barbifrons Fallén in Coe (1953)

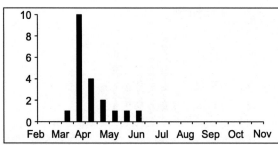

Biology
The larvae are aphidophagous, members of this genus appearing usually to have close associations with one, or a few, aphid species. Adults usually occur in broad-leaved woodland, and are among the species which can be found visiting *Salix* blossom in the early spring.

Distribution
There are scattered records throughout Great Britain. This is likely to be an under-recorded species on account of its early emergence period.

Melangyna cincta (Fallén, 1817)

Syrphus cinctus Fallén in Coe (1953)

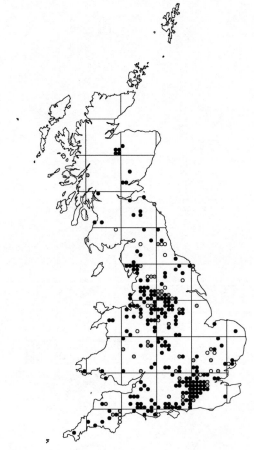

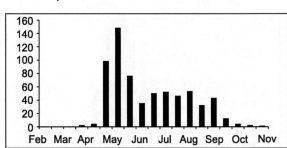

Biology
The larvae are aphidophagous, appearing to have a clear preference for *Phyllaphis fagi* on *Fagus*, but with records from aphids on *Quercus*, *Acer* and *Tilia*. This is a species of broad-leaved woodlands, typically found in glades, rides and edges, but can also occur around scrub and mature hedges. Adults are usually seen visiting flowers and are especially fond of white umbels along wooded tracksides. Males hover at some height over tracks and clearings in woodland.

Distribution
Widespread and locally common.

Melangyna compositarum (Verrall, 1873)

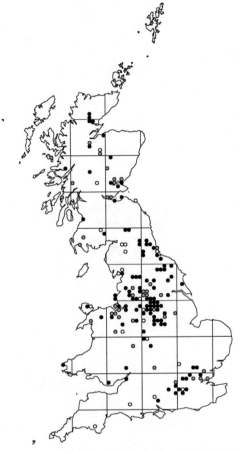

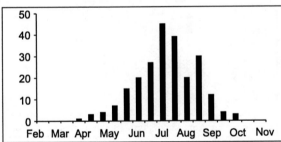

Biology
The larva is unknown. Adults are associated with coniferous woodlands and plantations where they can be found visiting flowers, especially *Heracleum* and *Angelica*, in rides and glades. Males hover fairly high at the edges of stands of trees.

Distribution
There is considerable confusion between this species and *M. labiatarum* and many recorders do not attempt to distinguish between the two. This species is said to be the more northerly of the pair, with fewer records from southern England and Wales.

Melangyna ericarum (Collin, 1946)

Syrphus ericarum Collin in Coe (1953)

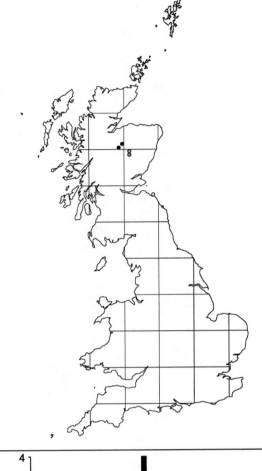

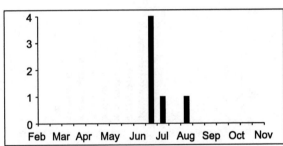

Biology
The larva is unknown. Associated with native *Pinus* woodlands in the Scottish Highlands. Adults can be swept or found visiting flowers in open rides where they fly low down over the bare edges of tracks and clearings.

Distribution
A species of the Caledonian pine forests.

Melangyna labiatarum (Verrall, 1901)

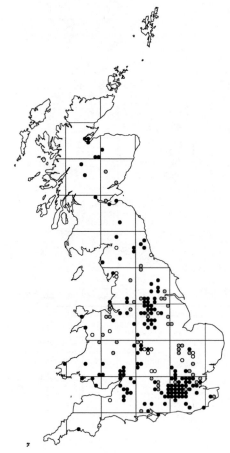

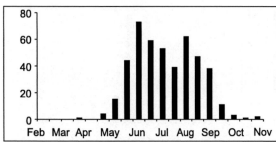

Biology
The larvae are aphidophagous, members of this genus appearing usually to have close associations with one, or a few, aphid species. Adults are usually found in woodland where they visit flowers, especially *Heracleum* and *Angelica*, in open glades and rides.

Distribution
There is considerable confusion between this species and *M. compositarum* and many recorders do not attempt to separate them. This species is believed to have the more southerly distribution of the two, and is common in well-wooded lowland districts of England and Wales. There are scattered Scottish records, but their validity is open to question.

Melangyna lasiophthalma (Zetterstedt, 1843)

Syrphus lasiophthalmus Zetterstedt in Coe (1953)

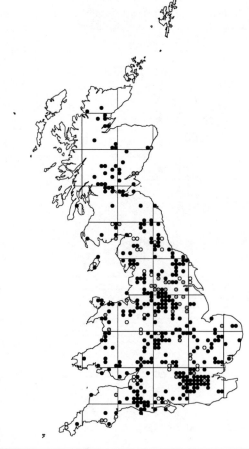

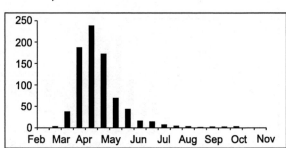

Biology
The larvae are aphidophagous. This is a characteristic species of woods, both broad-leaved and coniferous, in the early spring, where they visit the flowers of trees, such as *Salix*, and ground layer species, like yellow composites, *Ranunculus* and *Allium*. Males hover in clearings and over tracks. Both sexes can be found settled on sunlit tree trunks.

Distribution
Widely distributed in well-wooded areas throughout Britain. Often abundant where it occurs.

Melangyna quadrimaculata (Verrall, 1873)

Syrphus quadrimaculatus Verrall in Coe (1953)

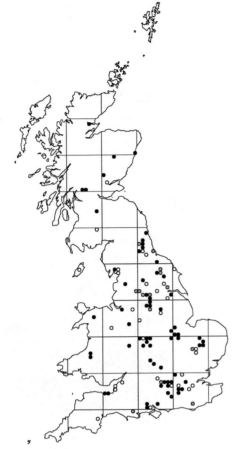

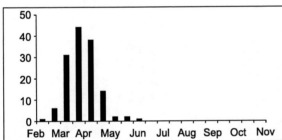

Biology

The larvae are aphidophagous, and appear to have a clear preference for adelgids on *Abies*. A woodland species which overwinters as a puparium. Adults are active very early in the spring when they usually visit flowering trees such as *Salix* and *Corylus* catkins in clearings and rides. According to Speight (1998) they are associated with mature broad-leaved woodland where overmature trees are present and normally visit taller trees in flower when these are available.

Distribution

Scarce but widely distributed. Possibly under-recorded because of its early flight period.

Melangyna umbellatarum (Fabricius, 1787)

Syrphus umbellatarum Fabricius in Coe (1953)

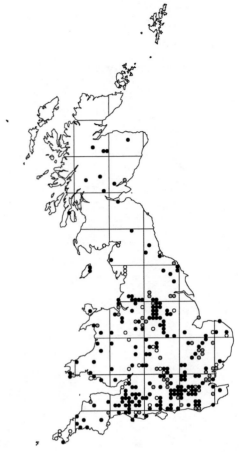

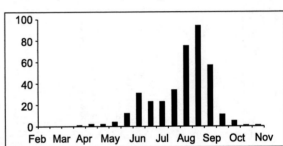

Biology

The larvae are aphidophagous, and appear to have a clear preference for *Cavariella* aphids on white umbels. Adults are usually found in or near woodland, especially on the flowers of *Heracleum* and *Angelica*. Males hover high over paths and clearings. Speight (1998) states that this species is associated with wet woodland: 'forest streams with *Salix*; *Salix* carr; beside streams and rivers fringed with *Salix*'.

Distribution

Scarce in the southern half of Britain, rare in northern England, but extending into central Scotland. This species can be confused with *M. compositarum* and *M. labiatarum* and is very difficult to separate from *M. ericarum*, so care is needed.

Melanogaster aerosa (Loew, 1843)

Chrysogaster macquarti Loew in Stubbs and Falk (1983)

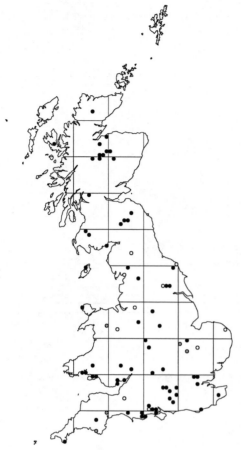

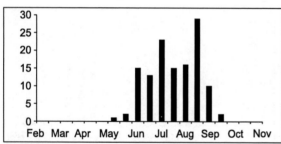

Biology

The larvae are aquatic living beneath the surface of semi-liquid, enriched mud near plant roots where there is no water movement. Larvae typically occur in acid bogs and flushes and around small moorland streams, although they may also be associated with ditches on alluvial levels. Adults are usually swept, or found visiting flowers, close to water.

Distribution

This mainly northern and western species is widespread in acid areas but rarely abundant. Care is needed with identification, as this species is difficult to separate from *M. hirtella*, which often occurs in similar places but flies later in the year.

Melanogaster hirtella Loew, 1843

Chrysogaster hirtella (Loew) in Stubbs and Falk (1983)

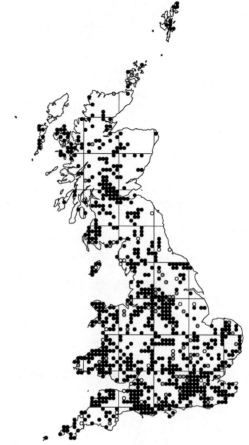

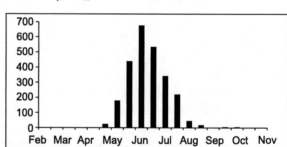

Biology

The larvae are aquatic, inhabiting mud adjacent to emergent plants such as *Typha* and *Glyceria*, but especially favouring *Caltha palustris*, usually at the edges of running water. They have modified hind spiracles which are used to gain access to the air spaces in the submerged parts of emergent plants. Found in marshes or near the margins of running water where there is lush emergent vegetation. Adults are usually swept from waterside vegetation or found visiting flowers, especially white umbels, *Caltha*, *Iris*, *Menyanthes*, *Ranunculus*, etc.

Distribution

Widespread and common. According to Speight (1998) this is very much an Atlantic seaboard species which is quite scarce in central and southern Europe.

Melanostoma dubium (Zetterstedt, 1838)

Melanostoma mellinum var. *dubium* Verrall *nec* Zetterstedt in Coe (1953)

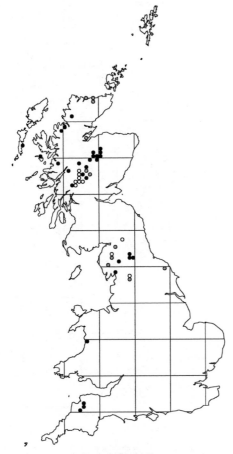

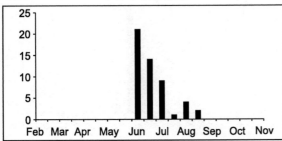

Biology
The larvae remain unknown, but other members of this genus are suspected to be general predators in leaf litter. Adults are found in mountainous areas, and recent work by MacGowan and Rotheray (quoted in Stubbs (1996)) suggests that there is an altitudinal cline between *M. mellinum* at lower altitude and *M. dubium* higher up. This might suggest that these are ecotypes of the same species, but opinion among European workers is divided.

Distribution
This is an upland species which occurs above about 460 m in northern and western Britain.

Melanostoma mellinum (Linnaeus, 1758)

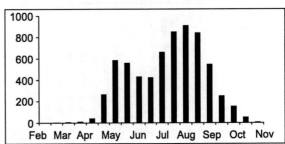

Biology
There are isolated observations of larval feeding on a wide range of prey species, including torpid adult flies *Musca domestica* and *Paregle cinerella*. They have been reared on aphids in the laboratory, but when these are not available they will readily take other prey, including *Tortrix* larvae, and even rotting chickweed! The normal habits of larvae in the field remain unknown, but they are suspected to be general predators in leaf litter, and are reported to be nocturnal. Occurs in a variety of grassy situations, preferring damp locations, and gravid females show a preference for shady places. Adults fly low among the vegetation and can be found visiting flowers, usually near ground level. Frequent at wind-pollinated flowers such as Poaceae and *Plantago*.

Distribution
One of the most abundant and widespread hoverflies throughout Britain, occurring in all types of grassy situation, including in the uplands, where it is often abundant in damp places such as flushes and damp meadows.

Melanostoma scalare (Fabricius, 1794)

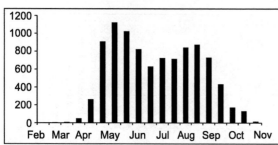

Biology
Although the larvae have been reared on aphids in the laboratory, their normal habits in the field remain unknown. They are suspected, however, to be general predators in leaf litter. Occurs in a variety of open grassy situations, preferring damper places. Adults are found flying low down amongst ground vegetation and visiting a wide range of flowers, including wind-pollinated flowers such as Poaceae and *Plantago*.

Distribution
Widespread and common in grassy situations throughout Britain, but not normally found in mountainous or moorland locations.

Melanostoma form A *sensu* Stubbs (1983)

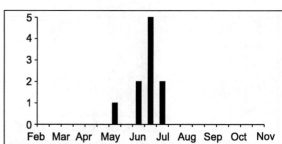

Biology
Biology unknown. Suggested by MacGowan and Rotheray (quoted in Stubbs (1996)) to be part of an altitudinal cline between *M. mellinum* at low altitude and *M. dubium* at high altitude, this form representing an intermediate ecotype.

Distribution
Based on a series taken in the Cairngorms along the tree line in Glen Einich, but there are a few similar specimens in the Natural History Museum collection from central Scotland. There is a museum specimen, apparently labelled as this species, collected from Lancashire.

Meligramma euchromum (Kowarz, 1885)

Syrphus euchromus Kowarz in Coe (1953), *Epistrophe euchroma* (Kowarz) in Stubbs and Falk (1983)

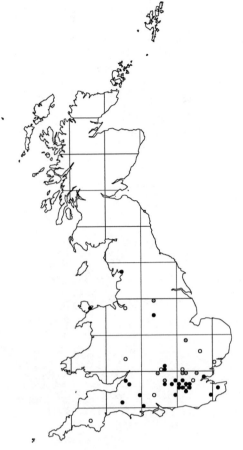

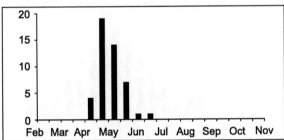

Biology
The larvae are aphidophagous, and are mainly associated with trees (particularly fruit trees) and shrubs. Adults are usually found in or around woodland or scrub, and are most often seen basking on sunlit foliage, especially *Acer pseudoplatanus* and *Aesculus hippocastanum* leaves. A specimen was reared from a puparium found in a suburban garden in Surrey (G Collins, pers. comm.).

Distribution
A rare species with few records, mainly from the south-east, but extending north to north-west England. Although possibly overlooked amongst other black and yellow species, this appears to be a genuinely elusive hoverfly and it is possible that adults spend much of their time out of reach in the canopy.

Meligramma guttatum (Fallén, 1817)

Syrphus guttatus Fallén in Coe (1953), *Melangyna guttata* (Fallén) in Stubbs and Falk (1983)

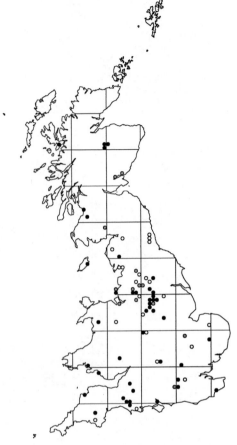

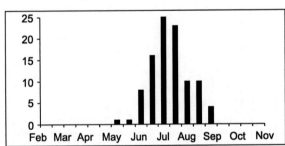

Biology
The larvae are aphidophagous, and have been reared from aphids on *Acer pseudoplatanus*. Usually found in woodland, especially wooded river banks, wet woodland and carr, where *Salix* or *Alnus* occurs. Adults are found in clearings where they visit flowers, especially white umbels.

Distribution
Records are few but widely scattered. In the field, this species appears very similar to common *Platycheirus* species (eg *P. albimanus*, *P. scutatus*) and is probably overlooked.

Meligramma trianguliferum (Zetterstedt, 1843)

Syrphus triangulifer Zetterstedt in Coe (1953), *Melangyna triangulifera* (Zetterstedt) in Stubbs and Falk (1983)

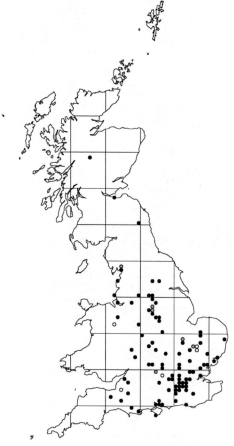

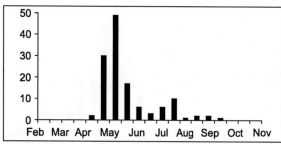

Biology
The larvae, which are convincingly camouflaged as bird droppings (see photograph in Rotheray (1994)), feed on a range of aphids on trees, especially fruit trees and shrubs. Generally found around trees along woodland rides and edges or amongst scrub, including isolated patches of scrub on heathland and moorland. Adults are elusive and may be arboreal, but can be found visiting flowers, especially white umbels.

Distribution
Scarce but widely distributed in England, with a tendency to be more frequent in the south. There are very few, widely scattered records in northern England, Wales and Scotland.

Meliscaeva auricollis (Meigen, 1822)

Syrphus auricollis Meigen in Coe (1953)

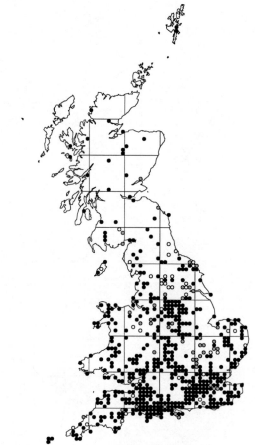

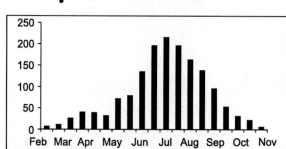

Biology
The larvae can be found feeding on aphids on shrubs such as *Berberis* and *Sarothamnus*, and also on the flowers and stems of white umbels. They have also been found with the psyllid *Psylla alni* on *Alnus glutinosa*. Typically found near trees (broad-leaved and coniferous) along woodland rides and edges, large hedgerows, in mature gardens, etc. Adults are found at a wide range of flowers, but are perhaps equally frequently seen settled on sunlit foliage. Males hover over tracks and around projecting, sunlit branches of trees.

Distribution
Common and widely distributed in the south, becoming scarcer further north, but recorded from Scotland.

Meliscaeva cinctella (Zetterstedt, 1843)

Syrphus cinctellus Zetterstedt in Coe (1953)

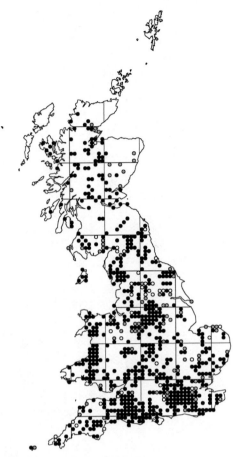

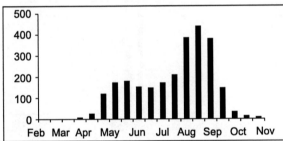

Biology

The larvae feed on aphids on a variety of tree species including *Quercus*, *Picea*, *Pinus*, *Malus* and *Sambucus*. Normally found near trees (broad-leaved and coniferous) along woodland rides and edges, in open scrub, etc, where they visit flowers, including tree blossoms in the spring and white umbels, amongst many others, in the summer.

Distribution

A widespread and common species, perhaps more abundant in the south.

Merodon equestris (Fabricius, 1794)

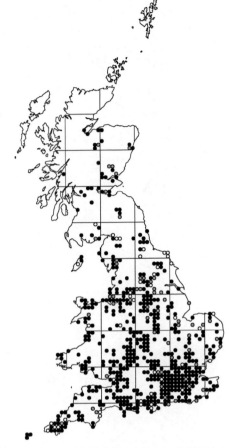

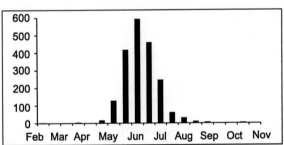

Biology

The larvae of this species (the 'greater bulb fly'), tunnel in the bulbs of many plants, especially cultivated daffodils *Narcissus*, and are regarded as a pest by some gardeners. Adults visit flowers close to breeding sites and can often be seen resting and mating on the leaves of larval foodplants. Frequently settles on stones or patches of bare ground in the sunshine. Several colour forms are recognised.

Distribution

This species is widespread and common in gardens. Whilst the distribution shows an urban tendency, this fly is not restricted to synanthropic habitats; wild bluebell *Hyacinthoides non-scripta* bulbs, for example, provide an equally acceptable larval food. It is believed to have been accidentally introduced in imported bulbs some time towards the end of the last century; Bloomfield (1895) states that it 'used to be considered a very rare British insect, but is now becoming common'. R McLachlan, in a footnote to that paper, noted that a horticulturist friend introduced it to his garden by an 'unlucky purchase' of a bag of bulbs from the south of Europe. It belongs to a large genus with many other European species, especially in the eastern Mediterranean, and it is quite possible that other species could arrive by a similar route (see Speight (1988a) for a discussion of the possibilities).

Microdon analis (Macquart, 1842)

Microdon eggeri Mik in Stubbs and Falk (1983)

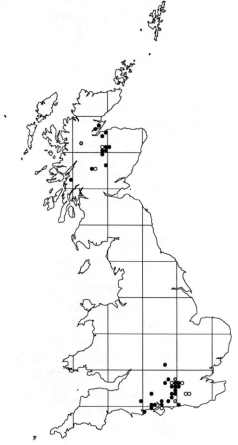

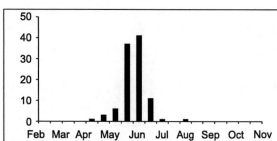

Biology

The very distinctive larvae live in ant nests. They are hemispherical in shape and heavily armoured, and prey on the eggs and larvae of *Lasius niger* or ants of the *Formica rufa* group, under the bark of stumps or decaying trunks of *Betula* or *Pinus*, usually on heathland. Their feeding behaviour is described by Barr (1995). The pupae are of a similar shape and are also armoured. Adults are rarely seen, and the species is most frequently recorded by searching for larvae and pupae.

Distribution

This species has a disjunct distribution. It occurs in the south of England on the heaths of the London Basin, the Weald, the New Forest and Dorset, and also in heathy valleys in Central Scotland.

Microdon devius (Linnaeus, 1761)

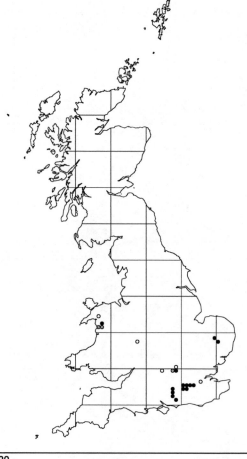

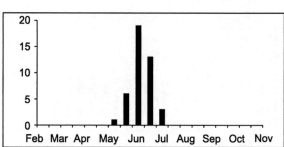

Biology

The very distinctive larvae live in ant nests. They are hemispherical in shape and heavily armoured, and prey on the eggs and larvae of *Lasius flavus* in nests usually on chalk grassland. The pupae are of similar shape and are also armoured. Adults are elusive and usually encountered as single specimens when sweeping chalk grassland.

Distribution

A rare species mainly found on chalk grassland in southern England, especially the Downs of Surrey and Hampshire, from which the great majority of records originate. It has also been recorded from fens at Cothill in Oxfordshire, and Redgrave and Middle Harling in Suffolk, with a number of records both old and recent from the first two localities suggesting well established populations. There are a few records from North Wales, including one recent, and a 19th century specimen in The Natural History Museum collection from Wyre Forest.

Microdon mutabilis (Linnaeus, 1758)

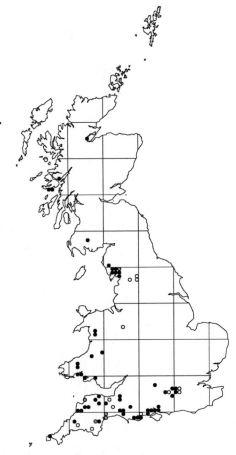

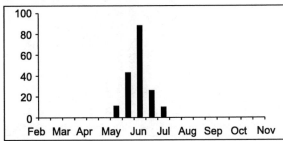

Biology
The very distinctive larvae live in ant nests. They are hemispherical in shape, heavily armoured and prey on the eggs and larvae of a variety of ant species including *Formica lemani* Bondroit, *F. fusca* Linnaeus, *Lasius niger* Linnaeus and *Myrmica ruginodis* Nylander often, but not exclusively, in wet or boggy situations. Their feeding behaviour is described by Barr (1995). On Mull, an average of 5.5 larvae per nest of *F. lemani* were recorded over a 10 year period (Barr 1995). The pupae are of similar shape and are also armoured. Adults are usually seen hovering low over paths or other bare areas in boggy heathland, wet meadows and dune slacks.

Distribution
The most widely distributed species of the genus, occurring down the west coast of Britain from Scotland through north-west England and Wales to the south-west peninsula, where it is perhaps most frequent. It also occurs on wet heath in Surrey, the New Forest and Dorset.

Myathropa florea (Linnaeus, 1758)

Myiatropa florea Linnaeus in Coe (1953)

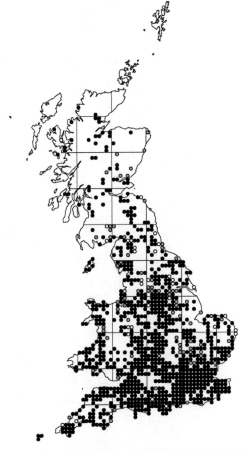

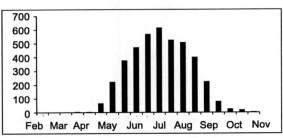

Biology
This is the most abundant and least choosy of the hoverflies associated with decaying wood. The larvae, which are of the 'long-tailed' aquatic type, occur in any situation where wet wood debris are present, such as water-filled hollows containing decaying leaf and wood detritus, and decaying roots deep underground. They can also develop in cow-dung. They will readily use artificial breeding sites consisting of containers of water mixed with rotted sawdust or woodland litter. Adults disperse widely and visit a variety of flowers. Males hover in the canopy, making a loud, high-pitched buzz. They are often seen in gardens.

Distribution
Widespread and common throughout Britain.

Myolepta dubia (Fabricius, 1805)

Myolepta luteola (Gmelin) in Stubbs and Falk (1983)

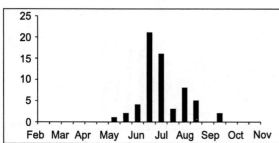

Biology

The larvae live in rot-holes in broad-leaved trees, including *Fagus* and *Quercus*. The larvae in a given rot-hole may be of very mixed sizes, suggesting they require more than one year to complete development. Tends to be found in or near ancient broad-leaved woodland, but has also been found in fenland in East Anglia (eg Wicken Fen) and a chalk-pit in Essex. This suggests that isolated trees in hedgerows and similar situations can provide suitable larval habitat. Adults can be found visiting flowers such as white umbels, usually in partial shade, and also sitting on leaves in dappled sunshine. Overwinters as larvae.

Distribution

A scarce species recorded from south and south-east England, from Somerset and Dorset to East Anglia.

Myolepta potens (Harris, 1780)

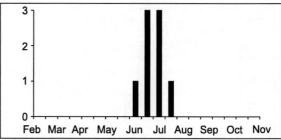

Biology

The larvae live in water-filled rot-holes in ancient broad-leaved trees, including *Fagus*, *Quercus* and *Populus* and probably take several years to reach maturity. Little is known of the adult habits, but they are presumed to be similar to *M. dubia*.

Distribution

See introduction for a summary of the history of this very rare species in Britain. Only known from two very restricted areas in Somerset and most of the 20 known British specimens date from the 1940s. It was last found in 1961 and is feared extinct. Appears to be a rare species throughout its known range.

Neoascia geniculata (Meigen, 1822)

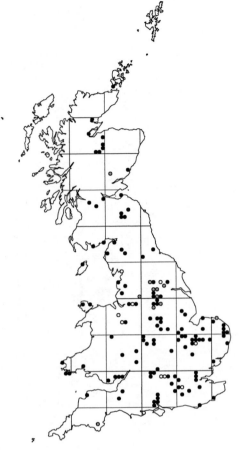

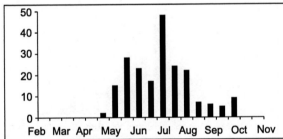

Biology
The small, semi-aquatic larvae have been found in decaying vegetation around the margins of ponds. Usually swept from lush emergent vegetation, such as *Glyceria*, around ponds and ditches. Adults visit flowers, especially *Ranunculus*, but do not seem to move far from larval habitat.

Distribution
This is a difficult species to identify and may be under-recorded. It appears to be widely distributed and is often abundant in suitable habitat.

Neoascia interrupta (Meigen, 1822)

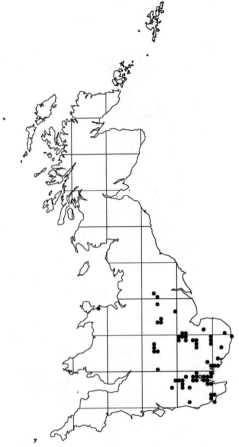

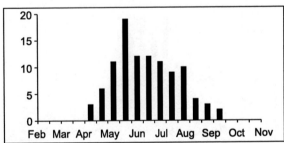

Biology
The larva of this species remains unknown, but other members of the genus are semi-aquatic, inhabiting wet organic matter. Adults are usually swept from lush vegetation around ponds and ditches, especially *Typha*. They have been found around mildly brackish ditches in grazing levels, in fenland and around richer ponds and ditches well inland. Speight (1998) notes that this species is largely coastal in the northern part of its European range.

Distribution
This species was only added to the British list in 1981, but has subsequently been recorded quite widely in the south-east of England, including East Anglia, and northwards to north Wales, Lincolnshire and South Yorkshire.

Neoascia meticulosa (Scopoli, 1763)

Neoascia aenea (Meigen, 1822) in Coe (1953) and Kloet and Hincks (1976)

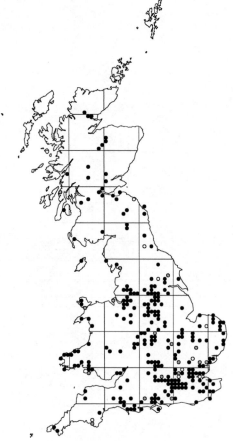

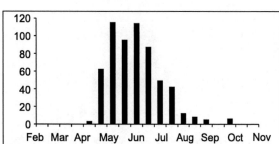

Biology
Both larvae and pupae have been found on *Typha*, the larvae between the submerged leaf sheaths, the pupae on plants growing on a floating mat of vegetation. Aduls are normally found among lush vegetation such as *Typha* and *Glyceria*, fringing wetlands and visit a variety of flowers.

Distribution
Widespread and locally abundant in suitable habitat, with a tendency for records to be more frequent from eastern Britain.

Neoascia obliqua Coe, 1940

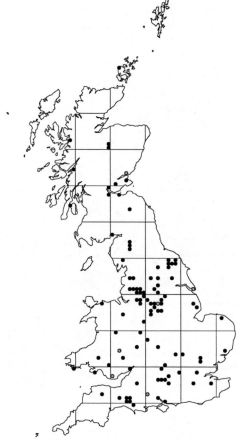

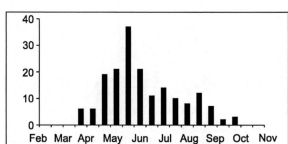

Biology
The larva of this species remains unknown, but other members of the genus are semi-aquatic, inhabiting accumulations of wet, organic matter. Found amongst lush vegetation in marshes and water margins in sheltered locations, such as at the edges of wet woods and wooded streams.

Distribution
Widely distributed but generally scarce, with most records from northern England and Scotland. Recent observations suggest that this can be the most frequently encountered member of the genus in some parts of Derbyshire and Yorkshire, where it is possibly associated with beds of *Petasites* (D Whiteley, pers. comm.; Stubbs 1996).

Neoascia podagrica (Fabricius, 1775)

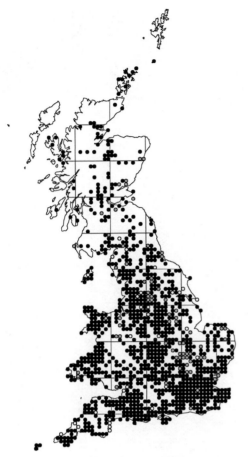

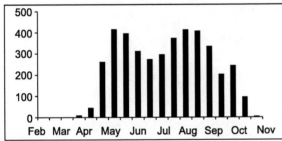

Biology
The small, semi-aquatic larvae have been found in wet manure in a farmyard, cow-dung and wet compost. They seem to be able to utilise a wide range of situations where highly nutrient-enriched, semi-aquatic conditions are present. Adults can be found in any habitat where there is lush vegetation, typically in hedgerows, woodland edges, gardens (where it is presumably breeding in compost heaps) and around the margins of water. They are typically found by sweeping, but will visit a wide range of flowers. Males hover near to flowers in bloom.

Distribution
A widespread and very common species.

Neoascia tenur (Harris, 1780)

Neoascia dispar (Meigen, 1822) in Coe (1953) and Kloet and Hincks (1976)

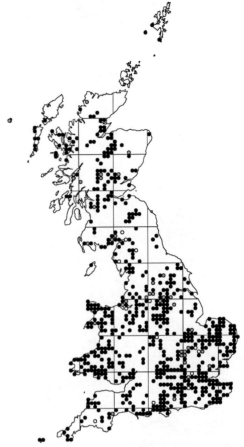

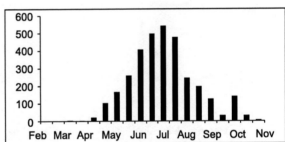

Biology
Larvae have been found at about the level of the water surface within the stem sheaths of dead *Typha* in a slow flowing stream. As an adult, this is probably the most frequently encountered member of the genus, occurring in lush vegetation around the margins of all types of water body, especially where beds of emergent plants such as *Glyceria*, *Typha* or *Phragmites* are present. Adults are most often found by sweeping such vegetation, but will visit a wide range of flowers.

Distribution
Widespread in wetlands throughout Britain, and often extremely abundant in suitable habitat.

Orthonevra brevicornis Loew, 1843

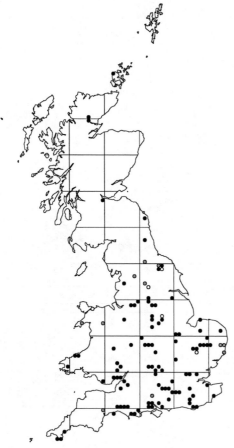

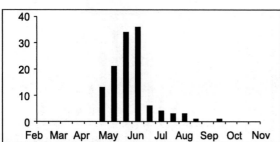

Biology
The larvae are aquatic, living in accumulations of decaying vegetation, especially in mesotrophic or base-rich seepages in fens, meadows and occasionally woods. Adults can be found in marshes and fens.

Distribution
This scarce species is widely distributed in England, though possibly more frequent towards the south and east. There are scattered records from both Scotland and Wales.

Orthonevra geniculata Meigen, 1830

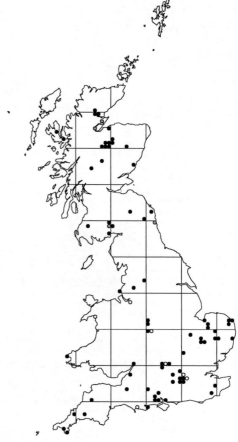

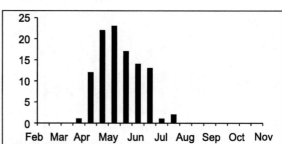

Biology
The larva of this species remains unknown, but is presumed to be aquatic like others of the genus. Generally found in mildly acid, boggy areas in Scotland, but also in fens in East Anglia and on heathland with base influences in southern Britain. Adults are usually found close to water where they will visit flowers, but also settle on bare patches and dead vegetation in the sun.

Distribution
A scarce species, found most frequently in central Scotland, but with scattered records in England. It appears to be closely associated with acid heaths in Surrey (Morris 1998).

Orthonevra nobilis (Fallén, 1817)

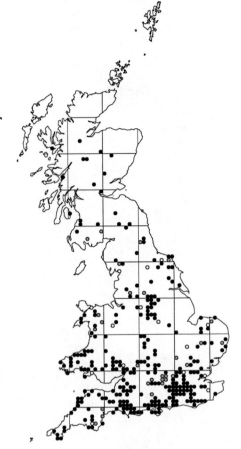

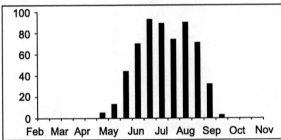

Biology

The larvae are aquatic and have been found in organically enriched mud in springs and flushes. Adults are usually found by sweeping lush vegetation in marshes and fens, but they can also be seen visiting flowers. Occasionally found well away from wetlands.

Distribution

Widespread in wetlands throughout Britain, but most frequent in southern lowland areas. Adults appear to be very mobile and can be found well away from wet sites.

Paragus albifrons (Fallén, 1817)

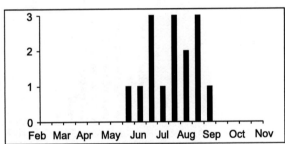

Biology

The larvae feed on a range of ground layer and arboreal aphids and have been found on *Cirsium arvense*, *Carduus* and *Onopordon*. Torp (1994) also mentions *Ononis repens* as a plant on which larvae have been found. Adults are secretive and hard to find, but have generally been taken in coastal localities, including flood embankments around grazing marsh and coastal shingle. Speight (1998) states that it is only active in early morning or late evening, under warm conditions, and flies within stands of taller grasses etc, along the edges of paths and in clearings.

Distribution

A rare species. The very few records are from the south coast between Dorset and Essex, with a 19th century record from near Ipswich, Suffolk. There are apparently inland specimens from Guildford (19th century) and Salisbury (1950) in the Hope Museum collection. The most recent records come from the Thames Marshes (in both Essex and Kent) and Hythe (Hampshire). This species was present on the Isle of Portland between 1890 and 1950, but recent attempts to re-locate it there have so far been unsuccessful.

Paragus haemorrhous Meigen, 1822

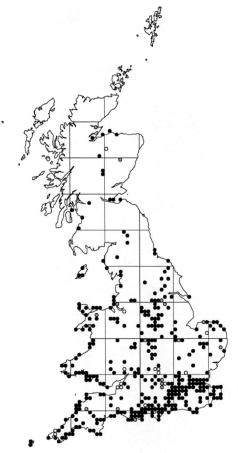

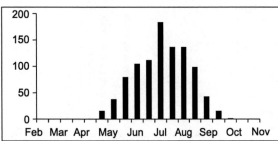

Biology

The larvae feed on a range of ground layer and arboreal aphids. Adults are generally found resting on, or hovering above, bare ground along tracks and paths in a variety of situations including grassland, sandy heath, dunes and coastal cliffs. They can occasionally be seen visiting flowers. Males patrol sunny patches and stands of flowers.

Distribution

Much the commonest member of the genus, but probably overlooked by many recorders. It is perhaps most frequent on chalk grassland in southern England, and in coastal habitats all around southern Britain. It is scarcer elsewhere, but with records extending to northern Scotland.

Paragus tibialis (Fallén, 1817)

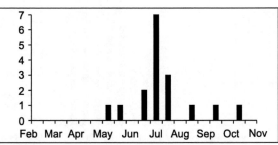

Biology

The larvae feed on a range of ground layer and arboreal aphids. In Britain, adults appear to be restricted to dry heathland, where they behave in a very similar way to *P. haemorrhous*, the two species sometimes occurring together. A very similar species, *P. constrictus* Simic, has recently been recognised from limestone pavement in the Burren, Ireland (mentioned under *P. tibialis* in Stubbs and Falk (1983)), and any specimens from limestone pavement in north-west England should be checked for this species.

Distribution

A rare species of dry heathland in southern Britain, which may be overlooked amongst the much commoner *P. haemorrhous*. Before the revision by Speight (1978), the only species recognised in this genus in Britain were *P. albifrons* and *P. tibialis*, but earlier specimens which have been checked have mostly proved to be *P. haemorrhous*. Consequently, all pre-1978 records must be considered suspect unless specimens are available and have been re-examined.

Parasyrphus annulatus (Zetterstedt, 1838)

Syrphus annulatus Zetterstedt in Coe (1953)

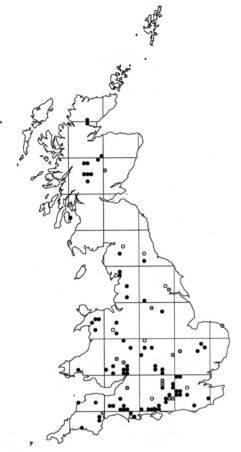

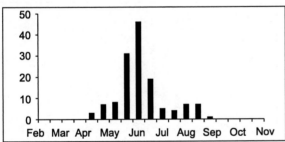

Biology

The larva is not described, but those of this genus are usually arboreal predators on adelgids and pine aphids. Normally found in larger woods, usually with some coniferisation. Adults are generally found visiting flowers, or settled on sunlit vegetation and are fairly distinctive, being noticeably smaller than other black and yellow syrphines.

Distribution

Very local (but sometimes abundant where it occurs) in woods in southern and central England, with scattered records throughout most of mainland Britain, north to south-east Sutherland.

Parasyrphus lineola (Zetterstedt, 1843)

Syrphus lineola Zetterstedt in Coe (1953)

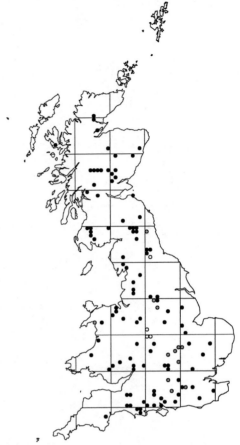

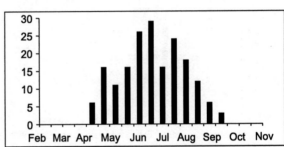

Biology

The larvae are arboreal predators on adelgids and aphids and have been found in the crowns of *Picea*. It has also been bred from a puparium found under the bark of *Picea abies*. Adults are usually found in or near conifer forests and plantations (*Pinus*, *Picea* and *Abies*) where they may be largely arboreal, but descend to feed on flowers in rides and clearings.

Distribution

Widespread and locally common. This species is probably more frequent in the north and west, extending to northern Scotland, but also occurs in conifer plantations in the Midlands and the south.

Parasyrphus malinellus (Collin, 1952)

Syrphus malinellus Collin in Coe (1953)

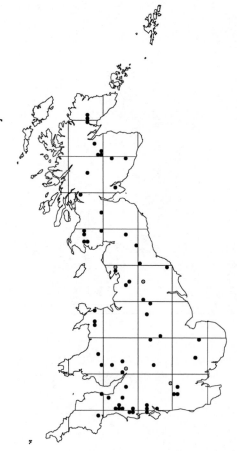

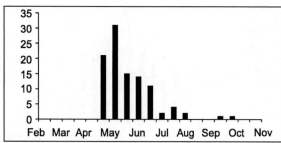

Biology

The larva of this species is undescribed, but those of other members of this genus are usually arboreal predators on adelgids and pine aphids. Adults are found along rides in conifer plantations, and in partially-coniferised broad-leaved woodland, where they fly amongst the conifer foliage at some height, descending to visit flowers.

Distribution

Described new to science in 1952 on the basis of British material caught between 1932 and 1942, this species has subsequently been found at widely scattered localities throughout mainland Britain, although most frequently in central-southern England. It has recently been found in numerous conifer plantations in Somerset (Dean quoted in Stubbs (1996)).

Parasyrphus nigritarsis (Zetterstedt, 1843)

Syrphus nigritarsis Zetterstedt in Coe (1953)

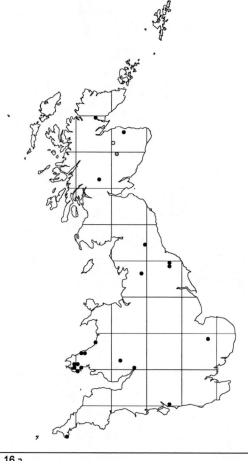

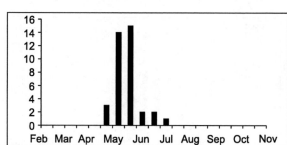

Biology

The larvae feed on the eggs, larvae and pupae of leaf-beetles (Coleoptera, Chrysomelidae) associated with *Alnus, Populus* and *Salix*. Adults have been found resting on the foliage of trees and scrub, often close to wet woodland or waterside trees, and males were recorded in three consecutive years sitting on a plastic coated washing line in the garden of Adrian Fowles in west Wales, adjoining a wooded valley with *Salix cinerea* and *Populus tremula*.

Distribution

The status and distribution were reviewed by MacGowan and Watt (1994), although the recording scheme holds some additional records. It was originally described from specimens taken in central Scotland, and, although there are recent records from a number of Scottish localities, these are outnumbered by records from south and west Wales. It has also been reported from Cornwall, northern England, Suffolk and Hampshire. It is possibly overlooked because of its resemblance (especially in the female) to the common *Syrphus* species.

Parasyrphus punctulatus (Verrall, 1873)

Syrphus punctulatus Verrall in Coe (1953)

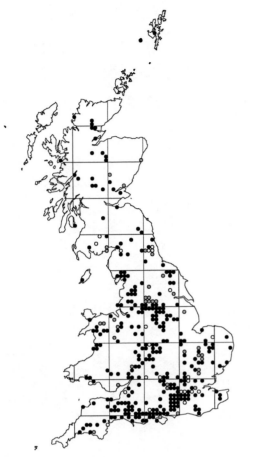

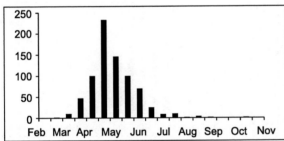

Biology

The larvae are illustrated by Rotheray (1994). Although females of this species have been seen laying eggs on young shoots of *Picea*, their range of prey is known to include aphids on broad-leaved shrubs and trees including *Rosa* and *Fagus*. Adults can be found visiting a variety of spring flowers in open areas in or around woodland, both broad-leaved and coniferous and occasionally in parks and large gardens with mature trees. Males hover close to tree foliage and both sexes are found settled on sunlit foliage, usually at some height.

Distribution

A widespread and common early spring species in woods throughout Britain, with records north to Shetland.

Parasyrphus vittiger (Zetterstedt, 1843)

Syrphus vittiger Zetterstedt in Coe (1953)

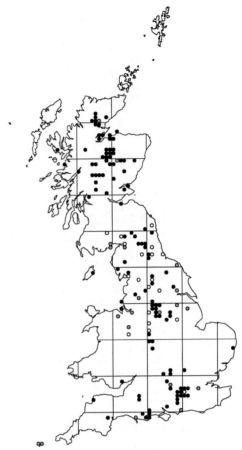

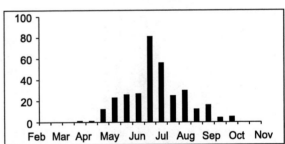

Biology

The aphidophagous larvae have been found mainly on conifers (*Abies*, *Picea* and *Pinus*), but also on *Fagus* and, in Switzerland, on *Ribes nigrum*. Adults are usually found in woodland (either broad-leaved or coniferous), but they are often taken on heathland in southern England, where they are probably associated with invading *Pinus*. They appear to be largely arboreal, but will descend to visit flowers in rides and clearings.

Distribution

This species appears to be most frequent in northern Britain, especially the Scottish Highlands, but there are also records from the heathlands of central-southern England. There are few recent records from Wales, the south-west peninsula or eastern England.

Parhelophilus consimilis (Malm, 1863)

Helophilus consimilis Malm in Coe (1953)

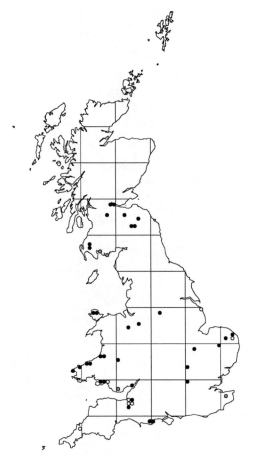

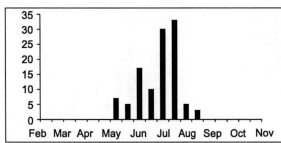

Biology

The larva is undescribed. Adults are associated with accumulations of wet, decaying matter, particularly *Typha*, in eutrophic bogs, but also occasionally in fens in eastern England. Adults are generally found in lush vegetation fringing water bodies and rarely stray far from water. They fly around rapidly, and settle on, emergent vegetation and visit flowers such as *Menyanthes*, *Ranunculus* and *Potentilla palustris*.

Distribution

Although the scarcest of the three *Parhelophilus* species, it has proved to be much less rare than previously thought, being found at widely scattered localities from Dorset to southern Scotland, sometimes in abundance.

Parhelophilus frutetorum (Fabricius, 1775)

Helophilus frutetorum Fabricius in Coe (1953)

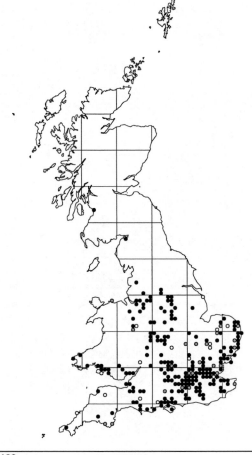

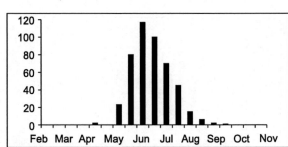

Biology

Larvae and puparia have been found in organic rich mud at the edge of a woodland pond. Adults are usually found around pools in fen and wet woodland. They are normally found in lush vegetation near standing water, but both sexes will visit nearby tree flowers and settle on sunlit tree foliage. Visits a wide range of flowers, especially white umbels and yellow composites.

Distribution

Locally abundant in suitable habitat in south-east England, with scattered records from south-west England, south Wales and the Midlands north to Ayr. It is scarce in the more northerly parts of its range.

Parhelophilus versicolor (Fabricius, 1787)

Helophilus versicolor Fabricius in Coe (1953)

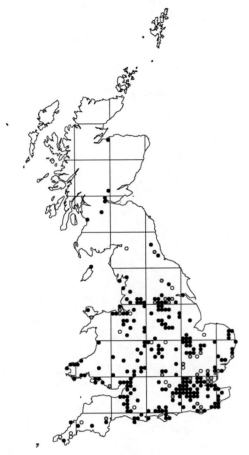

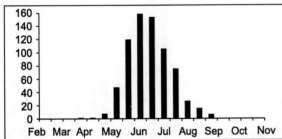

Biology

The larvae have been found in the decaying rhizomes of *Typha* in a pond and puparia have been found between the leaf sheaths of the plant. There seems to be a strong association with *Typha* and adults are often found resting on the stems and leaves of the plant. Occurs in wetlands of all types where there are pools and water-filled ditches with stands of tall, emergent vegetation. Adults are usually swept from such vegetation, or found visiting flowers nearby.

Distribution

Locally abundant in suitable habitat in the lowlands of southern Britain, and occurring northwards to Nairn. Scarce in the northern part of its range.

Pelecocera tricincta Meigen, 1822

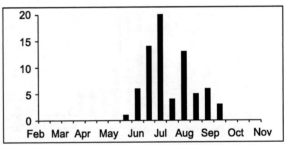

Biology

The larva of this species remains unknown. It is restricted to heathland (including clearings in wooded heath and the tracks and rides of conifer plantations which have been planted on heathland). Adults are usually found by sweeping low flowery vegetation bordering tracks and rides, but can also be seen visiting a range of flowers. *Potentilla erecta* and yellow composites are often abundant in such situations and are particularly favoured.

Distribution

This species has mainly been recorded from the extensive heathland sites of Dorset and Hampshire, but there are recent records from Devon, the Isle of Wight, Sussex and at least four localities in Surrey. It can be reasonably abundant at some localities.

Pipiza austriaca Meigen, 1822

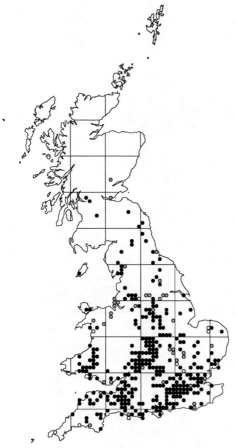

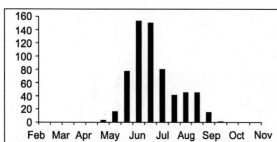

Biology
The larvae of this genus are aphidophagous, appearing to favour aphids which secrete a waxy flocculence (woolly aphids). They have also been reared on *Cavariella* aphids on *Heracleum sphondylium*. Adults are usually found resting on vegetation along woodland margins, although they occasionally visit flowers.

Distribution
Widespread but local in southern England, apparently becoming scarcer to the west and north, with records extending into southern Scotland.

Pipiza bimaculata Meigen, 1822

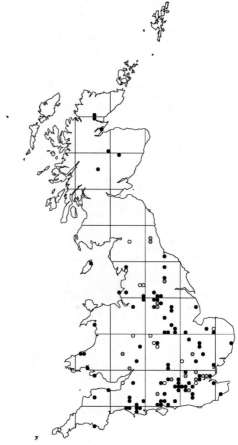

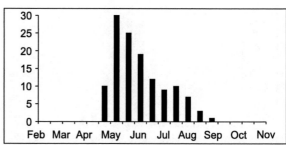

Biology
The larva of this species remains unknown, but those of other members of this genus are aphidophagous, appearing to favour aphids which secrete a waxy flocculence (woolly aphids). Adults are usually found resting on vegetation along woodland margins, occasionally visiting flowers.

Distribution
P. bimaculata, *P. fenestrata*, *P. lugubris* and *P. noctiluca* are justifiably seen as comprising a difficult species complex by many recorders, and are often ignored. Consequently, they must be regarded as under-recorded and probably subject to frequent misidentification. Records are widely scattered, though most frequent in southern England.

Pipiza fenestrata Meigen, 1822

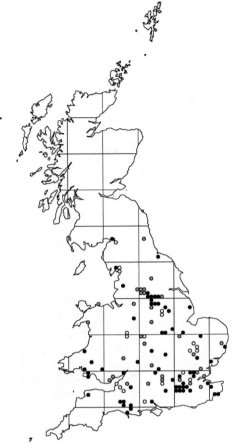

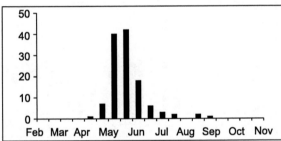

Biology

The larva of this species remains unknown, but other members of the genus are aphidophagous, appearing to favour aphids which secrete a waxy flocculence (woolly aphids). Adults are usually found resting on vegetation along woodland margins, occasionally visiting flowers such as *Ranunculus*.

Distribution

P. bimaculata, P. fenestrata, P. lugubris and
P. noctiluca are justifiably seen as comprising a difficult species complex by many recorders, and are often ignored. Consequently, they must be regarded as under-recorded and probably subject to frequent misidentification. There are few, mainly old records, these extending north to the Scottish border.

Pipiza lugubris (Fabricius, 1775)

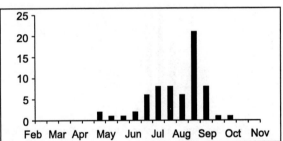

Biology

The larva of this species remains unknown, but other members of the genus are aphidophagous, appearing to favour aphids which secrete a waxy flocculence (woolly aphids). Adults are usually found resting on vegetation along woodland margins, occasionally visiting flowers, but also in wetland situations, especially where *Filipendula ulmaria* occurs.

Distribution

P. bimaculata, P. fenestrata, P. lugubris and
P. noctiluca are justifiably seen as comprising a difficult species complex by many recorders and are often ignored. Consequently, they must be regarded as under-recorded and probably subject to frequent misidentification. Records are few, and appear to be more frequent in older collections. They are widely scattered in the southern half of Britain, with very few north of the Humber.

Pipiza luteitarsis Zetterstedt, 1843

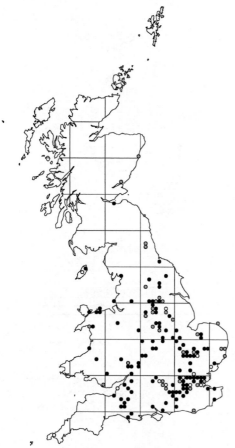

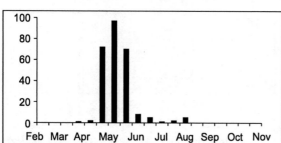

Biology

The larvae feed on *Schizoneura* aphids, which curl the leaves of *Ulmus*. This species is associated with broad-leaved woodland, and adults are often found resting on foliage along the edges of rides and clearings. Males defend patches of sunlight, hovering a few metres above the ground.

Distribution

The most distinctive member of the genus, and not difficult to identify reliably. This is a scarce but widespread species in the southern half of Britain, tending to be recorded more frequently from the east. Whilst its range extends northwards to Scotland, it is rare in the northern part of its range. Although listed by Stubbs (1982) as a 'good' primary woodland indicator, recent records suggest that it is not confined to ancient woodlands, and the presence of *Ulmus* may be a more significant factor.

Pipiza noctiluca (Linnaeus, 1758)

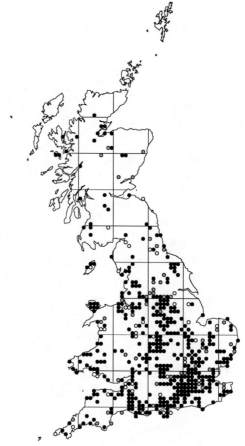

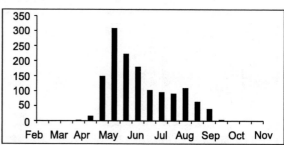

Biology

The larvae are aphidophagous, and have been reared on a variety of ground layer and arboreal species, including *Cavariella* on white umbels. Adults are usually found resting on vegetation along woodland margins, hedgerows and similar situations, or visiting flowers.

Distribution

P. bimaculata, P. fenestrata, P. lugubris and *P. noctiluca* are justifiably seen as comprising a difficult species complex by many recorders, and are often ignored. Consequently, they must be regarded as under-recorded and probably subject to frequent misidentification. This is much the most frequently recorded member of this group, however, and records are widespread in the southern half of Britain, with scattered records to northern Scotland.

Pipizella maculipennis (Meigen, 1822)

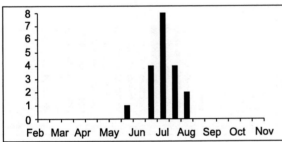

Biology
The larva of this species remains unknown, but other members of the genus prey on root-feeding aphids. It is mentioned as having been found with *Syrphus* larvae on a variety of aphids, but it is not clear whether the aphids were being used as prey. About half the records of adults appear to come from coastal situations, but it is also recorded from inland localities, including a woodland ride. According to Speight (1998) it is associated with dry, unimproved grassland areas in scrub or woodland.

Distribution
A very rare species with widely scattered records from southern England north to southern Scotland. In Europe, this species has been confused with the very similar *P. zeneggenensis* Goeldlin (which is not yet known in Britain, but occurs in Belgium and France), so the few British specimens should be re-examined with this in mind. The male terminalia are figured by van der Goot (1981).

Pipizella viduata (Meigen, 1822)

Pipizella varipes (Meigen) in Stubbs and Falk (1983)

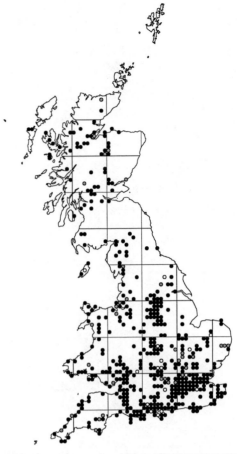

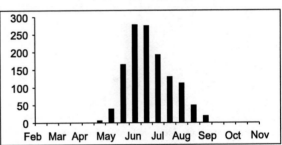

Biology
The larvae are associated with ant-attended, root-feeding aphids on umbels (eg *Anauraphis subterranea* attended by *Lasius niger* Linnaeus on the roots of *Pastinaca sativa*). Generally found by sweeping dry grassland (including calcareous and coastal grassland), dry heathland and woodland rides, or seen visiting low flowers, especially *Galium*, *Pastinaca* and other umbels. Adults will bask on sunlit leaves, but generally stay close to the ground.

Distribution
A widespread and common species found in suitable localities throughout Britain, although most frequent in the southern lowlands.

Pipizella virens (Fabricius, 1805)

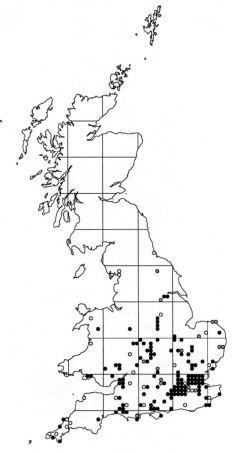

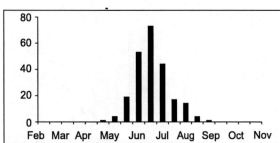

Biology
On the continent, the larvae are reported to be associated with aphids on the roots of white umbels. Found in taller and lusher vegetation than *P. viduata*, in a range of situations including woodland and scrub edges, the fringes of wetlands, and clifftop and other coastal grassland. Adults stay close to the ground and will bask on sunlit leaves, but are sometimes found visiting taller flowers including white umbels.

Distribution
Much scarcer than *P. viduata*, this species is largely restricted to the lowlands of south-east England, although there are a few records from northern England, south-west England and Wales. Separation from *P. viduata* requires care and is best done by examination of the male terminalia which are figured by van der Goot (1981).

Platycheirus albimanus (Fabricius, 1781)

Platycheirus cyaneus (Müller, 1776)

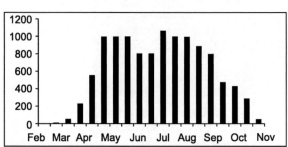

Biology
The early stages of this common species require further investigation. They appear to feed on aphids on low growing plants and bushes and have also been found on *Abies*, *Malus* and *Phragmites*. The species is multi-brooded, and adults can be found at almost any time of year, but they are particularly abundant at flowers in spring. Adults can be found in most habitats, but frequently in more humid, sheltered situations such as woodland edge, hedgerows, scrub and gardens.

Distribution
One of the commonest and most widespread of our smaller hoverflies.

Platycheirus ambiguus (Fallén, 1817)

Melanostoma ambiguus Fallén in Coe (1953)

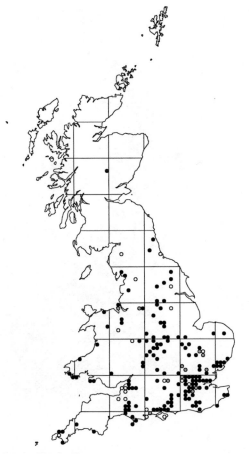

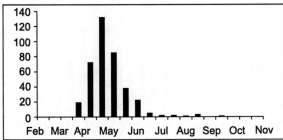

Biology

The larvae feed on aphids on trees and shrubs. They are most often found visiting spring blossom, especially *Prunus spinosa* and flowering *Salix* in sunny, sheltered situations such as woodland margins and large hedgerows. According to Speight (1998) there is a strong association with scrub; males hover close to flowering shrubs, often in amongst the branches, whilst females are found at the flowers or in the immediate vicinity.

Distribution

Although a very local species, it can be abundant in suitable localities. It is widespread in England and Wales north to central Scotland, but more frequent towards the south-east.

Platycheirus amplus Currant, 1927

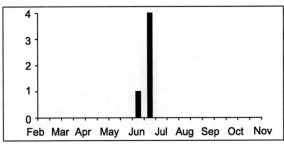

Biology

This is a comparatively recently described species and the larva is not yet known. Adults have been found in poor fens and around moorland flushes where they fly low down amongst sedges and other tall vegetation in the vicinity of water.

Distribution

Having already been found in Ireland (Speight & Vockeroth 1988), this species was added to the British list from Scotland in 1990. An older specimen, dated 1910 and previously identified as *P. peltatus*, was subsequently located in the collections of the Royal Museum of Scotland (Rotheray 1990). There are still few British records, all from Scotland.

Platycheirus angustatus (Zetterstedt, 1843)

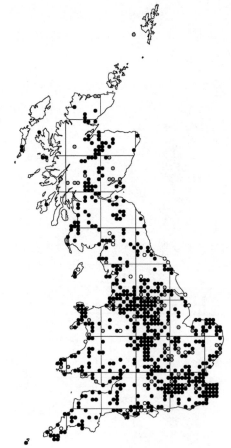

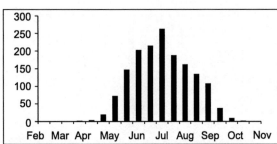

Biology
The larvae feed on aphids within the ground layer. Found in damp grassland situations such as marsh, fen and seasonally flooded, unimproved grassland. Adults fly low down amongst tall, emergent vegetation and are usually found by sweeping. They visit a range of flowers including the flower heads of sedges and grasses.

Distribution
Widespread and common throughout Britain.

Platycheirus clypeatus agg.

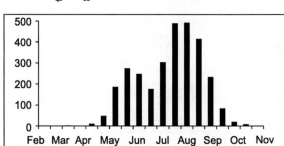

Biology
The *clypeatus* group, which has always presented identification difficulties, was recently 'split' by Speight and Goeldlin (1990) and Goeldlin *et al.* (1990), with three new species introduced (*P. occultus*, *P. europaeus*, *P. ramsarensis*). Old records of '*P. clypeatus*', for which no supporting specimens exist, have been mapped only as *P. clypeatus* agg. The map includes all records of the segregate species as well as the aggregate. All of the species in this complex are associated with wet habitats.

Distribution
Widely distributed and common.

Platycheirus clypeatus (Meigen, 1822)

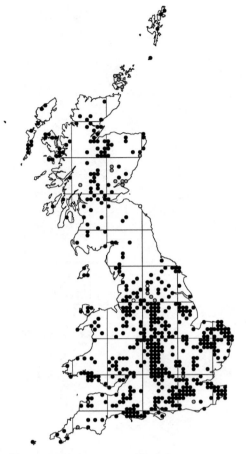

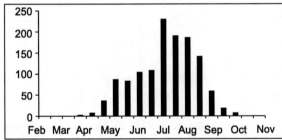

Biology

The early stages of this common species require further investigation. Larvae are rarely found at aphid colonies, and may be generalised predators within the litter layer. Since the splitting of this species complex by Speight and Goeldlin (1990) and Goeldlin *et al.* (1990), *P. clypeatus sensu stricto* has been by far the most frequently recorded segregate taxon. It is found in all sorts of grassy situations, but most abundantly in damp grassland including pond, stream and ditch margins. Adults fly low down amongst tall vegetation and are easily found by sweeping. They also visit a wide range of flowers including sedges and grasses.

Distribution

Widespread, occurring throughout Britain.

Platycheirus discimanus Loew, 1871

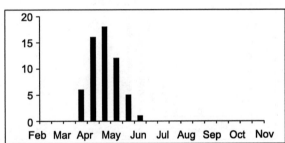

Biology

The larva is unknown. Adults are usually found around spring blossom, especially *Prunus spinosa* and *Salix*, in sheltered situations such as woodland edges (both broad-leaved and coniferous) and hedgerows. Adults can be found visiting the flowers, or resting in the immediate vicinity of flowering bushes where they sun themselves on dead grass tussocks, etc.

Distribution

This species may well be overlooked because of its early flight period and its resemblance to the very common *P. albimanus*, which occurs in similar situations. Records are scarce, but widely scattered; although they tend to be concentrated towards the lowlands of southern England, there are records from upland localities in northern England and Scotland.

Platycheirus europaeus Goeldlin, Maibach & Speight, 1990

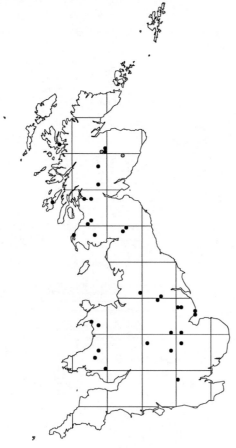

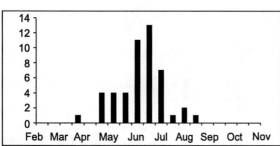

Biology

The larva is unknown. This is one of the species recently split from *P. clypeatus* by Speight and Goeldlin (1990) and Goeldlin *et al.* (1990), and as yet, few records have been received. Scottish records mainly refer to damp, open situations within woodland (including pine forest), whilst in England, the species is recorded from wet woodland rides, often on clay soils. In Wales it has been found in damp scrub in sand dunes. Adults fly low down amongst the vegetation and will visit the flowers of sedges and grasses.

Distribution

This appears to be a widespread but scarce species in Britain, although it can be abundant where it occurs.

Platycheirus fulviventris (Macquart, 1827-8)

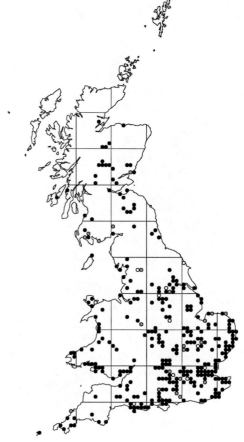

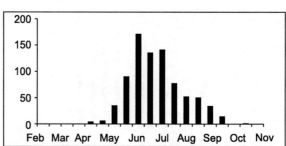

Biology

The larvae feed on the aphid *Hyalopterus pruni* on monocotyledonous plants in wetlands. It is usually found in marshes, by ponds, ditches or slow flowing rivers, usually where lush vegetation such as *Phragmites* or *Glyceria maxima* occurs. Adults fly amongst stands of reeds and sedges frequently settling on the stems and will visit flowers of sedges, grasses and *Plantago*.

Distribution

This species is very local, though often abundant where it occurs. It is most frequent in the lowlands of south-east Britain, especially wetlands along the east coast of England, but it is also widely scattered in the north and west. It becomes increasingly scarce further north, but occurs in reasonable numbers in some wetland localities in south-east Scotland (Stubbs 1996).

116

Platycheirus granditarsus (Forster, 1771)

Pyrophaena granditarsa (Forster) in Stubbs and Falk (1983)

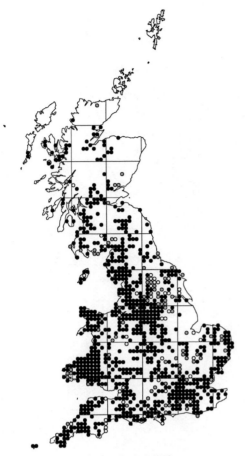

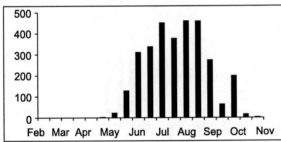

Biology

Larvae undescribed. Pupae have been found in wetland flood litter. It occurs in wet meadows and in the lush vegetation fringing marshes, ponds, lakes etc, including more acid habitats such as poor-fen and *Molinia* grassland. Adults fly amongst stands of tall vegetation such as *Juncus* and *Phragmites* and frequently settle on the stems. They visit a wide range of flowers, especially *Ranunculus*, and males can be found hovering over open areas such as paths.

Distribution

Widespread and common.

Platycheirus immarginatus (Zetterstedt, 1849)

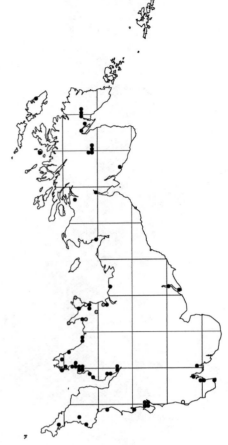

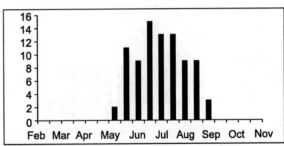

Biology

The larvae feed on the aphid *Trichocallis cyperi* on *Carex* in wetlands. In Britain, it is usually found in brackish marshes and saltmarsh, and Speight (1998) notes the tendency for it to be a coastal species towards the Atlantic margins of Europe. Adults fly low down amongst stands of tall vegetation and have been found at the flowers of *Bolboschoenus maritimus*. They are normally found by sweeping.

Distribution

Very localised, but can be abundant where it occurs. This is a problematic species in that identifications made using older keys (even by experienced workers), are frequently wrong, and do not take account of recent species splits (eg *P. occultus*). Although there are many inland records, especially in the older literature, it is not at all clear whether the species genuinely occurs away from brackish coastal localities in Britain. Most identification guides (eg Coe (1953); Stubbs and Falk (1983)) suggest that there are inland records, but records since 1990 from the most experienced and reliable recorders are almost exclusively coastal, and it is these which have been mapped here.

Platycheirus manicatus (Meigen, 1822)

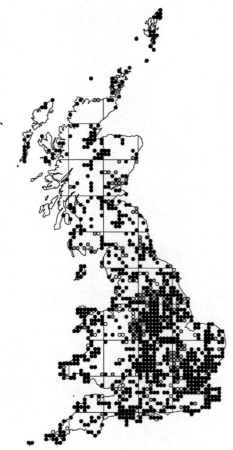

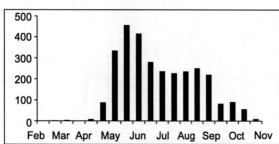

Biology

Larvae feed on aphids on low growing plants and bushes. According to Stubbs and Falk (1983) it is a grassland species, preferring drier grasslands on neutral to calcareous soils, but Speight (1998) describes it as a species of wet or humid open ground and Rotheray (1993) reports that gravid females seem to prefer moist shady situations. Our experience is that it is frequently swept from long grass in most habitats, but is especially abundant in coastal grasslands. Adults are often found visiting a wide range of flowers, especially white umbels.

Distribution

Widespread and common, including many of the Scottish islands.

Platycheirus melanopsis Loew, 1856

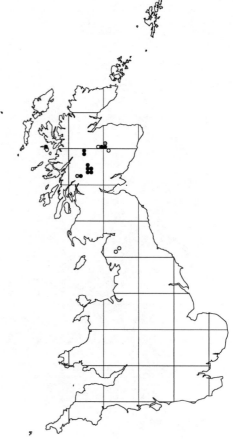

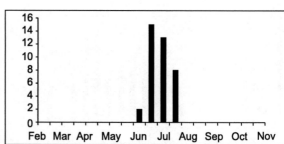

Biology

The larva of this species has recently been found by Rotheray (1997), who suggests that they may feed on the scale insect *Arctothesia cataphracta* (Homoptera: Ortheziidae) which is frequent amongst the roots of montane plants. It is found in mountains on calcareous rocks, at medium to high altitude in alpine grasslands and open structured *Pinus* woodland from about 260 to 300 m upwards. Males tend to hover low over roads or bare areas on tracks.

Distribution

Recent work by the Malloch Society suggests that this is quite a widespread species in the mountains of the Scottish Highlands, especially in Perth and the Cairngorms. It is also recorded from the Lake District. Records from Wales and southern England are probably misidentifications, although there seems no reason why the species should not occur on mountains in Snowdonia and the Pennines.

Platycheirus nielseni Vockeroth, 1990

Platycheirus species A in Stubbs and Falk (1983)

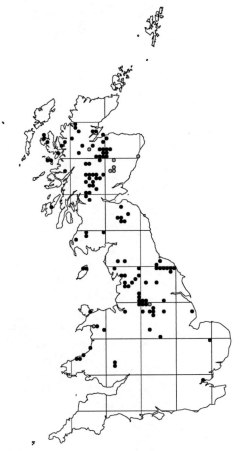

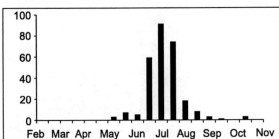

Biology

The larva is unknown. This species was split from
P. peltatus by Vockeroth (1990), and so far there are
relatively few records. It can be frequent in damp
places such as wet, rushy meadows and along stream
sides in upland areas, usually where there is some
shelter from scrub or trees. Males can be found
hovering in groups in clearings and over streams, in
dappled sunshine.

Distribution

This species appears to be widespread in the north
and west, including Scotland, Wales and northern
England, with some records from fairly high altitude
on moorland. In the south of England there are
records from Dorset, Somerset and Breckland, and one
confirmed record from the Thames marshes.

Platycheirus occultus Goeldlin, Maibach & Speight, 1990

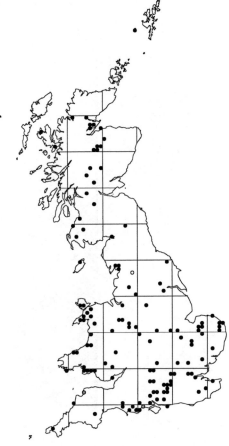

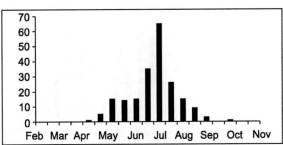

Biology

The larva is unknown. This is one of the species split
from *P. clypeatus* by Speight and Goeldlin (1990) and
Goeldlin *et al.* (1990), and as yet there are relatively
few records. It is found in peaty wetlands including
acid bog and moorland in the north and west;
calcareous fen in eastern England; and wet heathland
in central-southern England. Adults fly low down
amongst lush vegetation and are usually found by
sweeping, but also visit flowers.

Distribution

Records received so far suggest that this is a
widespread and locally abundant species in suitable
habitats. It can occur at fairly high altitude on
moorland in the north and west

Platycheirus peltatus agg.

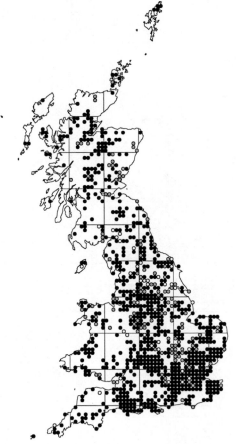

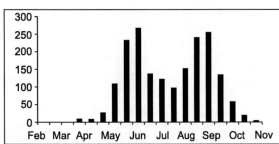

Biology

P. peltatus has been split into three species (*P. amplus*, *P. nielseni* and P. *peltatus s.s.*) by Vockeroth (1990). Old records of *'P. peltatus'* for which no supporting specimen exists, have been mapped only as *P. peltatus* agg. The map includes all records of the segregates as well as the aggregate.

Distribution

Widespread and common throughout Britain.

Platycheirus peltatus (Meigen, 1822)

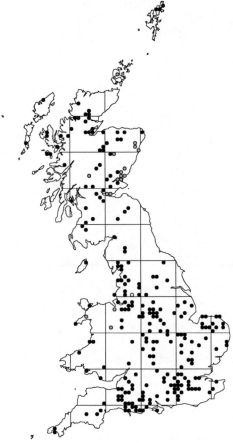

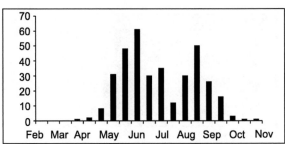

Biology

The early stages of this common species require further investigation because the identification of the specimens that have been described is open to doubt. The available data suggests that they prey on a range of aphids in shaded, moist sites. *'P. peltatus'* was split by Vockeroth (1990), and relatively few records have been received for *P. peltatus s.s.* It appears to be a more lowland species than *P. nielseni,* occurring in upland areas only along valley floors. It is found in damp, grassy situations along rivers and streams, in woodland rides and clearings and around large hedgerows. Adults fly low down amongst the vegetation and will settle on sunlit leaves. Males hover over bare patches.

Distribution

Widespread and common in lowlands throughout Britain.

Platycheirus perpallidus Verrall, 1901

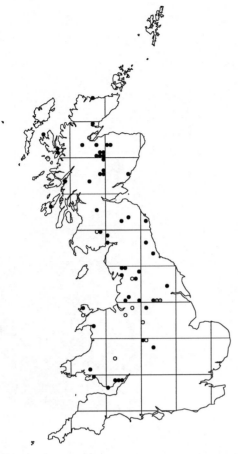

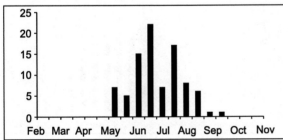

Biology

The larvae are associated with the aphid *Trichocallis cyperi* on *Carex* in wetlands. It occurs along the margins of ditches, ponds and rivers, especially in wet poor-fen where *Carex* occurs. Adults fly amongst stands of tall, emergent vegetation. Usually found by sweeping, but they seem to prefer the open-water side of vegetation stands, which can make them inaccessible.

Distribution

This is a very local species, which may nevertheless be abundant where it occurs. It is most frequent in Wales, northern England and Scotland, especially the central Highlands. It is rare in southern Britain.

Platycheirus podagratus (Zetterstedt, 1838)

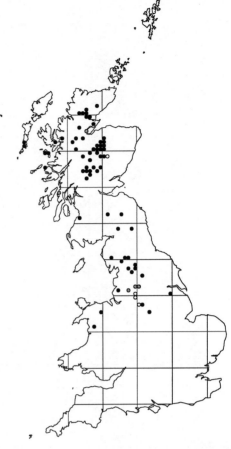

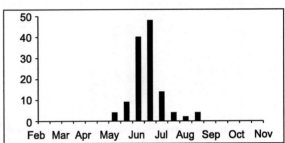

Biology

The larva is unknown. Occurs at the edges of oligotrophic lakes and in boggy areas on moorland at moderate altitudes, although it has been found at 700 m in the Pennines. Adults fly low amongst stands of vegetation such as *Carex* or *Juncus*, usually close to water, and are often found by sweeping. It has been found visiting sedge flowers.

Distribution

A scarce and local species of northern England and Scotland, with most records from the Scottish Highlands. There are records from North Wales. Some older records, which do not take into account recent species splits, may refer to *P. occultus*.

Platycheirus ramsarensis Goeldlin, Maibach & Speight, 1990

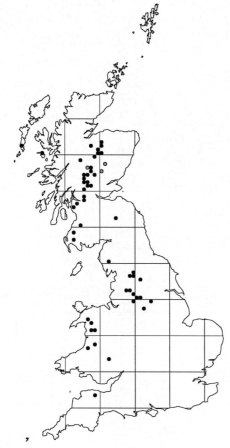

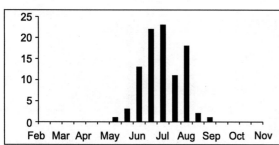

Biology
The larva is unknown. This species was split from *P. clypeatus* by Speight and Goeldlin (1990) and Goeldlin *et al.* (1990), and there are relatively few records as yet. It has been found in oligotrophic, wet situations beside moorland streams and lakes, usually where there are small flushes with abundant *Carex* or *Juncus*. Adults fly low down amongst stands of vegetation and will visit flowers such as *Caltha*.

Distribution
From the relatively few records received so far, this appears to be a widespread and relatively frequent species in moorland areas of Wales, the Pennines, Scotland and Exmoor. It is often abundant where it occurs.

Platycheirus rosarum (Fabricius, 1787)

Pyrophaena rosarum (Fabricius) in Stubbs and Falk (1983)

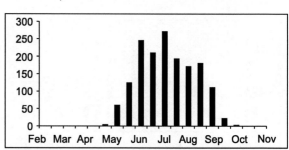

Biology
Larvae unknown, but are presumed to feed on aphids in wetland situations. Pupae have been found in fenland flood refuse. It occurs in wet meadows and in the lush vegetation fringing marshes, ponds, lakes, etc. Adults fly amongst stands of tall vegetation such as *Juncus* and *Phragmites* and frequently settle on the stems. They visit a wide range of flowers and males can be found hovering over more open areas. Generally occurs in the same habitats as *P. granditarsa*, and the two are often found together.

Distribution
Generally less abundant than *P. granditarsa*, but similarly widespread.

Platycheirus scambus (Staeger, 1843)

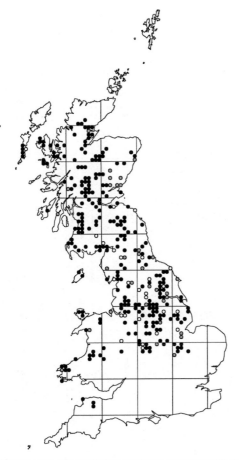

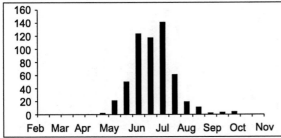

Biology
The larvae feed on aphids within the ground layer. Found in damp grassland including saltmarsh, poor-fen and the fringes of marshes, often where there is some shelter from trees or scrub. Adults fly amongst stands of tall vegetation and are rarely found far from the edges of water. They will visit a wide range of flowers and males hover near flowering shrubs, such as *Salix*, near water.

Distribution
Locally abundant in Scotland and northern England, and more widespread than was thought in the south, including the Midlands, west Wales and south-west England. Records from southern England need careful scrutiny as misidentification is possible.

Platycheirus scutatus (Meigen, 1822)

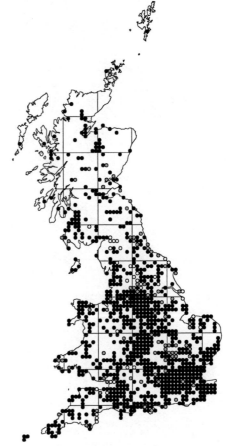

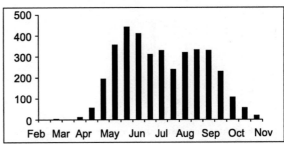

Biology
The larvae prey on a variety of aphid species on low growing plants, bushes and small trees. A species of woodland edge (both coniferous and broad-leaved) and scrub, including hedgerows, parks and mature gardens. Adults are usually found resting on sunlit vegetation or visiting a wide range of flowers in clearings, tracksides, etc. It is multiple brooded and has a long flight period.

Distribution
Widespread and common. Until very recently, two species were confused under the name *P. scutatus* in Britain. Records preceding the separation of *P. splendens* and *P. scutatus s.s.* by Rotheray (1998) could refer to either taxon. However, records of adults from July onwards are likely to be of *P. scutatus s.s.* whilst earlier records are mixed. It appears likely that both are frequent and widespread, but *P. scutatus s.s.* will still turn out to be one of our commonest species.

Platycheirus splendens Rotheray, 1998

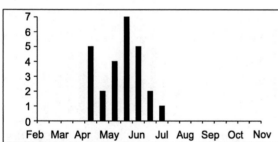

Biology

Newly described by Rotheray (1998). Bred from larvae collected from leaf-curl galls of *Schizoneura ulmi* on *Ulmus glabra* and also *Brachycaudus* sp. on *Silene dioca*. Adults closely resemble *P. scutatus* with which it was previously confused. Rotheray (1998) found that larvae enter diapause (unlike *P. scutatus*) not forming a puparium until the following spring and the few records of adults available so far support this, suggesting it has a short flight period early in the season.

Distribution

Rotheray (1998) examined material under the name of *P. scutatus* in several museum collections and found specimens from all over Britain which proved to be this species, suggesting it will turn out to be frequent and widespread. Several specimens came from city parks in Edinburgh and Oxford.

Platycheirus sticticus (Meigen, 1822)

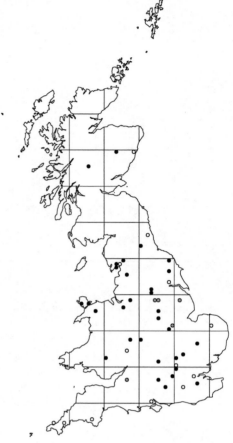

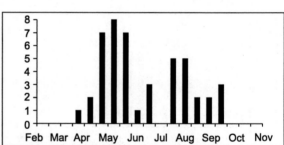

Biology

The larva is unknown. The habitat preferences of adults are little known, but the species has been taken in rough grassland, along woodland edges and hedgerows at altitudes of up to 240 m. This is a little known and poorly recorded species and more information would be welcome.

Distribution

There are few records, widely scattered from southern England to northern Scotland. It appears to be scarce, but may well be overlooked amongst commoner grey-marked *Platycheirus* species.

Platycheirus tarsalis (Schummel, 1836)

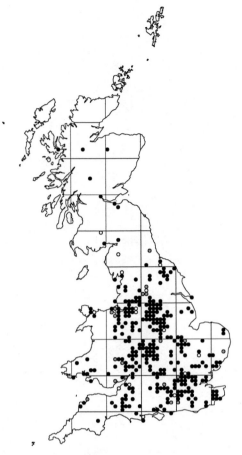

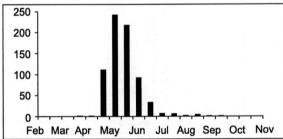

Biology
The larva is unknown. A woodland species, typically found along herb-rich rides, woodland edges or hedgerows. In spring it is most often found visiting the flowers of *Alliaria petiolata*, but will visit a range of other flowers.

Distribution
This was believed to be a scarce species, but recent records suggest it is a widespread and often abundant woodland hoverfly in the southern lowlands and Midlands where it appears to prefer woodlands on clay. There are scattered records throughout the north and west extending north to Inverness-shire.

Pocota personata (Harris, 1780)

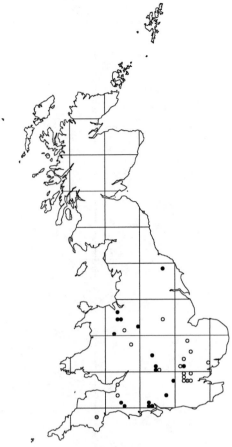

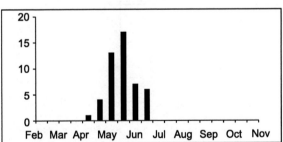

Biology
The larvae are found in rot-holes high up in various trees, but most frequently *Fagus* and *Populus*. Larval development probably takes a few years and larvae of different size classes can be found together in the same rot-hole. Adults are good bumblebee mimics and are seldom found, but can sometimes be seen visiting flowers, especially *Crataegus* blossom, near larval habitat. They have also been observed hovering about the entrances to rot-holes.

Distribution
A rare species, restricted to woodlands and parklands with ancient trees, although there are (mostly old) records from urban localities like Hampstead Heath and Blackheath in London, and Banbury Road, Oxford. It is mainly recorded from the forest belt of central-southern England, with the majority of records coming from 'classic dead-wood localities' like Windsor Forest and the New Forest. There is a scatter of records elsewhere in southern Britain, extending northwards through the Welsh border counties to the Wirral. Duncombe Park in North Yorkshire is rather isolated locally and the most northerly locality known. Records from the eastern side of Engalnd mostly date from the 1930s and 40s or earlier.

Portevinia maculata (Fallén, 1817)

Cheilosia maculata Fallén in Coe (1953)

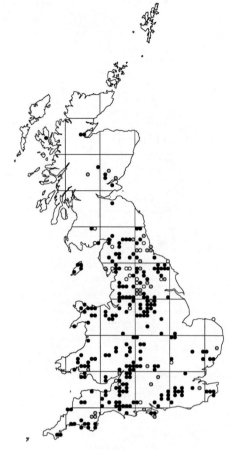

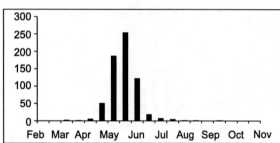

Biology

The larvae tunnel in the bulbs of *Allium ursinum*. During its rather short flight period, males are often abundant around stands of the larval foodplant, where they can be seen visiting the flowers and resting on the foliage. Females are surprisingly elusive, but are presumably also present, though making themselves less conspicuous.

Distribution

Widespread and often abundant wherever the larval food-plant grows (usually, but not exclusively, in woodland). It has recently been recorded from northern Scotland.

Psilota anthracina Meigen, 1822

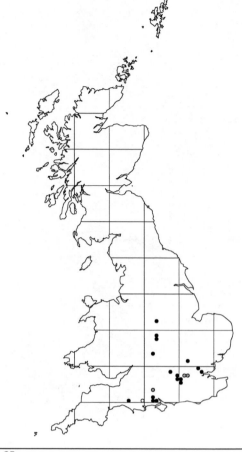

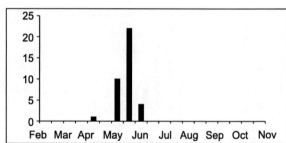

Biology

On the continent, the larvae have been found in sap-runs on trees (Stubbs 1996) and the female has been observed to oviposit in the exit hole of *Cerambyx cerdo* Linnaeus in an ancient living *Quercus* (Speight, 1998 quoting Doczkal, pers. comm.). In Britain, it is restricted to sites with large numbers of ancient trees. Adults are elusive, but are sometimes found visiting *Crataegus* or *Salix* flowers.

Distribution

The great majority of records are from a few sites with large populations of ancient trees, such as Windsor Forest, the New Forest and Richmond Park, but there are recent records from Essex, Worcestershire, Warwickshire and Derbyshire. The adults are possibly overlooked by hoverfly recorders because of their close resemblance to shining blue-black muscids (eg *Hydrotaea* spp.).

Rhingia campestris Meigen, 1822

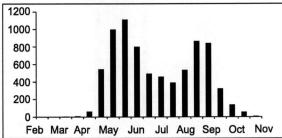

Biology
The larvae live in cow-dung, fragments of which adhere to their bodies, ensuring that they are well camouflaged. However, adults are found in areas where cattle are absent, raising the possibility that dung of other species, or even other media such as wet compost, may be used. Occurs in meadows, gardens, hedgerows, woodland edges, etc. Adults are usually seen visiting flowers, especially pink or purple flowers with concealed nectar sources, or resting on vegetation. The long extension to the face, and the long proboscis sited beneath, gives access to deep flowers, such as *Silene*, which other hoverflies cannot exploit.

Distribution
Widespread and very common throughout Britain, including many of the islands, but the numbers of records received per year has fluctuated widely and there is a possibility that they are scarcer in the year following a dry season.

Rhingia rostrata (Linnaeus, 1758)

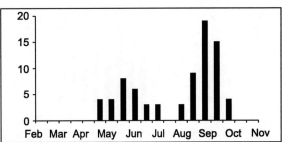

Biology
The larva is unknown. Many records are associated with broad-leaved woodland and Speight (1998) states that adults fly 'within woodland, visiting flowers in small glades and dappled sunlight'. Like *R. campestris*, it has two flight periods; in May/June and again in early autumn. Autumn records are much more numerous.

Distribution
A rare and enigmatic species which is sometimes found in great abundance at a locality and then disappears. Records are concentrated in south-east England, especially in the woods of the Weald and the Chilterns, and in South Wales. Records from the latter area have increased, especially in the autumn.

Riponnensia splendens (Meigen, 1822)

Orthonevra splendens (Meigen) in Stubbs and Falk (1983)

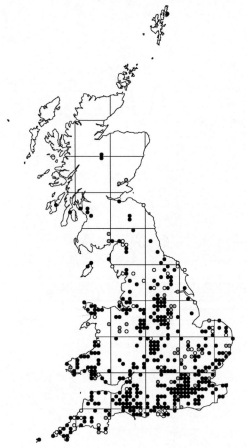

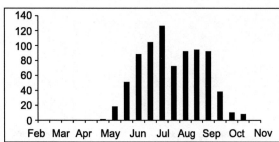

Biology
The larvae are aquatic, occurring in very shallow, slow moving water with accumulations of woody debris. It is found in marshes and fens (especially close to trees or scrub), springs and seepages in woodland and along farm ditches beside hedgerows. Adults are found amongst vegetation close to water or settled on the foliage of trees and bushes. They frequently visit flowers, especially *Ranunculus* and white umbels, but also a variety of others.

Distribution
Widespread and common in the lowlands of the southern half of Britain, scarcer in the north, although extending to central Scotland.

Scaeva albomaculata (Macquart, 1842)

Biology
Little known. In Greece, it visits flowers such as *Cytisus* in dry grassland.

Distribution
A Mediterranean species, one specimen of which was taken in Sussex in August 1938. A second, taken in 1949 on the Isle of Wight, has recently been discovered in a museum collection (Palmer 1996).

Scaeva mecogramma (Bigot, 1860)

Syrphus mecogramma Bigot in Coe (1953)

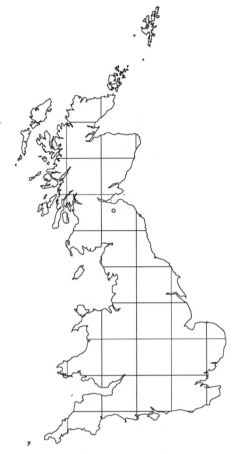

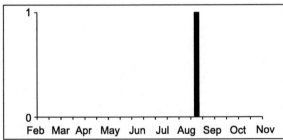

Biology
According to Speight (1998), this is a species of *Quercus ilex/Q. suber* forest, olive groves and citrus orchards. Highly migratory.

Distribution
A southern European species recorded from Spain, southern France, Corsica, Italy and Switzerland (Speight 1998). A single male was taken in Arniston, Lothian in August 1905. This seems an unusual place for a vagrant to turn up, and it was possibly an accidental import.

Scaeva pyrastri (Linnaeus, 1758)

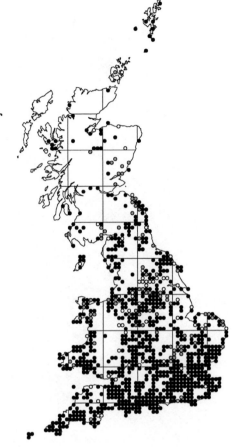

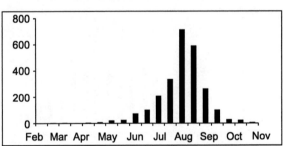

Biology
The larvae feed on a wide range of ground layer and (less frequently) arboreal aphids. Adults are often seen visiting flowers such as white umbels, *Cirsium* and *Carduus*. This is a migrant which reaches Britain around June from southern and central Europe, breeding here to give a generation in late summer. Although it is known to overwinter in central Europe, there is little evidence of this from western Europe suggesting that its annual occurrences are totally dependent on immigration (Speight 1998). In Ireland and western Scotland, the earliest records are in July, suggesting that it does not usually manage to breed in these areas.

Distribution
Widespread in the lowlands of the southern half of Britain. In northern England and southern Scotland records are noticeably clustered along the east coast, as one might expect for a migrant species. It seems to be scarce further north in Scotland, although it is recorded north to Shetland. The numbers of records received vary greatly between years.

Scaeva selenitica (Meigen, 1822)

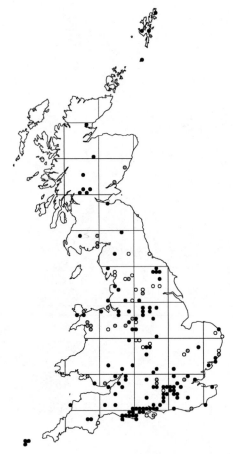

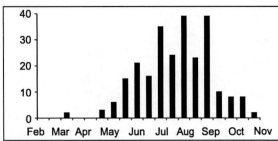

Biology
The larvae feed on aphids on *Pinus* and *Picea*. A puparium has been found under the bark of *Picea*. Records that make reference to habitat most frequently specify woodland (including both broad-leaved and coniferous), although open habitats, such as chalk grassland, are also mentioned. In the south of England this species is mainly associated with *Pinus* on heathland. Adults are often seen visiting flowers, such as white umbels, along woodland rides and edges. Males hover in clearings.

Distribution
Scarce but widely scattered. Whilst Stubbs and Falk (1983) state that it is at least a partial migrant, Falk (1991b) argues that it is resident. It is quite possible that a resident population receives reinforcement by migration from the continent.

Sericomyia lappona (Linnaeus, 1758)

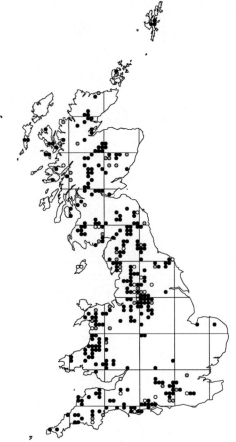

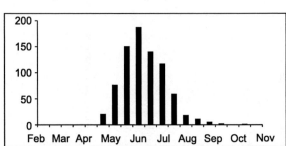

Biology
The larvae are of the 'long-tailed' aquatic type, and are associated with peaty pools and boggy stream-sides in moorland and with wet woodland, such as *Salix* carr. Adults are usually seen visiting flowers, or basking on sunlit foliage, rocks etc, near larval habitat. In southern England, this species is associated with sandy, acid heathland, not always in wet areas. It tends to occur earlier in the year than *S. silentis*, although they are not infrequently seen together.

Distribution
Very similar in distribution to *S. silentis* (the two species often occurring together), but less abundant and more strictly confined to bogs, especially in southern Britain.

Sericomyia silentis (Harris, 1776)

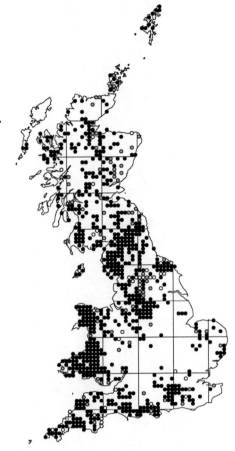

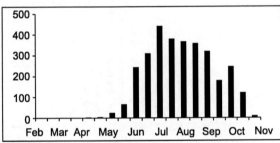

Biology

The larvae are of the 'long-tailed' aquatic type and have been found amongst old, wet, rotting wood fragments in a sawmill and from a water-filled drainage ditch on a cut-over peat bog. It is associated with peaty pools in moorland and acid habitats, including bogs on heathlands in the south and east of Britain, poor-fen and wet woodland, including *Salix* and *Alnus* carr. Adults are usually found along tracksides or woodland edges, visiting flowers or settled in sunlight on vegetation or bare areas of ground. They are very strong and active fliers and appear to disperse widely, often being found far from water.

Distribution

Widespread and abundant in northern and western Britain, especially west Wales, the Pennines and other upland areas of northern England, and in upland Scotland. In the lowlands of southern and eastern England it is much scarcer, probably breeding on heathland and other more acid habitats, although adults may be found some distance from such localities. It is almost absent from most of the English Midlands and rather local in East Anglia.

Sphaerophoria bankowskae Goeldlin, 1989

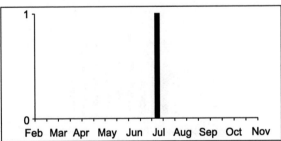

Biology

The larva is unknown. Adults have been found in open areas in woods where they will visit low growing flowers such as *Potentilla*.

Distribution

This rare species was added to the British list from Canfield Hart, North Essex in 1986 by Plant (1990), and is so far recorded elsewhere only from a wood in Northamptonshire (not mapped). A new key to the British members of the genus is given by Stubbs (1996). Although this recently described species is widely recorded in Europe (Speight (1998) lists Denmark, Britain, France, Germany, Switzerland and Italy) it is poorly known as yet.

Sphaerophoria batava Goeldlin de Tiefenau, 1974

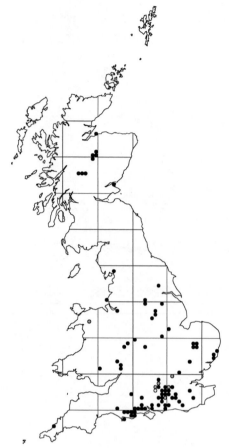

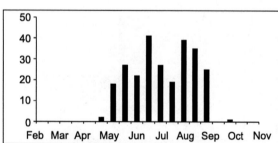

Biology

The larva is unknown. Records which give habitat details most frequently refer to heathland or open rides in conifer woods (including native *Pinus* woods in Scotland, and conifers planted on dunes on Anglesey) where specimens have been swept from heather or found on flowers such as *Potentilla erecta*. A few records mention broad-leaved woodland. Adults are usually swept from tracksides or clearings or found visiting flowers.

Distribution

A scarce but widely distributed species, with the majority of records from southern England, but extending to northern Scotland.

Sphaerophoria fatarum Goeldlin, 1989

Sphaerophoria abbreviata Zetterstedt in Kloet and Hincks (1976) and Stubbs and Falk (1983); see Speight (1989a)

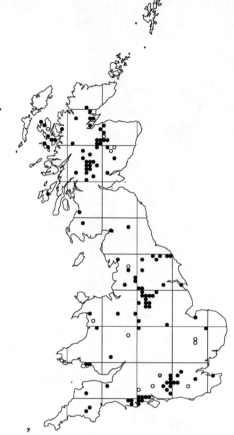

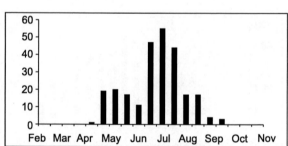

Biology

The larva is unknown. Adults are usually found in open, heathy vegetation, and in the Scottish Highlands this is one of the characteristic species of wet areas on open moorland and heathland. It also occurs in heathy rides in conifer plantation and other woodland. Adults fly low down amongst the vegetation, and are usually found by sweeping, but also visit flowers such as *Potentilla erecta* and *Ranunculus*.

Distribution

'*S. abbreviata*' has recently been split; the true *S. abbreviata* Zetterstedt is a Scandinavian species apparently confined to Lapland. British material is attributed to *S. fatarum*. This is a frequent species in Scotland and northern England where it is often the commonest member of the genus. It also occurs in Wales and on heathland in southern England, where it is scarce.

Sphaerophoria interrupta (Fabricius, 1805)

Sphaerophoria menthastri (Linnaeus) *sensu* Vockeroth in Stubbs and Falk (1983)

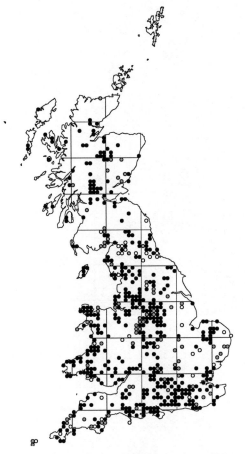

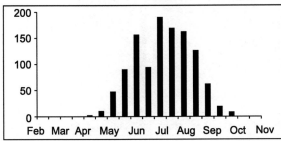

Biology

The larvae feed on aphids and other small, soft-bodied Homoptera in the ground layer, and have been found with aphids on *Silene dioica* and *Cerastium fontanum* ssp. *holosteoides* (Stubbs 1996). It is typically found in open, wet or moist grassland such the edges of fen, coastal dunes, and unimproved wet meadows, but it also occurs in damp grassy woodland clearings. Occasionally recorded from chalk grassland. Adults fly low amongst the vegetation and visit a wide range of flowers.

Distribution

Described in Stubbs and Falk (1983) as 'one of the commonest and most widespread species in grassland habitats', recent records suggest that this species must be considered rather more local, and quite scarce in parts of eastern Britain. Lowlands in the west seem to provide the best habitat.

Sphaerophoria loewi Zetterstedt, 1843

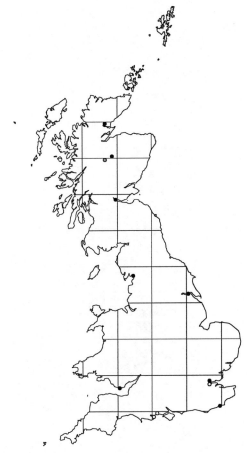

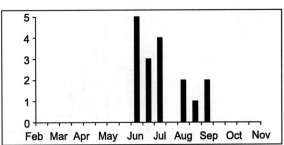

Biology

The larva is unknown. Adults have been found in brackish reed-beds (usually *Phragmites*, but also *Bolboschoenus maritimus* at Leighton Moss) at a few coastal localities. It is likely that the larvae feed on aphids or other soft-bodied Homoptera in this habitat. It has been suggested that the adult is active very early in the morning, but there are several recent records made in the middle of the day. Adults fly amongst stands of tall vegetation, usually remaining over the water, but they occasionally visit flowers.

Distribution

A very rare species known only from a few widely separated coastal localities. The common feature in these localities seems to be the presence of brackish marsh. There is one inland record, of an adult swept from *Phragmites* on a marshy loch side near Aviemore in central Scotland. Normally found as isolated single specimens, it is, however, reported to be reasonably frequent at Leighton Moss and the Tay Reedbeds.

Sphaerophoria philanthus (Meigen, 1822)

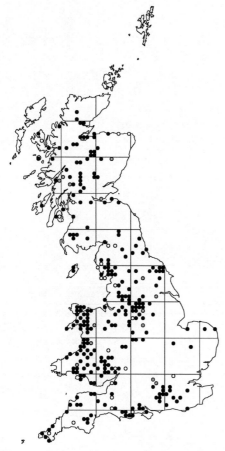

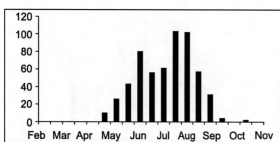

Biology
Although the larvae has not been found in Europe, a species with the same name is well known in North America where it is an aphid predator in crops such as *Brassica*. However, the habits and biology described in American literature do not fit at all well with what is known of this species in Europe, so it is probable that the two are not conspecific (Speight 1998). In Britain it is found in dry heath and moorland situations and also in heathy rides in conifer plantations. Adults fly low amongst the vegetation where they may visit flowers such as *Potentilla erecta*.

Distribution
Widespread and frequent in suitable localities in the north and west of Britain. Scarce in southern England and East Anglia where it is confined to the major heathlands.

Sphaerophoria potentillae Claussen, 1984

Biology
The larva is unknown. Occurs in wet, unimproved grassland where adults have been found visiting *Achillea*, *Potentilla erecta* and *Ranunculus*.

Distribution
This species was added to the British list from wet grasslands in North Devon by Stubbs (1989), and so far has only been recorded from a few sites in the immediate vicinity of the original discovery. The occurrence of this species in Britain was predicted by Speight (1988a), who illustrates the male genitalia. A new key to the British members of the genus is given by Stubbs (1996). It was originally described from a series of bogs in northern Germany and has so far only been found in Denmark, the Netherlands and Britain (Speight 1998), but there are few records as yet.

Sphaerophoria rueppellii (Wiedemann, 1820)

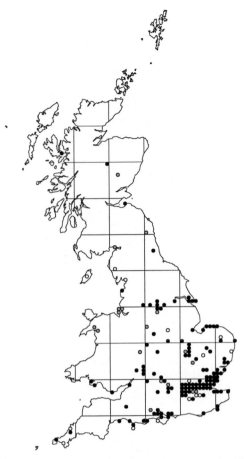

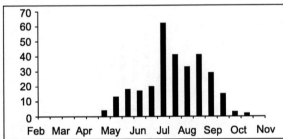

Biology

Larvae feed on aphids on plants such as *Brassica* and *Sonchus*. It can be found in dry, rank grassland and other open, dry situations such as ruderal communities, although females have been observed ovipositing on *Epilobium hirsutum*, which is more typical of damper situations. According to Speight (1998), it occurs in open fringes of wetlands, including salt-marsh on the western edge of its European range, and also on exposed, vegetated, sand and gravel beds beside rivers. Adults fly amongst tall vegetation and visit flowers, especially yellow composites.

Distribution

Locally abundant in south-east England, and especially frequent in the marshes around the Thames where it is characteristically found on grassy flood banks. It is also frequent on dry heathland edges in Surrey, Hampshire and Dorset. There are scattered records from elsewhere in the southern half of Britain, and north to Skye; it has recently been found near Edinburgh (Stubbs 1996).

Sphaerophoria scripta (Linnaeus, 1758)

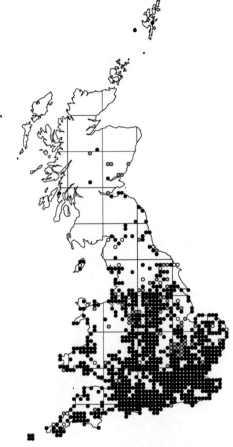

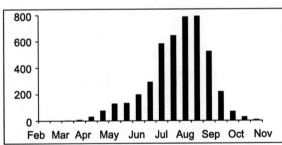

Biology

The larvae, which overwinter, feed on aphids and other small, soft-bodied Homoptera in the ground layer including various crop-aphids. It is found in open grassland, woodland edges, hedgerows, urban waste ground and gardens and, according to Speight (1998), tends to be coastal towards the northern edge of its European range and distinctly anthropogenic further south. Adults fly low down amongst, or just above, the vegetation and frequently visit flowers, especially *Achillea,* white umbels and yellow composites. However, many other flowers, including garden varieties, are utilised.

Distribution

Very common and widespread in the lowlands of southern Britain, north to a line between the Humber and the Mersey. There are scattered records north to southern Scotland, but it is scarce, and may occur only as a migrant here.

Sphaerophoria taeniata (Meigen, 1822)

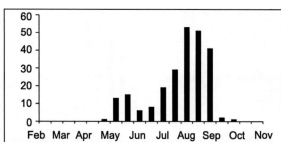

Biology
The larvae are unknown, but it has been reared from a puparium found on a *Phragmites* stem. It is generally found in rich, unimproved, damp grassland, often with *Juncus*, but also in open areas in damp woodland and scrub. Adults fly low amongst the vegetation and visit flowers such as *Ranunculus* and yellow composites.

Distribution
A rather scarce and local species of southern Britain, with a few records in the Welsh borders, the fens of Anglesey and northern Scotland, including a relatively recent record from north of Inverness.

Sphaerophoria virgata Goeldlin de Tiefenau, 1974

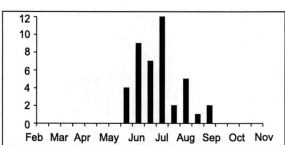

Biology
The larva is unknown. The adults appear to prefer sheltered, heathy locations, most records referring to heathy rides in conifer plantations, mixed woods or Scottish *Pinus* wood, though one mentions *Quercus* woodland, and another open *Betula*. It has been found on the flowers of heathers and *Potentilla erecta*, and has also been taken in water traps on heathland.

Distribution
A scarce and little known species, with few, widely scattered records extending from the New Forest to northern Scotland.

Sphaerophoria form A *sensu* Stubbs (1983)

Sphaerophoria species B *sensu* Stubbs (1991)

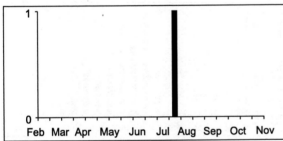

Biology
Unknown.

Distribution
A single male taken by Steven Falk in Hampshire may be an unusual variety of *S. interrupta*, which it closely resembles. More material is required to clarify the situation.

Biology
Unknown.

Distribution
A single male was taken by Alan Stubbs in Blean Woods, Kent in 1976. Further searches in the same area have failed to provide any more records. The male genitalia are very distinctive, but more material is required to show that this is not merely an aberrant individual. A new key to the British members of the genus is given by Stubbs (1996).

Sphegina clunipes (Fallén, 1816)

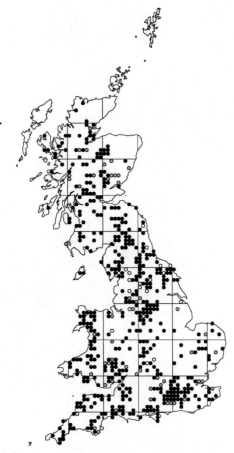

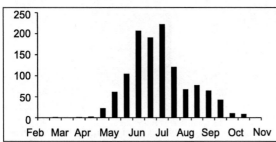

Biology
The larvae are found in sap-runs and other accumulations of decaying sap under bark, usually in damp shaded places. It is found in lush, damp undergrowth in broad-leaved woodland, including carr woodland, wooded river banks and fenland scrub. Adults seem to prefer shady situations and are rarely found outside the shade of woodland canopy and are normally taken by sweeping, but occasionally visit flowers in dappled sunlight.

Distribution
This is the most frequent member of the genus (with more than twice as many records received by the Recording Scheme for this species than for *S. elegans*, and nearly eight times as many than for *S. verecunda*), found in woodland throughout Britain. Curiously, northern specimens are much more colourful.

Sphegina elegans Schummel, 1843

Sphegina kimakowiczii Strobl in Stubbs and Falk (1983)

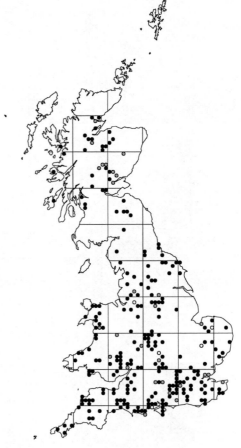

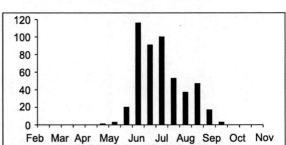

Biology
The larvae are found in accumulations of decaying sap under bark, usually in damp shaded places including under the bark of partially submerged logs in streams. Found in wet, shady woodland, generally in much wetter situations than is typical for *S. clunipes* and not usually far from water. Adults appear to stay in the shade of the canopy and very few records mention adults visiting flowers.

Distribution
Although both species are widely distributed throughout Britain, this species is much more patchily distributed than *S. clunipes*, although it is the more frequent species at some localities in the West Midlands.

Sphegina sibirica Stackelberg, 1953

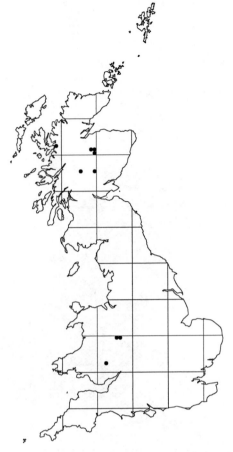

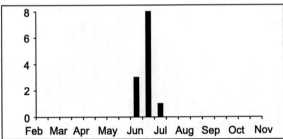

Biology

Larvae unknown, but females have been observed ovipositing on the underside of a cut *Picea* trunk lying across a stream (Speight 1998). In continental Europe, adults are found in *Picea* forests along the edges of paths and streams, where they often hover around freshly cut logs (Speight 1988a). So far in Britain, records come from grassy areas and stream-sides in or near *Picea* plantations.

Distribution

This species was added to the British list by Stubbs (1994) from Loch Duich in 1991, and has been found subsequently in several localities in south Wales, Shropshire and central Scotland. The occurrence of this species in Britain was predicted by Speight (1988a) and this work, and Stubbs (1996), should be consulted for separation from other British members of the genus. On the continent, it appears to be spreading rapidly westwards from Scandinavia and European Russia, and can be expected to turn up more frequently in the future.

Sphegina verecunda Collin, 1937

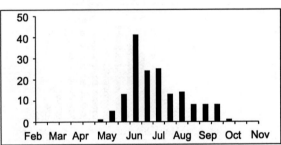

Biology

The larvae have been found in the exudates from a sap-run on *Ulmus*. It is found in wet shady situations in woodland and carr. Adults are found in shade, or dappled sunshine, usually close to wet areas or streams, and are occasionally found visiting flowers.

Distribution

This is much the scarcest member of the genus (leaving aside the newly discovered *S. sibirica*), with scattered records in the southern half of Britain, but a marked increase in frequency westwards. There are a few records from northern England and Scotland.

Syritta pipiens (Linnaeus, 1758)

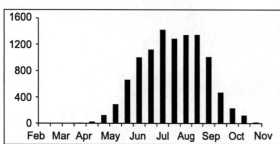

Biology

The larvae are found, often in large numbers, in wet decaying organic matter including compost heaps, manure heaps, cow-dung and silage, but not in pools and ponds. A ubiquitous species in lowland areas including anthropogenic habitats such as farmland, parks and gardens. Usually found flying low down amongst the vegetation or visiting flowers. It is very prominent at the end of the season when large numbers visit ivy flowers. Males patrol around flowers, manoeuvring slowly and with great agility, and engage in confrontations, where two males hover head to head, with one hovering backwards as the other approaches. It is not clear how the contest is decided, but one suddenly darts away whilst the other resumes patrolling.

Distribution

Widely distributed and very common throughout lowland Britain, but scarcer in upland areas and the more remote parts of Scotland.

Syrphus ribesii (Linnaeus, 1758)

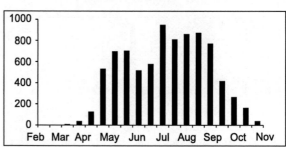

Biology

The larvae are commonly found feeding at all sorts of ground layer and arboreal aphid colonies. Overwintering larvae can often be found in leaf litter below aphid-infested *Acer pseudoplatanus* trees. Occur in most habitats, including woodland of all types, farmland, parks and gardens and urban areas. Adults can be found resting on sunny vegetation and visiting flowers of all sorts. The males hover amongst the canopy of woodlands and are responsible for the audible whine that can be heard in woodlands in mid-summer. This species is multiple-brooded, and so has a long season. It can be abundant in urban areas and gardens.

Distribution

One of the most widespread and abundant hoverflies throughout Britain.

Syrphus torvus Osten-Sacken, 1875

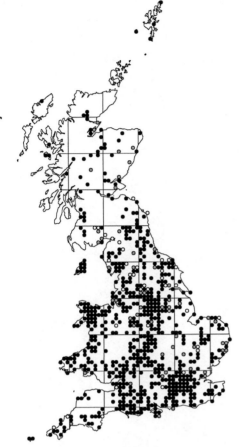

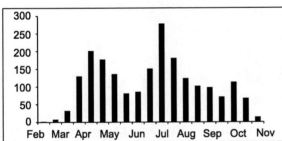

Biology

The larvae feed on a wide range of ground layer and arboreal aphids. Adults are usually, but not always, found around trees, with woodland edges, hedgerows, orchards and mature gardens being typical situations. They visit a wide range of flowers. Like *S. ribesii*, it is multiple-brooded and has a long flight season, but it tends to show marked, and quite brief peaks of abundance in the spring and again in mid-summer.

Distribution

This hoverfly (especially the female) is probably overlooked amongst other *Syrphus* species. There has been a tendency to think of this as a southern species, but recent records suggest that it is also common in Scotland. The records possibly indicate an increase in abundance westwards.

Syrphus vitripennis Meigen, 1822

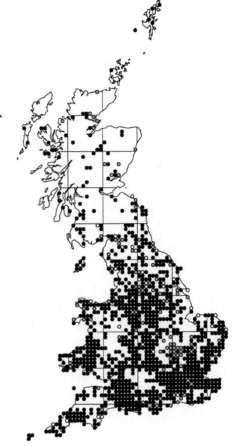

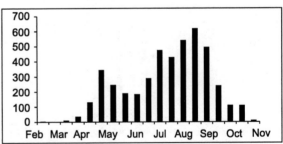

Biology

The larvae feed on aphids on a wide range of trees and shrubs. It is found in all types of woodland, scrub and hedgerow situations including urban parks and gardens. Adults visit a wide range of flowers and males hover high in the canopy. It is believed to be highly migratory and numbers are probably reinforced in some years by immigrants from the continent.

Distribution

Common and widespread throughout Britain.

Trichopsomyia flavitarsis (Meigen, 1822)

Parapenium flavitarsis (Meigen, 1822) in Coe (1953) and Kloet and Hincks (1976)

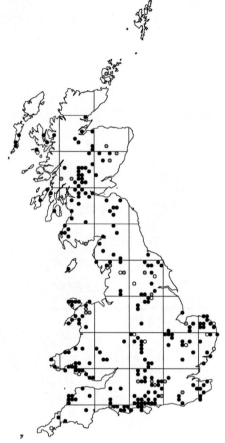

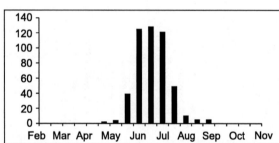

Biology

The larvae have been recorded feeding on the psyllid *Livia juncorum* in the galls that this insect forms on *Juncus articulatus*, but it may have additional predation strategies. Found in wet situations including fen, rushy meadows and boggy areas in moorland including *Myrica* stands and *Molinia* grasslands. Adults fly low amongst dense vegetation and visit low-growing flowers, such as *Potentilla erecta* and *Narthecium*. Males hover in small groups near shelter, such as bushes.

Distribution

Locally abundant where suitable habitat occurs, extending well above the tree line in the Scottish Highlands. Field experience suggests that this species is more frequent in the north and west of Britain, but this is not obvious from the map, which may reflect lower levels of recording in these areas. In southern Britain it is much more restricted by the availability of its habitat, but can still be found in suitable localities.

Triglyphus primus Loew, 1840

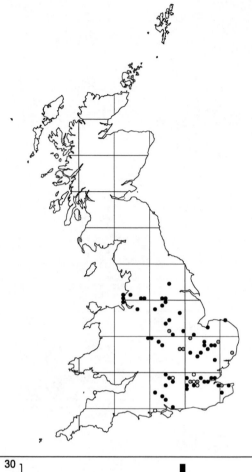

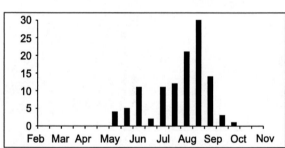

Biology

The larvae are aphidophagous, and appear to be specific to the galls induced by *Cryptosiphum artimisae* on *Artemisia vulgaris*. Adults are elusive, but tend to be found visiting flowers such as white umbels or resting on sunny foliage in the sorts of places that *Artemisia* grows. These include urban waste ground, abandoned quarries and disused railway lines, but also semi-natural grassland with an element of disturbance. For example, they have been found on Salisbury Plain near tank-damaged areas.

Distribution

Rather scarce and local in south-east Britain from around Dorset and Wiltshire eastwards, and north to about a line between the Mersey and the Humber. A number of recent records are associated with urban waste ground, for example in Sheffield and East London.

Tropidia scita (Harris, 1780)

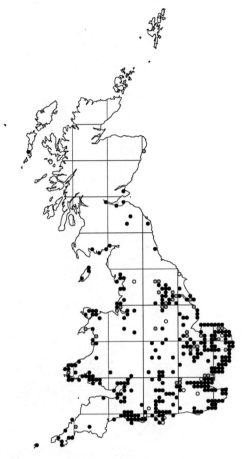

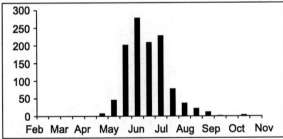

Biology
Mature larvae and puparia have been found between
the basal leaf sheaths of *Typha*. The larvae will
probably be found living in the wet plant debris
around the base of such emergent plants. It is found
among emergent vegetation, especially *Phragmites* and
Typha, in fens, ponds, drainage ditches and the edges
of slow rivers. Adults fly amongst stands of such
plants, settle on the stems and leaves and visit nearby
flowers including white umbels, *Ranunculus, Mentha*
and *Iris*. Males hover, sometimes for extended periods,
close to a leaf or stem.

Distribution
Locally abundant in wetlands throughout the lowlands
of England and Wales, but most frequent in coastal
wetlands and grazing levels, where it can be one of
the most abundant hoverflies. In the areas that used to
be occupied by fens in Cambridgeshire and south
Lincolnshire, it can still be found in ditches between
intensively managed cereal fields, providing that some
emergent vegetation is present, even if the water
quality appears very poor. In Scotland it is present in
the south, and has also recently been found on South
Uist in the Outer Hebrides.

Volucella bombylans (Linnaeus, 1758)

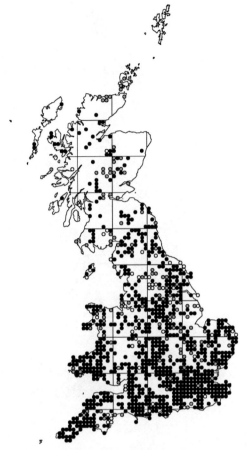

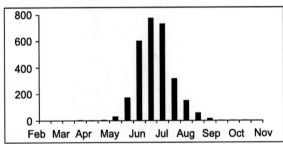

Biology
The larvae are scavengers and predators on the floor
of the nest cavity of social wasps (including the hornet
Vespa crabro Linnaeus) and bumblebees, where they
probably feed on larvae and pupae. The adults are
convincing bumblebee mimics, occurring in two main
colour forms, one of which mimics red-tailed, the
other white-tailed bumblebees. They are often found
visiting flowers or resting on sunny vegetation along
woodland edges, rides and glades, mature hedgerows
or in scrub. This species occurs rather earlier in the
season than other members of the genus.

Distribution
Widespread and common throughout Britain,
including several of the Scottish islands.

Volucella inanis (Linnaeus, 1758)

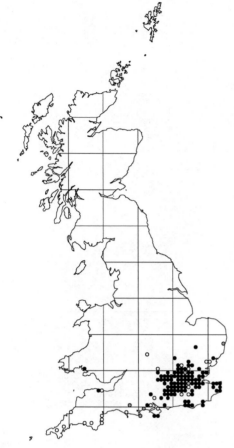

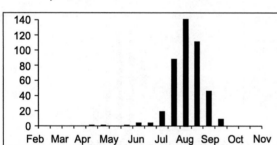

Biology

The larvae are ectoparasites of social wasp larvae, and have been found in association with *Vespula germanica* (Fabricius) and *Vespa crabro* Linnaeus. They are, unlike any other member of the genus, very flattened so that they fit into the larval cells beside the wasp larvae on which they feed. Found in open areas in woodland and scrub and, most frequently, in suburban areas, in parks and gardens. Adults are usually seen visiting flowers, especially white umbels and *Buddleja*.

Distribution

Locally abundant in the outer suburbs of London and the surrounding countryside. There are a few records away from this area, including scattered localities along the south coast from Kent to Cornwall, the Exmoor coast, South Wales and Oxfordshire.

Volucella inflata (Fabricius, 1794)

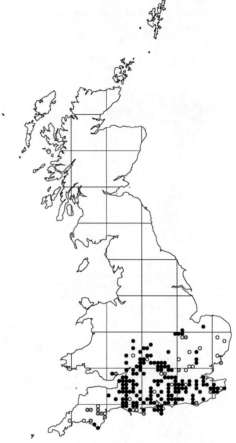

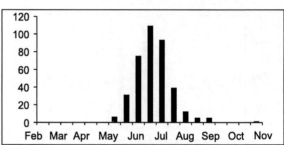

Biology

A larva has been found in a sap-run on *Quercus*, where it was probably feeding on other insect larvae. Females have been observed ovipositing in sap-runs, including those caused by goat moth caterpillars *Cossus cossus* (Linnaeus). It is generally found in or near woodland with overmature trees, where adults visit flowers such as *Rubus*, *Rosa* and *Heracleum* in sunny, open rides and glades.

Distribution

Locally frequent in heavily-wooded areas in the south of Britain, mainly south-east of a line from the Severn to the Wash. It is scarce in the more northerly parts of its range, and also in the East Midlands and East Anglia, probably because these areas are not well-wooded.

Volucella pellucens (Linnaeus, 1758)

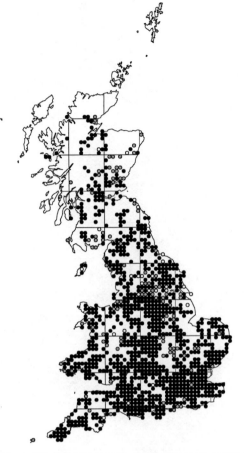

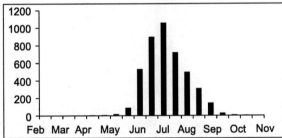

Biology
The larvae are scavengers and predators on the floor of the nest cavity of social wasps (including the hornet *Vespa crabro* Linnaeus), where they probably feed on wasp larvae and pupae. It is found in all sorts of woodland, in scrub and around large hedgerows. Also occurs in suburban parks and large, mature gardens. Adults are characteristically found visiting a wide range of flowers, but especially *Heracleum sphondylium*. Males are frequently seen hovering high up in a sunbeam over tracks in woodland rides and glades.

Distribution
Widespread and common throughout Britain, especially near woodland or scrub.

Volucella zonaria (Poda, 1761)

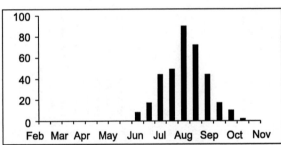

Biology
The larvae are scavengers and predators in the nests of social wasps (including the hornet *Vespa crabro* Linnaeus), where they probably feed on larvae and pupae. This, our largest and most spectacular hoverfly, seems to be almost entirely anthropogenic in Britain. It is usually seen visiting flowers in suburban areas where it occurs in parks and gardens. Many recent records come from civic amenity plantings around car-parks and urban roads.

Distribution
Verrall (1901) knew of only two specimens, and until about 1940 it was regarded as a rare vagrant to the south coast of England, and greatly prized by collectors. Then, during the 1940s, it began to become established in the London area and is now quite frequent, especially in the outer suburbs and in northern Kent. Its distribution elsewhere is remarkably similar to that of *V. inanis*, with a few scattered records along the south coast from Kent to Cornwall and also in the Bristol area. Records outside the London area seem to be increasingly frequent, so it may be spreading.

Xanthandrus comtus (Harris, 1780)

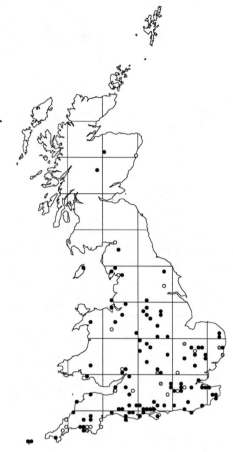

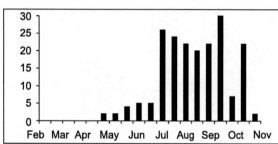

Biology

The larvae prey on gregarious caterpillars of yponomeutid and tortricid micro-moths. It occurs in woodland edges (broad-leaved and coniferous) and scrub where adults are usually found visiting flowers or resting on vegetation in clearings or along tracks.

Distribution

Although relatively frequent in older collections, this species underwent a period of decline and came to be regarded as a great rarity. It has evidently recovered, as there are numerous recent records at widely scattered localities throughout the southern half of Britain, and it has recently been re-found in Scotland (Rotheray 1992). Records remain very erratic, however, and there are few sites where it occurs regularly. This could possibly indicate that this species is a migrant.

Xanthogramma citrofasciatum (De Geer, 1776)

Xanthogramma festivum (Linnaeus, 1758)

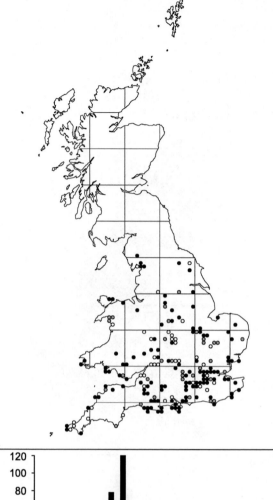

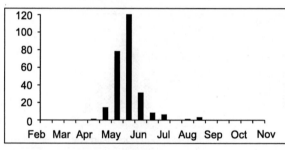

Biology

The larva has been found under turf and stones, and in *Lasius* nests, where it was once claimed they were fed by worker ants. In fact, it is more likely that they feed on ant-attended root aphids. It is generally found in grassy places including meadows, coastal grazing marsh, large gardens and woodland rides, and is usually associated with well drained situations such as occur on calcareous or sandy soils. This suggests that *Lasius flavus* (Fabricius) may be a likely host species. Adults fly low amongst the vegetation and visit a variety of flowers.

Distribution

This is much the least frequent of the two *Xanthogramma* species, and whilst widely scattered over the southern half of Britain north to Westmorland, it remains rather scarce. The majority of records are from downland in southern England.

Xanthogramma pedissequum (Harris, 1776)

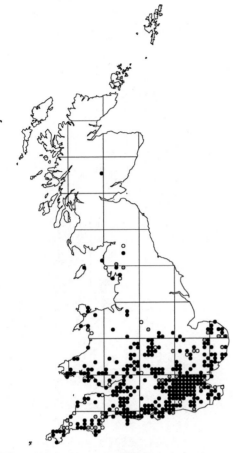

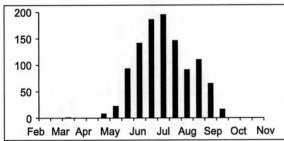

Biology

The larvae have been found in the galleries of the ant *Lasius niger* under a stone in a limestone quarry, in which the root aphid *Forda formicaria* was also present (Foster 1987). Another record from a nest of the same ant species records the presence of a different root aphid, *Trama* sp. (Dixon 1960). The species overwinters in the larval stage. It is found in flowery and grassy places including waste ground, disused railways, canal banks, gardens and woodland rides and edges. It appears to be associated with less well drained sites than *X. citrofasciatum* and there are a few records from acid grassland and wetlands.

Distribution

Local and usually scarce. About three times as many records have been submitted to the recording scheme for this species than for *X. citrofasciatum*, these being concentrated in southern England south of a line from the Severn to the Wash, and in South Wales. There are scattered records north of this, but it must be regarded as scarce in North Wales and northern England. There is a recent Scottish record from a shingle island in the River Tay in central Scotland.

Xylota abiens Meigen, 1822

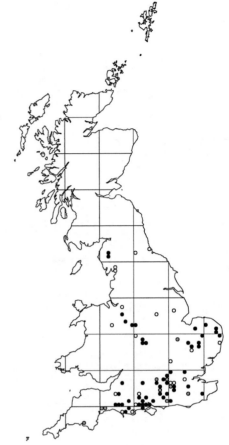

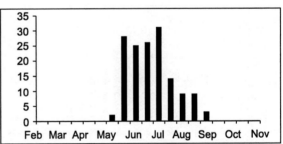

Biology

The larva has been found in the wet, decaying roots of a *Fagus* stump. It is associated with over-mature, broad-leaved woodland and usually occurs close to water. Adults bask on stumps and fallen logs in small clearings or can be found running about over vegetation in dappled sunlight. As with many of the species of this genus, it is not often found visiting flowers.

Distribution

A scarce species recorded mainly from south-east England, but with scattered records north to Cumberland and Durham.

Xylota coeruleiventris Zetterstedt, 1838

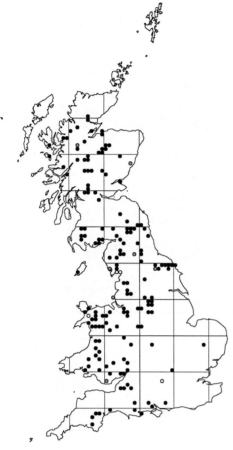

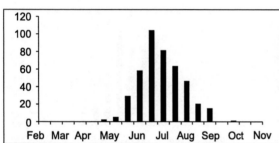

Biology

The larvae are found in sap-filled tunnels of the bark weevil *Hylobius abietis* (Linnaeus) (Rotheray & Stuke 1998). It is associated with conifer plantations, and unlike most members of the genus, can frequently be found visiting flowers, especially *Ranunculus*, in open spaces such as rides, fire-breaks and wayleaves. It is particularly abundant in areas felled 2–3 years previously, after which time the stumps become suitable for the weevil larvae.

Distribution

Although there are museum specimens from Caledonian pine forest in the Highlands of Scotland going back to the end of the last century, recent records extend throughout northern and western Britain. It seems to have spread southwards into conifer plantations, and to be continuing to do so, with recent records from Dartmoor, the Mendips, Kent (record not mapped) and Breckland. If this trend continues, it will be found in most parts of Britain before too long, except perhaps for the East Midlands and the Fens.

Xylota florum (Fabricius, 1805)

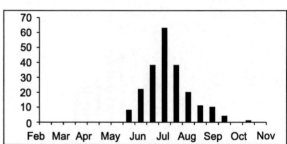

Biology

The larvae are associated with decaying wood and sap. An association with *Populus nigra* has been claimed, based on rearing records, but this dates from before it was separated from *X. coeruleiventris* and *X. meigeniana* so the identity of these records must be in some doubt. Adults are usually found in damp places in woodland such as stream-sides, where they can be seen sunning on logs, including those partially submerged in water. There would appear to be a strong concentration of records on the acid heaths of south-east England.

Distribution

A scarce species of southern Britain with scattered records extending northwards to Cumbria and Durham, but with most records from well-wooded areas of central-southern England, and also from South Wales.

Xylota segnis (Linnaeus, 1758)

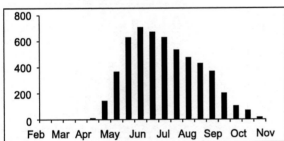

Biology
The larvae have been found in decaying sap under the bark of trees, and in sap-runs created by the bark weevil *Hylobius abietis* (Linnaeus), but also in habitats not associated with trees, such as silage and decomposing potatoes. It occurs in all sorts of woodland and scrub, but also along hedgerows and in parks and gardens. Adults are typically seen running rapidly backwards and forwards over sunlit foliage. They rarely visit flowers.

Distribution
Widespread and common in woodland and scrub of all kinds throughout Britain

Xylota sylvarum (Linnaeus, 1758)

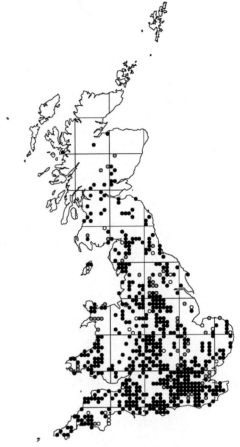

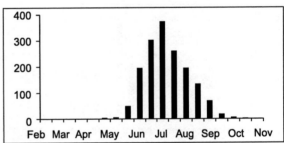

Biology
The larvae feed in the soft, decaying heartwood of various trees (*Abies, Fagus, Quercus*) including deep underground in the roots. They have also been reared from decaying sawdust. It occurs in woodland and scrub, including large hedgerows. Adults are typically seen running rapidly backwards and forwards over sunlit foliage or basking on stumps and fallen branches. They rarely visit flowers.

Distribution
Widespread and common in wooded districts throughout England and Wales, but becoming scarcer further north. In Scotland it is rather local, although widespread south of the Highlands and extends northwards to Aberdeenshire (Stubbs 1996).

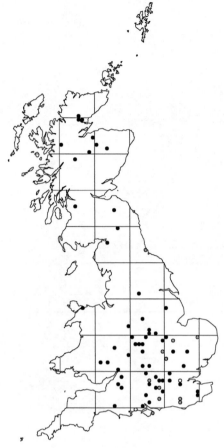

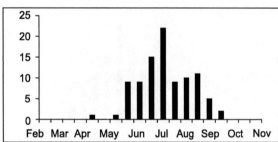

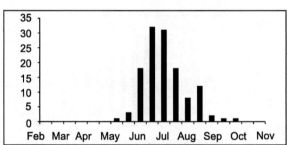

Biology

The larvae have been found in a sap-run near the base of *Populus tremula*. They are usually found in damp situations in woodland, at the edges of wet woodland, or near streams, but nearly always where over-mature trees are present. Adults run rapidly over sunlit foliage of bushes and trees or bask on stumps and bare ground. Rarely visits flowers.

Distribution

A scarce species mainly found in the Midlands and central-southern England, but with scattered records north to the Scottish Highlands.

Biology

The larvae have been found in rot-holes of *Taxus*. It usually occurs in or near ancient broad-leaved woodland, although, according to Speight (1998) it favours sites with well-drained soils. Adults are found running rapidly over foliage or basking on sunlit trunks in clearings. There appear to be no records of this species visiting flowers.

Distribution

Rare and largely confined to the southern half of Britain, but also found in old woodland on limestone in Yorkshire (Stubbs 1996). It was found to be locally abundant in some woods near Coventry by staff of the Herbert Art Gallery & Museum in the early 1980s.

ACKNOWLEDGEMENTS

No atlas project can be achieved without the help of a large number of recorders and we are indebted to all who have contributed to the scheme. We are particularly grateful to the recorders who have consistently sent large numbers of records on a yearly basis, but also to those who undertook the immense task of computerising records for their recording area and have supplied these in machine-readable form. Owing to this range of sources the list below represents all recorders listed on the database, including long-dead dipterists whose records have been trawled from museum specimens, notebooks and the published literature. We hope that this atlas, which represents the combined efforts of many hundreds of dipterists, will stimulate renewed activity and interest in hoverfly recording.

A A Abbott, D M Ackland, F C Adams, J H Adams, J E Addey, M V Albertini, M Aldridge, Dr K N A Alexander, P B M Allan, A A Allen, G W Allen, R H Allen, M Amphlett, R H Andrew, Sir C H Andrewes, H W Andrews, D Ansati, D M Appleton, Dr M E Archer, R Archer, J S Armitage, G Armstrong, V Arnold, C D Ash, J H Ashworth, R R Askew, R S Atkins, A E Atmore, E W Aubrook, L F H Audcent, E Austen, J Avery, J S Badmin, J E Bailey, M P Bailey, P R Bailey, W E Bailey, C Bain, Dr S G Ball, T Balmer, F Bancroft, C J Banks, D Barker, A Barlow, C Barlow, R M Barnes, R J Barnett, S L Barnett, B Barr, M Barr, P J Barraud, J D Barringer, P L Barringer, W L Barringer, A Barron, C Bartlett, J Bartlett, S Bates, D M Bayne, G Beasley, A J Beattie, A Beaumont, R A Beaver, I C Beavis, J E Bebbington, Rev W Becher, S Beck, F C Bedwell, D H Beech, B P Beirne, P Bellamy, R M Belringer, P Belton, F H Bendorf, C Bennett, R B Benson, C Bentley, E Benton, T Benton, R Bergin, D S Bertram, A K Best, N Best, P L Th Beuk, Z Bhatia, J Biglin, M Bigmore, A Binding, A E Binding, Miss J E Binding, C Bindon, T Bindon, T Bird, Dr N L Birkett, P Black, T Blackburn, Dr K G Blair, J Blair, K Bland, I Blatchley, Rev E N Bloomfield, M G Bloxham, D Bolton, O C Boon, R F Botterill, J Bowden, J P Bowdrey, J W Bowhill, J J Bowley, D C Boyce, C W Bracken, A Brackenbury, A Brackenridge, M D Bradford, A E Bradley, P G Bradley, R C Bradley, J H Bratton, M C Brian, B Brigden, A Brindle, R K Brinklow, H J Britten, T Brock, D Bromwich, M T Brooke, M G Broome, M O Broome, R R Broome, A J Brown, C R Brown, E S Brown, J D H Brown, P Brown, P Brown, J M Brummitt, J Bryant, A Buckham, A S Buckhurst, P Buckland, G G Buckley, E J Bunnett, A Burbridge, J H Burkill, J Burn, H L Burrows, E Burt, J F Burton, R J L Burton, R Busbridge, P Butcher, R Butterfield, W K Butterfield, P Cameron, J M Campbell, W Cane, G D H Carpenter, J W Carr, L A Carr, D Carstairs, A E J Carter, H Carter, J W Carter, G Cartwright, K M Catley, D Cawthorne, E A Chadderton, J Chadwick, A Chalkley, J M Chalmers-Hunt, S J Chambers, C G Champion, P J Chandler, G S Channer, R A Chapman, A O Chater, C A Cheetham, Prof J M Cherrett, E Christie, I C Christie, Dr S E Christmas, H F Church, S P Clancey,

Dr M Claridge, D I Clark, D J Clark, Prof J Clark, S Clark, A Clarke, D J Clarke, W E Clarke, K Clarkson, P Clarkson, E W Classey, G Clayton, T M Clegg, Dr D K Clements, L Clemons, J Clifton, J A Clifton, R Clinging, W Clynes, P R Cobb, N Cobley, Dr W P Cocks, R L Coe, E Coetzee, A Coker, S J Coker, J D Coldwell, J H Cole, R Cole, W S Cole, S R Colenutt, C L Collenette, J E Collin, G A Collins, J J Collins, C N Colyer, M A Common, M Conway, B D Cooke, H Cooke, F W Coombes, A E Cooper, J E Cooter, P J Copson, H H Corbett, P Corkhill, F S Cotton, F J Coulson, T Coult, W S Cowin, J Cowley, L V Crellin, S M Crellin, M Crick, M Crittenden, R Cropper, I Cross, S Cross, W Cross, R Crossley, P N Crow, E Crozier, J Cudworth, S B Cull, P W Currie, D Cuthbertson, M J D'Oyly, C W Dale, J C Dale, A A Dallman, H W Daltry, H V Danks, A S Davidson, J W Davidson, W F Davidson, A M Davies, Miss B Davies, B N K Davies, J E Davies, Dr L Davies, W G Davis, N Davison, W Davison, Dr C D Day, F H Day, M C Day, Ade Porochin, W F Dean, A Dearden, Dr K Decleer, J C Deeming, Dr D Denman, Dr J S Denton, H G Denvil, S Derry, C J Devlin, J R Dibb, T Dickenson, Dr G H L Dicker, J A Dickinson, Dr R H L Disney, Capt C Diver, J Dobson, S Dobson, H Dodds, M H Dolling, H St J K Donisthorpe, E A Douglas, P Douglas, D Down, P Downey, P Doyle, E Drabble, H Drabble, R A Drahe, Dr C M Drake, R A Drake, E Dransfield, I Draycott, D J Dredge, J Driver, A G Duff, E A Duffey, R D Dumbrell, Sir A B Duncan, G A Dunlop, C Dunn, T C Dunn, W R Dunstan, K C Durrant, R Eades, T R Eagles, M Edgington, H Edmunds, B Edwards, F W Edwards, J Edwards, K Edwards, M Edwards, R E Edwards, R L Edwards, S R E Edwards, T G Edwards, D Element, J H Elliott, E A Ellis, J Ellis, T Ellis, A C Else, G R Else, Dr W Elstow, W A Ely, D W Emley, P F Entwhistle, G H Evans, S Evans, W Evans, H Eve, B C Eversham, Dr M D Eyre, W Fairhead, S J Falk, H Falkener, D Farrar, L Farrel, T Faulds, C Faulkner, C Felton, J C Felton, A Ferguson, K Ferguson, E H Fielding, Dr M G Fitton, V Fitton, J Flannagan, H E Flint, J H Flint, P W H Flint, D S Fluum, C Flynn, P Follett, E C M d'Assis Fonseca, J B Ford, L T Ford, R L E Ford, W K Ford, W J Fordham, G Forester, J B Formstone, A Forsyth, A P Foster, S Foster, J A Fowler, A P Fowles, A Fox, D G Fox, H L Fox, G Fox-Wilson, Rev E E Frampton, Dr I S Francis, N Frankel, J P L Franks, P Franks, N D Frankum, P Freeman, Miss T Freeman, Dr C N French, R French, J S Frost, R Fry, D T Fryer, R Gabrielle, A Galt, J J M Gammack, L Gander, M Gandy, A E Gardener, B Gardiner, S P Garland, P Garner, W J Garnett, L S Garrad, G Garratt-Jones, A Garside, C Gaskin, J Gendall, R S George, W S George, A E Gibbs, D J Gibbs, M R Gibbs, R Gibbs, C Gibson, J Gibson, D Gilbert, F S Gilbert, Dr O Gilbert, M W Gilchrist, J P Gill, B Gillam, E F Gilmour, S Ginley, M R Gipson, G Glombeck, P Goddard, A Godfrey, N Goff, Capt E R Goffe, J Goldsmith, M Goldthorp, B Goodey, R Goodier, R Goodier, R Goodwin, I J Gordon, C Gorham, M S Gorham, L Gorman, N Gowing, A Grace, G Grace, M de V Graham, P Grainger, W R O Grant, N C Grattan, G R Gray, J R A Gray, A Grayson, J N Greatorex-Davies, D M Green, M Green, S V Green, A Greensmith, J L Gregory, S Gregory, L W Grensted, A Grieve, C F Griffith, G C D Griffiths, Dr P

Griffiths, M A Grimes, P H Grimshaw, S J Grove, E W
Groves, K M Guichard, B Gummer, C M Gummer,
A Gunn, D Hackett, E C M Haes, F H Haines,
B Hakwood, H Halkyard, Dr M Hall, P Hall, S E Hall,
D H Hall-Smith, J Halliburton, A J Halstead, K H
Halstead, S Hamilton, A H Hamm, C O Hammond,
D Hance, J Hancell, E G Hancock, M Hancox, M W
Hanson, J A Hardman, L W Hardwick, T W Harman,
D J Harries, G J Harris, Rev H A Harris, P L Harris,
R Harris, F Harrison, C Hart, B G Harthon, J C Hartley,
A Harvey, M C Harvey, P R Harvey, B S Harwood,
P Harwood, R Harwood, W H Harwood, G Haslehurst,
Dr J Haslett, C N Hasnip, R B Hastings, F L Hatcher,
Miss K Hawkins, R D Hawkins, R Hawley, N A Hayes,
S J Hayhow, W H Haywood, G A Hazelhurst,
J Hazelhurst, J R Heal, D J Heaver, D G Hemingway,
D Henderson, R Henderson, J Herbert, G H Herrich,
W C Hewitson, S M Hewitt, T Hextell, B Hider, K Hill,
R Hillier, H W Hills, W D Hincks, S H Hind, L W
Hinxman, B M Hitching, J Hobart, B M Hobby, P J
Hodge, J Hodgson, W G Hoff, A Hold, J A Hollier, G J
Holloway, D Holmes, Dr P R Holmes, S Holyfield,
M Hooley, P Hope Jones, A J Hopkins, G W Hopkins,
D A Horne, E C Horrell, E G Horrocks, H Horsfall,
D Horsfield, G Hosie, D Houlihan, V Howard, Dr M A
Howe, Dr E A Howe, P Howe, C A Howes, A C
Hubbard, I R Hudson, C F Huggins, H C Huggins, M O
Hughes, Dr M Hull, A Humphries, R J Hunt, D Hunter,
C Hutchinson, J Hutchinson, Dr P Hyman, A Idle, D A
Iliff, S F Imber, P Inchbald, A J Innes, Dr A G Irwin,
Dr J W Ismay, Miss D A Iveson, B E Jackson,
E Jackson, F A Jackson, L H Jackson, S N A Jacobs,
M J James, T James, Dr N F Janes, M G Jefferies, D J
Jeffers, F H Jenkinson, J H Jenkinson, J H A Jenner,
M Jenner, F B Jennings, M Jermyn, R O Jermyn, Col T
Jermyn, J B Jobe, Dr B Johnson, C Johnson, E J
Johnson, R Johnson, D R Jolley, A W Jones, C J Jones,
C M Jones, D Jones, N F Jones, N P Jones, R A Jones,
R A Jones, R E Jones, R G Jones, S Jones, V Jones, R J
Juckes, S Judd, P G Keates, D Keen, S Kelly, D A
Kendall, P Kendall, D Kendrick, A Kennard,
J Kennaugh, W B Kenneth-Booker, S Kent-Francis,
G Kernings, G B Kershaw, L Kett, D K Kevan, Dr R S
Key, B M Keywood, L N Kidd, F J Killington, G J King,
J J F X King, S King, N Kingett, Dr P Kirby, S J Kirby,
T W Kirkpatrick, T B Kitchen, D B Kloet, G S Kloet,
G Knight, R Knight, S A Knill-Jones, J Kramer, J Kydd,
J Laczo, Dr C G Lamb, S J Lambert, F Lancaster, S A
Lane, M R Langden, R Langdon, M Langston, B Last,
H Last, T Latham, P Latus, B R Laurence, R I Lawson,
A Lazenby, R Leagas, R Learett, R L Leavett, M J
Lebane, M Lee, W J Lee, R C Leeke, R S Leeke, D Lees,
R Lees, A Leftwick, A E LeGros, B J Lempke,
D Leonard, L Lester, T P Levett, D A Levy, E T Levy,
J E Levy, R Lewington, D Lewis, J W Lewis, K Limb,
M Limbert, C Lines, K Lines, J Linton Smith, R J
Livingston, D S Lloyd, S M Lloyd, Dr L Lloyd-Evans,
K Loney, Dr A G Long, G B Longstaff, I Lorimer, D A
Lott, D Loughlin, A M Low, Dr E E Lowe, D M Lownie,
H Lucas, Dr J Lucas, S P P Lucas, Dr M L Luff, Dr B
MacClean, I C MacDonald, S MacDonald,
I MacGowan, J Maiden, S Malcolm, D Malone, D J
Mann, S A Manning, W Mansbridge, P Mapplebeck,
K W Mardle, C Marjot, N Marks, T A Marshall,
N Marven, J E Maskrey, G Mason, R L Mason, J R
Mather, G Matthes, C Matthews, M G Matthews, T H
Mawdesley, S May, D Maylam, P Maynard,
A McCallum, J A J McCleary, I McClenaghan,

J McCracken, D McCutcheon, J McDonald, M McEwan,
I McGillan, G Y McInnes, Dr I F G McLean,
I McLenaghan, N F McMillan, S J McWilliams, Dr R H
Meade, A V Measday, P Mellor, C Melvill, R K
Merrifield, A J Merrill, D G Merry, H N Michaelis,
M Middler, H W Miles, J Miles, S R Miles, D Miller, J E
Miller, J E Millett, R Mills, E Milne-Redhead, E Milner,
A V Moon, A Moore, D Moore, J Moore, S A Moran,
I K Morgan, M J Morgan, B Morley, C Morley,
A Morris, Dr M G Morris, P Morris, Dr R Morris, R K A
Morris, S T Morris, S L Moseley, E H Moss, J Mouseley,
S Muddiman, J G Murgatroyd, J H Murgatroyd,
M Murgatroyd, M D Murphy, J Murray, D Musson,
L Nathan, G R Naylor, R Naylor, G Neale, J M Nelson,
S Nelson, Dr C Neville, J A Newbould, M J Newcombe,
E Newman, S Newman, S A Newsome, M Newstead,
Dr A H Newton, J Newton, C Nicholson, G E Nixon,
H Noble, F Norgate, G M Norman, R Normand,
I Norrington, E R Nye, W O'Dwyer, M A O'Neill,
C O'Toole, M Oates, W R Ogilvie-Grant, D Okines,
T Oldfield, N Onslow, G W Ord, D F Owen, J Owen,
Prof J A Owen, L Packer, J Pain, D E M Paish, Dr C J
Palmer, S M Palmer, H S Papworth, A R Parker, J B
Parker, L Parker, M J Parker, W Parker, S Parkin,
L Parmenter, A J Parr, J D Parrack, C Parry, A J
Parsons, M S Parsons, T Parsons, M W J Paskin, V S
Paton, I J Patterson, P M Pavett, K G Payne, R G
Payne, R M Payne, R Peacock, E K Pearce, N D F
Pearce, A W Pearcey, D Peasegood, M N Peckham,
E C Pelham-Clinton, M Pennington, T H Pennington,
F Pepper, R C L Perkins, V R Perkins, I Perry, J F Perry,
B Peterek, L M Peters, Prof W Peters, R Petley-Jones,
W Philips, J Phillips, R Phillips, E G Philp, A Philpot,
J Piekarczyk, F N Pierce, A Piffard, B Pinchen, N Pipe,
R Pitt, D M Pittkin, A R Plant, C W Plant, S Pollard, A C
Pont, Dr J Pontin, D G Pope, J Pope, N Pope, G T
Porritt, D A Porter, J Porter, Dr K Porter, P Porter, S P J
Potter, T Potter, W Potter, G Potts, R H Poulding,
M Poulton, T Prater, C B Pratt, P J Precey, E V
Prendergast, S Price, J A Prichard, G Prior, J A
Pritchard, M C Probert, D A Procter, C H W Pugh, M N
Pugh, K A Pyefinch, G Pyman, G A Pymen, J Quigley,
S Rae, L Raeburn, G Ramel, S Randolf, E B Rands, A C
Rapson, D R Ratcliffe, F Ratter, N O M Ravenscroft,
R W J Read, N D Redgate, P J Reeve, C A M Reid,
D Reid, M C Reid, R Reid, S Reid, T Rheinhalt, J D
Rhodes, J P Richards, O W Richards, E Richardson,
N R Richardson, N J Riddiford, E C Riggall, G Riley,
J Riley, T H Riley, E Rivenhall, T Robathan, J Robbins,
R Robbins, A S Roberts, K A S Roberts, Dr M J Roberts,
P Roberts, S P M Roberts, D M Robertson, E Robertson,
R B Robertson, Dr J Robinson, Dr W Robinson, W D
Roebuck, R H Rogers, T D Rogers, W A Rollason,
P Roper, Dr G E Rotheray, N C Rothschild, G Rottger,
G B Routledge, R W Rowe, K Rowland, K M Rowland,
M Rowland, C Rowse, J Ruffle, B Russell, D Russell,
H M Russell, R Russell, C I Rutherford, G B Rutlidge,
P W Ryan, Dr M A Salmon, M Samworth, A G
Sandford, J Sankey, C Sargeant, T Saunders, J W Saunt,
R Saville, B Sawford, N Sawyer, M M Schofield, J Scott,
S Scrivens, L A Searle, A Sestakovs, M Shaffer, Dr D
Sharp, R Sharples, E Shaw, Dr M R Shaw, R Shaw,
S Shaw, Dr D A Sheppard, C Sherringham, J F Shillito,
G Shingleton, P R Shirley, Dr D B Shirt, A Shooter, G E
Shreeves, K C Side, E H Sills, F Sills, M Simmonds,
A Simmons, K Simmons, M J Simmons, C Simms,
Dr A N B Simpson, G Simpson, Dr P Skidmore, S W
Skillman, J F Skinner, L Slack, G C Slawson, H D Smart,

M J Smart, A Smith, Dr A H V Smith, A J Smith, B D S
Smith, C J Smith, D A Smith, D H Smith, E J Smith,
G Smith, G Smith, G A Smith, I F Smith, K G V Smith,
L Smith, M J M Smith, M N Smith, Dr P H Smith,
A Sneddon, P Sokoloff, K Sorensen, R South,
A Spalding, Dr M C D Speight, A G Spencer, B Sperry,
Dr C R Spilling, Dr B M Spooner, G M Spooner,
V Spouge, W H Spreadbury, W Stanley, S Stares,
Dr R E Stebbings, D Steel, A Steele, J Steer, A W
Stelfox, P G Stenton, B Stephens, J F Stephens,
P Stephenson, D Stevens, F Stewart, R Stewart,
B Stobart, DA Stone, MW Storey, Dr DJ Stradling,
D Streeter, H M Stuart, A E Stubbs, M Sullivan,
D Summers, D P Sumner, S E Surl, S L Sutton, H D
Swain, M C Swan, Dr N R Sweet, S M Swift, P R Symes,
E E Syms, R J Tallack, Col W G Teagle, D Telfer, R K
Templeton, P Terry, J H Theaker, J A Thickitt, C D
Thomas, C F Thomas, D G Thomas, N Thomas,
O Thomas, R Thomas, A T Thompson, J E Thompson,
M H Thompson, M L Thompson, Rev A Thornley,
E Thorpe, J E Thorpe, E E Thoyts, P J Tilbrooke,
R Tomlinson, N Topham, C J Trant, L A C Truscott,
D Tucker, S M Turk, C Turner, J Turner, S J Turpin,
D W Twigg, J Tyler, R W J Uffen, Dr R Underwood,
D Unwin, W Urwin, J Valentine, D Vallance, B van
Peperzel, M van Veen, R Vandersteen, Prof G C Varley,
A Vaughan Jones, R Veal, Dr B Verdcourt, P W
Verdon, G H Verrall, W A Vice, J R Vokeroth, A Waas,
R O Wace, A Waddington, K G Wagstaff, R Wagstaffe,
C J Wainwright, J C Wainwright, A Wake, S Wakely,
Dr A Walker, B J Walker, F A Walker, B D Wallace,
Dr I D Wallace, G Waller, J Wallis-Kew, G B Walsh,
C L Walton, H F Walton, J D Ward, P H Ward,
J Wardrope, M Warhurst, Dr P Waring, Dr A C Warne,
D F Warren, A Wass, M Waterhouse, J Waterston, M G
Watkins, C Watson, J A Watson, J F Watson, J H
Watson, S Watson, K R Watt, W E L Wattam, L E Watts,
M V Watts, O Watts, R E Waugh, R D Weal, J Webster,
M Weir, R C Welch, A R Welstead, B Wetton, Dr P S
Whalley, C R Wheway, F C Whiston, D White, J H
White, I E Whitehead, P Whitehead, P F Whitehead,
D Whiteley, H Wickison, A Wight, M Wilcox, V Wilkin,
B Wilkinson, C Wilkinson, B Willers, A Williams, C J
Williams, D W Williams, H Williams, J Williams, M G
Williams, S A Williams, J Willis, E Wills, D Wilson, N M
Wilson, C W Wiltshire, D Winsland, P Q Winter, A J
Wise, P Withers, J Wollner, H Womersley, J H Wood,
T Wood, Rev A E Woodruffe-Peacock, Ms M
Wooldridge, S J Woolfall, L H Woollatt, P Wormell,
J Worth, A E Wright, B A Wright, G S Wright, J D
Wright, M Wright, R Wright, N Wyatt, P Wyett, I R
Wynne, C S Yeates, Col J W Yerbury, M R Young.

The maps were drawn using the DMAP computer
package developed by Dr Alan J. Morton.

Drafts were read and comments were received
from a number of people including Steve Crellin,
Peter Hodge, Dave and Ted Levy, Graham
Rotheray, Roger Payne, Ivan Perry, Colin Plant, Alan
Stubbs, Eilien Thorpe and Brian Wetton. We would
particularly like to thank Alan Stubbs for his help
and encouragement over the years without which
we would not even have begun this task.

Finally we are indebted to Paul Harding, Mark Telfer
and Henry Arnold of the Biological Records Centre,
CEH Monks Wood and Karen Threlfall of CEH
Publications for their help in editing and preparing
this atlas for publication.

REFERENCES

Barr, B. 1995. Feeding behaviour and mouthpart structure of larvae of *Microdon eggeri* and *Microdon mutabilis* (Diptera, Syrphidae). *Dipterists Digest*, New series, **2**, 31–36.

Barr, B. 1996. *Mallota cimbiciformis* (Diptera, Syrphidae) in Lanarkshire. *Dipterists Digest*, New series, **3**, 4.

Beuk, P.L.T. 1990. A hoverfly of the genus *Epistrophe* (Dipt., Syrphidae) new to Britain. *Entomologist's monthly Magazine*, **126**, 167–170.

Bloomfield, Rev. E.N. 1895. Rare British Diptera in the British Museum (Natural History), South Kensington. *Entomologist's monthly Magazine*, **31**, 113–115.

Brischke, C.G. 1880. Uber Fliegenmaden aus *Scrophularia nodosa* u. *Pteris aquilina*. *Entomologische Nachrichten Berlin*, **6**, 56.

Chandler, P.J. 1998. Checklist of Insects of the British Isles (New Series) Part 1: Diptera. *Handbooks for the Identification of British Insects*, **12**, 1–234.

Claussen, C. & Kassebeer, C.K. 1993. Eine neue Art de Gattung *Cheilosia* Meigen 1822 aus den Pyrenaen (Diptera: Syrphidae). *Ent. Z., Franf. a. M.*, **103**, 420–427.

Coe, R.L. 1953. Diptera, Syrphidae. *Handbooks for the Identification of British Insects*, **10**(1), 1–98.

Collin, J.E. 1918. A Dipteron new to the British List. *Transactions of the Entomological Society of London (Proceedings)*, 1918: lxxvii.

Collin, J.E. 1940. Notes on Syrphidae (Diptera). IV. *Entomologist's monthly Magazine*, **76**, 150–158.

Collin, J.E. 1950. A second species of *Myolepta* (Diptera, Syrphidae). *Journal of the Society of British Entomology*, **3**, 133–137.

Department of the Environment. 1995. *Biodiversity: the UK Steering Group report*. 2 volumes. London: HMSO.

Dobson, J. 1997. Oviposition in *Epistrophe diaphana* (Syrphidae). *Dipterists Digest*, New series, **4**, 47.

Doczkal, D. 1996. Observations host plants and behaviour of egg-laying females of *Cheilosia* Meigen (Diptera, Syrphidae) in central Europe. *Volucella*, **2**, 77–85.

Dixon, T.J. 1960. Key to and description of the third instar larvae of some species of Syrphidae (Diptera) occurring in Britain. *Transactions of the Royal Entomological Society of London*, **112**, 345–379.

Entwistle, P.F. 1995. Hoverflies north of Inverness. *Hoverfly Newsletter*, No. **20**, 2–5.

Entwistle, P.F. & Stubbs, A.E. 1983. *Preliminary atlas of the hoverflies (Diptera: Syrphidae) of the British Isles*. Huntingdon: Biological Records Centre.

Falk, S.J. 1990. *Eristalis pratorum* (Meigen, 1822): a new British hoverfly. *British Journal of Entomology and Natural History*, **3**, 139–141.

Falk, S.J. 1991a. *A review of the scarce and threatened flies of Great Britain* (Part 1). Research and Survey in Nature Conservation, No. 39. Peterborough: Nature Conservancy Council.

Falk, S.J. 1991b. *Scaeva selenitica* (Meigen) recorded in March with discussion of the overwintering status of *Scaeva* species in Britain. *Dipterists Digest*, **8**, 36–37.

Foster, A.P. 1987. *Xanthogramma pedissequum* (Harris) (Dip.: Syrphidae) bred from a *Lasius niger* (L.) (Hym.: Formicidae) nest. *Entomologists Record & Journal of Variation*, **99**, 44.

Gilbert, F.S. 1986. *Hoverflies*. Naturalists' Handbooks, No. 5. Cambridge: Cambridge University Press.

Goeldlin de Tiefenau, P., Maibach, A. & Speight, M.C.D. 1990. Sur quelques de *Platycheirus* (Diptera, Syrphidae) nouvelles ou méconnues. *Dipterists Digest*, **5**, 19–44.

Heaver, D. 1990. *Epistrophe ochrostoma*: new to Britain. *Hoverfly Newsletter*, No. **10**, 8.

Imhof, G. 1979. Arthropod communities connected with *Phragmites*. *Monographia biol.*, **37**, 389–405.

Kloet, G.S. & Hincks, W.D. 1976. A Check List of British Insects, Part 5: Diptera and Siphonaptera. *Handbooks for the Iidentification of British Insects*, **11**(5), 1–139.

Levy, E.T. & Levy, D.A. 1994. *Eoseristalis cryptarum* (Diptera, Syrphidae) on Dartmoor. *Dipterists Digest*, New Series, **1**, 86.

Levy, E.T. & Levy, D.A. 1998. *Somerset hoverflies*. Yeovil: Somerset Wildlife Trust.

Levy, E.T., Levy, D.A. & Dean, W.F. 1992. *Dorset hoverflies*. Dorchester: Dorset Environmental Records Centre.

MacGowan, I. 1994. Creating breeding sites for *Callicera rufa* Schummel (Diptera, Syrphidae) and a further host tree. *Dipterists Digest*, New Series, **1**, 6–8.

MacGowan, I. & Watt, K. 1994. A further record of *Parasyrphus nigritarsis* (Zetterstedt, 1843) (Diptera: Syrphidae), with a review of its known distribution in Britain. *Dipterists Digest*, New series, **1**, 26–28.

Morris, R.K.A. 1998. *Hoverflies of Surrey.* Woking: Surrey Wildlife Trust.

Palmer, C.J. 1985. *Hoverflies (Diptera: Syrphidae) in the collections of the Herbert Art Gallery & Museum, Coventry, U.K.* Coventry: Herbert Art Gallery & Museum.

Palmer, C. 1996. A further record of *Scaeva albomaculata* in Britain and a note on the K.G. Blair collection of British Diptera. *Dipterists Digest*, New Series, **2**, 97–99.

Plant, C.W. 1990. *Sphaerophoria bankowskae* Goeldlin, 1989 (Syrphidae) recorded in mainland Britain. *Dipterists Digest*, **3**, 32–33.

Rotheray, G.E. 1990. An old specimen of a new European *Platycheirus* species (Dipt., Syrphidae). *Entomologist's monthly Magazine*, **126**, 204.

Rotheray, G.E. 1992. *Xanthandrus comtus* (Harris) (Dipt., Syrphidae) breeding in Scotland. *Entomologist's monthly Magazine*, **128**, 57–58.

Rotheray, G.E. 1994. Colour guide to hoverfly larvae (Diptera, Syrphidae) in Britain and Europe. *Dipterists Digest*, **9**, 1–155.

Rotheray, G.E. 1996. The larvae of *Brachyopa scutellaris* Robineau-Desvoidy (Diptera, Syrphidae), with a key to and notes on the larvae of British *Brachyopa* species. *Entomologist's Gazette*, **47**, 199–205.

Rotheray, G.E. 1997. Larval stages of the predatory hoverflies *Trichopsomyia flavitarsis* (Meigen), *Platycheirus melanopsis* Loew and *Parasyrphus nigritarsis* (Zetterstedt) (Diptera, Syrphidae). *Entomologist's Gazette*, **48**, 127–134.

Rotheray, G.E. 1998. *Platycheirus splendens* sp. n. from Britain formerly confused with *Platycheirus scutatus* (Diptera, Syrphidae). *Entomologist's Gazette*, **49**, 271–276.

Rotheray, G.E. & MacGowan, I. 1990. Re-evaluation of the status of *Callicera rufa* Schummel (Dipt., Syrphidae) in the British Isles. *Entomologist*, **109**, 35–42.

Rotheray, G.E. & Stuke, J-H. 1998. Third stage larvae of four species of saproxylic Syrphidae (Diptera), with a key to the larvae of British *Criorhina* species. *Entomologist's Gazette*, **49**, 209–217.

Shirt, D.B. (ed.) 1987. *British Red Data Books 2: Insects.* Peterborough: Nature Conservancy Council.

Smith, K.G.V. 1989. An introduction to the immature stages of British flies. *Handbooks for the Identification of British Insects*, **10**(14), 1–280.

Speight, M.C.D. 1976. The puparium of *Chrysotoxum festivum* (L.) (Dipt., Syrphidae). *Entomologists Record & Journal of Variation*, **88**, 51–52.

Speight, M.C.D. 1978. The genus *Paragus* (Dipt.: Syrphidae) in the British Isles including a key to the known and possible British Isles species. *Entomologists Record & Journal of Variation*, **90**, 100–107.

Speight, M.C.D. 1985. Adjustments to the Irish hoverfly list (Diptera, Syrphidae). *Irish Naturalists Journal*, **21**, 385–391.

Speight, M.C.D. 1986. *Cheilosia argentifrons* (Diptera: Syrphidae) new to Ireland: *Donacia cinerea* (Coleoptera: Chrysomelidae) and *Palloptera muliebris* (Diptera: Pallopteridae), presence confirmed in Ireland. *Irish Naturalists Journal*, **22**, 159–160.

Speight, M.C.D. 1987. Redefinition of *Cheilosia ahenea* and *C. argentifrons* with records extending the known range of these species in western Europe (Diptera, Syrphidae). *Annales - Société Entomologique de France*, New series, **23**, 299–308.

Speight, M.C.D. 1988a. Syrphidae known from temperate Western Europe: potential additions to the fauna of Great Britain and Ireland and a provisional species list for N. France. *Dipterists Digest*, **1**, 2–35.

Speight, M.C.D. 1988b. *Doros destillatorius,* espèce nouvelle pour la France, avec désignation des types des deux espèces européennes du genre *Doros,* description de leurs pupes et clès de détermination des adultes et des pupes. *Bull. Soc. Ent. Fr.*, **92**, 193–200.

Speight, M.C.D. 1989a. *Sphaerophoria fatarum* in the British Isles (Syrphidae). *Dipterists Digest*, **2**, 34.

Speight, M.C.D. 1989b. *Saproxylic invertebrates and their conservation.* Nature and Environment series, No. 42. Strasbourg: Council of Europe.

Speight, M.C.D. 1991. *Callicera aenea, C. aurata, C. fagesii* and *C. macquartii* redefined, with a key to and note on the European *Callicera* species (Diptera: Syrphidae). *Dipterists Digest*, **10**, 1–25.

Speight, M.C.D. 1996. *Cheilosia psilophthalma* and *Odinia boletina*: insects new to Ireland and *Sapromyza sexpunctata* confirmed as an Irish species (Diptera: Syrphidae, Odiniidae and Lauxaniidae). *Irish Naturalists Journal*, **25**, 178–182.

Speight, M.C.D. 1998. *Species accounts of European Syrphidae (Diptera): the Atlantic zone species (revised).* Syrph the Net publications, Vol. 7. Dublin: Syrph the Net.

Speight, M.C.D. & Chandler, P.J. 1995. *Paragus constrictus, Pteromicra pecterosa & Stegana similis*: insects new to Ireland and *Stegana coleoptrata,* presence in Ireland confirmed. *Irish Naturalists Journal*, **25**, 28–32.

Speight, M.C.D. & Goeldlin de Tiefenau, P. 1990. Keys to distinguish *Platycheirus angustipes, P. europaeus, P. occultus* and *P. ramsarensis* (Dipt., Syrphidae) from other *clypeatus* group species known in Europe. *Dipterists Digest*, **5**, 5–18.

Speight, M.C.D. & Vockeroth, J.R. 1988. *Platycheirus amplus*: an insect new to Ireland not previously recorded from Europe (Diptera: Syrphidae). *Irish Naturalist Journal*, **22**, 447–452.

Stace, C. 1997. *New flora of the British Isles*. Second edition. Cambridge: Cambridge University Press.

Stubbs, A.E. 1980. The rearing of *Cheilosia paganus* and *Cheilosia fraterna* (Diptera: Syrphidae). *Entomologists Record & Journal of Variation*, **92**, 114-117.

Stubbs, A.E. 1981. *Anasimyia contracta* Claussen & Torp, 1980 and *A. interpuncta* (Harris, 1776) (Diptera: Syrphidae) in Britain. *Proceedings and Transactions of the British Entomological and Natural History Society*, **14**, 10–11.

Stubbs, A.E. 1982. Hoverflies as primary woodland indicators with reference to Wharncliffe Woods. *Sorby Record*, No. **20**, 62–67.

Stubbs, A.E. 1989. An additional British *Sphaerophoria* discovered in Devon. *Dipterists Digest*, **2**, 34–35.

Stubbs, A.E. 1990. The beginning of Diptera recording schemes in Britain. *Dipterists Digest*, **6**, 2–6.

Stubbs, A.E. 1994. *Sphegina* (*Asiosphegina*) *sibirica* Stackelberg, 1953 a new species and sub-genus of hoverfly (Diptera, Syrphidae) in Britain. *Dipterists Digest,* New Series, **1**(1), 23–25.

Stubbs, A.E. 1995. Advances to the British hoverfly list: 1901 - 1990. *Dipterists Digest*, New series, **2**, 13–23.

Stubbs, A.E. 1996. *British hoverflies: second (revised and enlarged) supplement*. London: British Entomological & Natural History Society.

Stubbs, A.E. & Falk, S.J. 1983. *British hoverflies: an illustrated identification guide*. London: British Entomological & Natural History Society.

Stuke, J.H. 1996. *Helophilus affinis* new to the British Isles (Diptera, Syrphidae). *Dipterists Digest*, New series, **3**(1), 45–46.

Torp, E. 1984. De danske svirrefleur. *Danmarks Dyreliv*, Bind 1, Fauna Boger, Copenhagen. [Danish Hoverflies - in Danish. 2nd edition:1994]

UK Biodiversity Group. 1998. *UK Biodiversity Group Tranche 2 Action Plans*. Peterborough: English Nature.

UK Biodiversity Steering Group. 1995. *Biodiversity: the UK Steering Group Report, Volume 2: Action Plans.* London: HMSO.

Van der Goot, V.S. 1981. De zweefvliegen van Noordwest – Europa en Europees Rusland, in het bijzonder van Benelux. KNNV, Utgave no 32. Amsterdam.

Verrall, G.H. 1901. *British Flies 8: Syrphidae, etc.* Reprinted 1969 edition. Faringdon: Classey.

Vockeroth, J.R. 1990. Revision of the Neararctic species of *Platycheirus* (Diptera, Syrphidae). *Canadian Entomologist*, **122**, 659–766.

Watt, K.R. and Robertson, D.M. 1990. *Eupeodes lundbecki* (Soot-Ryen) (Diptera, Syrphidae) new to Britain and its separation from related species. *Dipterists Digest*, **6**, 23–27.

Whiteley, D. 1988. *Cheilosia argentifrons* Hellen - a hoverfly new to Derbyshire and Great Britain. *Derbyshire Entomological Society Quarterly Journal*, No. **93**, 5.

Whiteley, D. 1995. Using Diptera for assessment of local wetlands. *Sorby Record*, **31**, 82–83.

SPECIES INDEX

This species index incorporates all species names used in the text, whether synonyms or currently accepted names. Synonyms are italicised. Bold page references refer to the map, histogram and species account.

A

abbreviata, Sphaerophoria 132
abiens, Xylota 11, **147**
abusivus, Eristalis **61**
aenea, Callicera 10, 22
aenea, Neoascia 98
aeneus, Eristalinus **60**
aeneus, Eristalis 60
aerosa, Melanogaster 11, **88**
affinis, Helophilus 6, **74**
ahenea, Cheilosia 5
albifrons, Paragus 11, **101**, 102
albimanus, Platycheirus 91, **112**, 115
albipila, Cheilosia **26**
albitarsis, Cheilosia **26**
albomaculata, Scaeva 6, **128**
albostriatus, Dasysyrphus **51**
albostriatus, Syrphus 51
alneti, Didea 6, 10, **54**
ambiguus, Melanostoma 113
ambiguus, Platycheirus **113**
amplus, Platycheirus **113**, 120
analis, Microdon 11, **94**
Anasimyia contracta **15**, 17
Anasimyia interpuncta 10, **15**, 16
Anasimyia lineata **16**
Anasimyia lunulata 10, **16**
Anasimyia transfuga 15, **17**
angustatus, Platycheirus **114**
annulatus, Parasyrphus **103**
annulatus, Syrphus 103
annulipes, Didea 59
annulipes, Megasyrphus 10, 59
annulipes, Syrphus 59
anthracina, Psilota 11, **126**
antiqua, Cheilosia **27**, 41
arbustorum, Eristalis **62**
arctica, Melangyna **83**
arcticus, Syrphus 83
Arctophila fulva 17
Arctophila mussitans 17
Arctophila superbiens **17**
arcuatum, Chrysotoxum **45**, 46

argentifrons, Cheilosia 39
asilica, Criorhina 10, **49**
aurata, Callicera 10, **22**
auricollis, Meliscaeva **92**
auricollis, Syrphus 92
austriaca, Pipiza **108**

B

Baccha elongata **18**
Baccha obscuripennis 18
balteatus, Episyrphus 6, **59**
balteatus, Syrphus 59
bankowskae, Sphaerophoria **131**
barbata, Cheilosia 10, **27**
barbifrons, Melangyna 11, **84**
barbifrons, Syrphus 84
batava, Sphaerophoria **132**
berberina, Criorhina 10, **49**
bergenstammi, Cheilosia **28**
bicinctum, Chrysotoxum **45**
bicolor, Brachyopa 10, **19**
bifasciatus, Syrphus 56
bimaculata, Pipiza **108**, 109, 110
bimaculatus, Brachypalpus 21
Blera fallax 6, 10, 13, **18**
bombylans, Volucella **143**
Brachyopa bicolor 10, **19**
Brachyopa insensilis 10, **19**
Brachyopa pilosa 10, **20**
Brachyopa scutellaris 10, **20**
Brachypalpoides lentus 10, **21**
Brachypalpus bimaculatus 21
Brachypalpus eunotus 24
Brachypalpus laphriformis 10, **21**, 24
brevicornis, Orthonevra 11, **100**
brevidens, Heringia 10, **77**
brevidens, Neocnemodon 10, 77

C

caledonicus, Chamaesyrphus 10, **25**
Caliprobola speciosa 10, **22**
Callicera aenea 10, 22

Callicera aurata 10, **22**

Callicera rufa 7, 10, **23**

Callicera spinolae 6, 10, 13, **23**

campestris, Rhingia **127**

carbonaria, Cheilosia 10, **28**

cautum, Chrysotoxum **46**

cemiteriorum, Chrysogaster **43**

Chalcosyrphus eunotus 10, **24**

Chalcosyrphus nemorum 10, **24**

chalybeata, Chrysogaster 43

Chamaesyrphus caledonicus 10, **25**

Chamaesyrphus lusitanicus 25

Chamaesyrphus scaevoides 10, **25**

Cheilosia ahenea 5

Cheilosia albipila **26**

Cheilosia albitarsis **26**

Cheilosia antiqua **27**, 41

Cheilosia argentifrons 39

Cheilosia barbata 10, **27**

Cheilosia bergenstammi **28**

Cheilosia carbonaria 10, **28**

Cheilosia chrysocoma 10, **29**

Cheilosia corydon 31

Cheilosia cynocephala 10, **29**

Cheilosia fasciata 38

Cheilosia fraterna **30**

Cheilosia globulipes 36

Cheilosia griseiventris **30**, 33

Cheilosia grossa **31**

Cheilosia honesta 10, 32

Cheilosia illustrata **31**

Cheilosia impressa **32**

Cheilosia intonsa 33

Cheilosia lasiopa 10, **32**

Cheilosia laskai 5

Cheilosia latifrons 30, **33**

Cheilosia latigens 5

Cheilosia longula **33**

Cheilosia maculata 126

Cheilosia mutabilis 5, 10, **34**

Cheilosia nasutula 41

Cheilosia nebulosa 10, **34**

Cheilosia nigripes 10, **35**

Cheilosia pagana **35**

Cheilosia praecox 5, **36**

Cheilosia proxima **36**, 40

Cheilosia psilophthalma 5

Cheilosia pubera 5, 10, **37**

Cheilosia ruffipes 39

Cheilosia sahlbergi 10, **37**

Cheilosia scutellata **38**

Cheilosia semifasciata 10, **38**

Cheilosia soror 10, **39**

Cheilosia species A **42**

Cheilosia species B 10, **43**

Cheilosia species C 30

Cheilosia species D 36

Cheilosia species E 36

Cheilosia uviformis **39**

Cheilosia variabilis **40**

Cheilosia velutina 10, **40**

Cheilosia vernalis **41**

Cheilosia vicina **41**

Cheilosia vulpina **42**

chrysocoma, Cheilosia 10, **29**

Chrysogaster cemiteriorum **43**

Chrysogaster chalybeata 43

Chrysogaster hirtella 88

Chrysogaster macquarti 11, 88

Chrysogaster solstitialis 43, **44**

Chrysogaster virescens **44**

Chrysotoxum arcuatum **45**, 46

Chrysotoxum bicinctum **45**

Chrysotoxum cautum **46**

Chrysotoxum elegans 8, 10, **46**

Chrysotoxum festivum **47**

Chrysotoxum octomaculatum 7, 8, 10, **47**

Chrysotoxum vernale 10, **48**

Chrysotoxum verralli 47, **48**

cimbiciformis, Mallota 11, **83**

cincta, Melangyna **84**

cinctella, Meliscaeva **93**

cinctellus, Syrphus 93

cinctus, Syrphus 84

citrofasciatum, Xanthogramma **146**, 147

clunipes, Sphegina 11, **138**

clypeatus agg., Platycheirus **114**

clypeatus, Platycheirus **115**, 116, 119, 122

Cnemodon latitarsis 78

Cnemodon verrucula 79

Cnemodon vitripennis 79

coeruleiventris, Xylota 5, 11, **148**

compositarum, Melangyna **85**, 86

comtus, Xanthandrus 6, 11, **146**

conopseus, Doros 10, 55

consimilis, Helophilus 106

consimilis, Parhelophilus 11, **106**

constrictus, Paragus 5, 102

contracta, Anasimyia **15**, 17

corollae, Eupeodes 6, **68**, 71

corollae, Metasyrphus 68

corollae, Syrphus 68

corydon, Cheilosia 31

Criorhina asilica 10, **49**

Criorhina berberina 10, **49**

Criorhina floccosa 10, **50**

Criorhina ranunculi 10, **50**

cryptarum, Eoseristalis 62

cryptarum, Eristalis 7, 10, **62**

cuprea, Ferdinandea 10, **73**

cyaneus, Platycheirus 112

cynocephala, Cheilosia 10, **29**

Cynorrhina fallax 18

D

Dasysyrphus albostriatus **51**

Dasysyrphus friuliensis 5, **51**, 52

Dasysyrphus hilaris **52**

Dasysyrphus lunulatus 52

Dasysyrphus pinastri **52**

Dasysyrphus tricinctus **53**

Dasysyrphus venustus 52, **53**

devius, Microdon 8, 11, **94**

diaphana, Epistrophe 10, **56**

diaphanus, Syrphus 56

Didea alneti 6, 10, **54**

Didea annulipes 59

Didea fasciata 10, **54**, 55

Didea intermedia 10, **55**

discimanus, Platycheirus 11, **115**

dispar, Neoascia 99

Doros conopseus 10, 55

Doros profuges 7, 8, 10, **55**

dubia, Myolepta 6, 11, **96**

dubium, Melanostoma 11, **89**, 90

dubium, Melanostoma mellinum var. 89

E

eggeri, Microdon 11, 94

elegans, Chrysotoxum 8, 10, **46**

elegans, Sphegina 11, **138**

eligans, Epistrophe **56**

eligans, Syrphus 56

elongata, Baccha **18**

Eoseristalis cryptarum 62

Epistrophe diaphana 10, **56**

Epistrophe eligans **56**

Epistrophe euchroma 11, 91

Epistrophe grossulariae 10, **57**

Epistrophe melanostoma **57**

Epistrophe nitidicollis 10, **58**

Epistrophe ochrostoma **58**

Episyrphus balteatus 6, **59**

equestris, Merodon 5, **93**

ericarum, Melangyna 11, **85**

ericarum, Syrphus 85

Eriozona erratica 5, 10, **59**

Eriozona syrphoides 5, **60**

Eristalinus aeneus **60**

Eristalinus sepulchralis **61**

Eristalis abusivus **61**

Eristalis aeneus 60

Eristalis arbustorum **62**

Eristalis cryptarum 7, 10, **62**

Eristalis horticola **63**, 65

Eristalis interruptus **63**, 65

Eristalis intricarius **64**

Eristalis nemorum 63

Eristalis pertinax **64**, 65

Eristalis pratorum 65

Eristalis rupium 10, 63, **65**

Eristalis sepulchralis 61

Eristalis similis **65**

Eristalis tenax 6, **66**

erratica, Eriozona 5, 10, **59**

euchroma, Epistrophe 11, 91

euchromum, Meligramma 11, **91**

euchromus, Syrphus 91

Eumerus ornatus 10, **66**

Eumerus sabulonum 10, **67**

Eumerus strigatus **67**

Eumerus tuberculatus 5, 67, **68**

eunotus, Brachypalpus 24

eunotus, Chalcosyrphus 10, **24**

Eupeodes corollae 6, **68**, 71

Eupeodes lapponicus 6, 10, **69**

Eupeodes latifasciatus **69**

Eupeodes latilunulatus 10, **70**

Eupeodes lundbecki 6, **70**

Eupeodes luniger **71**

Eupeodes nielseni 10, **71**

Eupeodes nitens 10, **72**

Eupeodes species A **72**

europaeus, Platycheirus 114, **116**

F

fallax, Blera 6, 10, 13, **18**

fallax, Cynorrhina 18

fasciata, Cheilosia 38

fasciata, Didea 10, **54**, 55

fatarum, Sphaerophoria **132**

fenestrata, Pipiza 108, **109**, 110

Ferdinandea cuprea 10, **73**

Ferdinandea ruficornis 10, **73**

ferruginea, Hammerschmidtia 7, 10, 13, **74**

festivum, Chrysotoxum **47**

festivum, Xanthogramma 146

flavitarsis, Parapenium 142

flavitarsis, Trichopsomyia **142**

floccosa, Criorhina 10, **50**

florea, Myathropa **95**

florea, Myiatropa 95

florum, Xylota 11, **148**

form A, Melanostoma **90**

form A, Sphaerophoria **137**

fraterna, Cheilosia **30**

friuliensis, Dasysyrphus 5, **51**, 52

frutetorum, Helophilus 106

frutetorum, Parhelophilus **106**

fulva, Arctophila 17

fulviventris, Platycheirus **116**

G

geniculata, Neoascia 11, **97**

geniculata, Orthonevra 11, **100**

glaucia, Leucozona **81**, 82

glaucius, Syrphus 81

globulipes, Cheilosia 36

granditarsa, Pyrophaena 117

granditarsus, Platycheirus **117**, 122

griseiventris, Cheilosia **30**, 33

groenlandicus, Helophilus 6, 10, **75**

grossa, Cheilosia **31**

grossulariae, Epistrophe 10, **57**

grossulariae, Syrphus 57

guttata, Melangyna 11, 91

guttatum, Meligramma 11, **91**

guttatus, Syrphus 91

H

haemorrhous, Paragus **102**

Hammerschmidtia ferruginea 7, 10, 13, **74**

Helophilus affinis 6, **74**

Helophilus consimilis 106

Helophilus frutetorum 106

Helophilus groenlandicus 6, 10, **75**

Helophilus hybridus 74, **75**

Helophilus lineatus 16

Helophilus lunulatus 16

Helophilus parallelus 76

Helophilus pendulus **76**

Helophilus transfuga 17

Helophilus trivittatus 6, **76**

Helophilus versicolor 107

Helophilus vittatus 81

heringi, Heringia **77**

Heringia brevidens 10, **77**

Heringia heringi **77**

Heringia latitarsis 10, **78**

Heringia pubescens 10, **78**, 79

Heringia verrucula 11, **79**

Heringia vitripennis **79**

hilaris, Dasysyrphus **52**

hirtella, Chrysogaster 88

hirtella, Melanogaster 27, **88**

honesta, Cheilosia 10, 32

horticola , Eristalis **63**, 65

hybridus, Helophilus 74, **75**

I

illustrata, Cheilosia **31**

immarginatus, Platycheirus 11, **117**

impressa, Cheilosia **32**

inanis, Volucella 11, **144**, 145

inflata, Volucella 11, **144**

insensilis, Brachyopa 10, **19**

intermedia, Didea 10, **55**

interpuncta, Anasimyia 10, **15**, 16

interrupta, Neoascia 11, **97**

interrupta, Sphaerophoria **133**, 137

interruptus, Eristalis **63**, 65

intonsa, Cheilosia 33

intricarius, Eristalis **64**

K

kimakowiczii, Sphegina 11, 138

L

labiatarum, Melangyna 85, **86**

laphriformis, Brachypalpus 10, **21**, 24

lappona, Sericomyia **130**

lapponicus, Eupeodes 6, 10, **69**

lapponicus, Metasyrphus 10, 69

lapponicus, Syrphus 69

lasiopa, Cheilosia 10, **32**

lasiophthalma, Melangyna **86**

lasiophthalmus, Syrphus 86

laskai, Cheilosia 5

laternaria, Leucozona 81, **82**

laternarius, Syrphus 82

latifasciatus, Eupeodes **69**

latifasciatus, Metasyrphus 69

latifasciatus, Syrphus 69

latifrons, Cheilosia 30, **33**

latigens, Cheilosia 5

latilunulatus , Metasyrphus 10, 70

latilunulatus, Eupeodes 10, **70**

latilunulatus, Syrphus 70

latitarsis, Cnemodon 78

latitarsis, Heringia 10, **78**

latitarsis, Neocnemodon 10, 78

Lejogaster metallina **80**

Lejogaster splendida 11, 80

Lejogaster tarsata **80**

Lejops vittatus 11, **81**

lenta, Xylota 21

lenta, Xylotomima 21

lentus, Brachypalpoides 10, **21**

Leucozona glaucia **81**, 82

Leucozona laternaria 81, **82**

Leucozona lucorum **82**

lineata, Anasimyia **16**

lineatus, Helophilus 16

lineola, Parasyrphus **103**

lineola, Syrphus 103

loewi, Sphaerophoria 11, **133**

longula, Cheilosia **33**

lucorum, Leucozona **82**

lugubris, Pipiza 11, 108, **109**, 110

lundbecki, Eupeodes 6, **70**

luniger, Eupeodes **71**

luniger, Metasyrphus 71

luniger, Syrphus 71

lunulata, Anasimyia 10, **16**

lunulatus, Dasysyrphus 52

lunulatus, Helophilus 16

lunulatus, Syrphus 52

lusitanicus, Chamaesyrphus 25

luteitarsis, Pipiza 11, **110**

luteola, Myolepta 11, 96

M

macquarti, Chrysogaster 11, 88

maculata, Cheilosia 126

maculata, Portevinia 11, **126**

maculipennis, Pipizella 11, **111**

malinellus, Parasyrphus **104**

malinellus, Syrphus 104

Mallota cimbiciformis 11, **83**

manicatus, Platycheirus **118**

mecogramma, Scaeva 6, **129**

mecogramma, Syrphus 129

Megasyrphus annulipes 10, 59

meigeniana, Xylota 148

Melangyna arctica **83**

Melangyna barbifrons 11, **84**

Melangyna cincta **84**

Melangyna compositarum **85**, 86

Melangyna ericarum 11, **85**

Melangyna guttata 11, 91

Melangyna labiatarum 85, **86**

Melangyna lasiophthalma **86**

Melangyna quadrimaculata **87**

Melangyna triangulifera 11, 92

Melangyna umbellatarum **87**

Melanogaster aerosa 11, **88**

Melanogaster hirtella 27, **88**

melanopsis, Platycheirus 11, **118**

Melanostoma ambiguus 113

Melanostoma dubium 11, **89**, 90

Melanostoma form A **90**

Melanostoma mellinum **89**, 90

Melanostoma mellinum var. dubium 89

Melanostoma scalare **90**

Melanostoma species A 11

melanostoma, Epistrophe **57**

Meligramma euchromum 11, **91**

Meligramma guttatum 11, **91**

Meligramma trianguliferum 11, **92**

Meliscaeva auricollis **92**

Meliscaeva cinctella **93**

mellinum var. dubium, Melanostoma 89

mellinum, Melanostoma **89**, 90

menthastri, Sphaerophoria 133

Merodon equestris 5, **93**

metallina, Lejogaster **80**

Metasyrphus corollae 68

Metasyrphus lapponicus 10, 69

Metasyrphus latifasciatus 69

Metasyrphus latilunulatus 10, 70

Metasyrphus luniger 71

Metasyrphus nielseni 10, 71

Metasyrphus nitens 10, 72

Metasyrphus species A 72

meticulosa, Neoascia **98**

Microdon analis 11, **94**

Microdon devius 8, 11, **94**

Microdon eggeri 11, 94

Microdon mutabilis 11, **95**

mussitans, Arctophila 17

mutabilis, Cheilosia 5, 10, **34**

mutabilis, Microdon 11, **95**

Myathropa florea **95**

Myiatropa florea 95

Myolepta dubia 6, 11, **96**

Myolepta luteola 11, 96

Myolepta potens 6, 11, **96**

N

nasutula, Cheilosia 41

nebulosa, Cheilosia 10, **34**

nemorum, Chalcosyrphus 10, **24**

nemorum, Eristalis 63

nemorum, Xylota 24

nemorum, Xylotomima 24

Neoascia aenea 98

Neoascia dispar 99

Neoascia geniculata 11, **97**

Neoascia interrupta 11, **97**

Neoascia meticulosa **98**

Neoascia obliqua 11, **98**

Neoascia podagrica **99**

Neoascia tenur **99**

Neocnemodon brevidens 10, 77

Neocnemodon latitarsis 10, 78

Neocnemodon pubescens 10, 78

Neocnemodon verrucula 11, 79

Neocnemodon vitripennis 79

nielseni, Eupeodes 10, **71**

nielseni, Metasyrphus 10, 71

nielseni, Platycheirus **119**, 120

nigripes, Cheilosia 10, **35**

nigritarsis, Parasyrphus 11, **104**

nigritarsis, Syrphus 104

nitens, Eupeodes 10, **72**

nitens, Metasyrphus 10, 72

nitidicollis, Epistrophe 10, **58**

nitidicollis, Syrphus 58

nobilis, Orthonevra **101**

noctiluca, Pipiza 108, 109, **110**

O

obliqua, Neoascia 11, **98**

obscuripennis, Baccha 18

occultus, Platycheirus 114, 117, **119**, 121

ochrostoma, Epistrophe **58**

octomaculatum, Chrysotoxum 7, 8, 10, **47**

ornatus, Eumerus 10, **66**

Orthonevra brevicornis 11, **100**

Orthonevra geniculata 11, **100**

Orthonevra nobilis **101**

Orthonevra splendens 128

P

pagana, Cheilosia **35**

Paragus albifrons 11, **101**, 102

Paragus constrictus 5, 102

Paragus haemorrhous **102**

Paragus tibialis 5, 11, **102**

parallelus, Helophilus 76

Parapenium flavitarsis 142

Parasyrphus annulatus **103**

Parasyrphus lineola **103**

Parasyrphus malinellus **104**

Parasyrphus nigritarsis 11, **104**

Parasyrphus punctulatus **105**

Parasyrphus vittiger **105**

Parhelophilus consimilis 11, **106**

Parhelophilus frutetorum **106**

Parhelophilus versicolor **107**

pedissequum, Xanthogramma **147**

Pelecocera tricincta 11, **107**

pellucens, Volucella **145**

peltatus agg., Platycheirus **120**

peltatus, Platycheirus 113, 119, **120**

pendulus, Helophilus **76**

perpallidus, Platycheirus 11, **121**

personata, Pocota 7, 11, **125**

pertinax, Eristalis **64**, 65

philanthus, Sphaerophoria **134**

pilosa, Brachyopa 10, **20**

pinastri, Dasysyrphus **52**

pipiens, Syritta **140**

Pipiza austriaca **108**

Pipiza bimaculata **108**, 109, 110

Pipiza fenestrata 108, **109**, 110

Pipiza lugubris 11, 108, **109**, 110

Pipiza luteitarsis 11, **110**

Pipiza noctiluca 108, 109, **110**

Pipizella maculipennis 11, **111**

Pipizella varipes 111

Pipizella viduata **111**, 112

Pipizella virens 11, **112**

Pipizella zeneggenensis 111

Platycheirus albimanus 91, **112**, 115

Platycheirus ambiguus **113**

Platycheirus amplus **113**, 120

Platycheirus angustatus **114**

Platycheirus clypeatus **115**, 116, 119, 122

Platycheirus clypeatus agg. **114**

Platycheirus cyaneus 112

Platycheirus discimanus 11, **115**

Platycheirus europaeus 114, **116**

Platycheirus fulviventris **116**

Platycheirus granditarsus **117**, 122

Platycheirus immarginatus 11, **117**

Platycheirus manicatus **118**

Platycheirus melanopsis 11, **118**

Platycheirus nielseni **119**, 120

Platycheirus occultus 114, 117, **119**, 121

Platycheirus peltatus 113, 119, **120**

Platycheirus peltatus agg. **120**

Platycheirus perpallidus 11, **121**

Platycheirus podagratus 11, **121**

Platycheirus ramsarensis 114, **122**

Platycheirus rosarum **122**

Platycheirus scambus **123**

Platycheirus scutatus 9, **123**, 124

Platycheirus species A 119

Platycheirus splendens 13, 123, **124**

Platycheirus sticticus 11, **124**

Platycheirus tarsalis 11, **125**

Pocota personata 7, 11, **125**

podagratus, Platycheirus 11, **121**

podagrica, Neoascia **99**

Portevinia maculata 11, **126**

potens, Myolepta 6, 11, **96**

potentillae, Sphaerophoria **134**

praecox, Cheilosia 5, **36**

pratorum, Eristalis 65

primus, Triglyphus 11, **142**

profuges, Doros 7, 8, 10, **55**

proxima, Cheilosia **36**, 40

psilophthalma, Cheilosia 5

Psilota anthracina 11, **126**

pubera, Cheilosia 5, 10, **37**

pubescens, Heringia 10, **78**, 79

pubescens, Neocnemodon 10, 78

punctulatus, Parasyrphus **105**

punctulatus, Syrphus 105

pyrastri, Scaeva 6, **129**

Pyrophaena granditarsa 117

Pyrophaena rosarum 122

Q

quadrimaculata, Melangyna **87**

quadrimaculatus, Syrphus 87

R

ramsarensis, Platycheirus 114, **122**

ranunculi, Criorhina 10, **50**

Rhingia campestris **127**

Rhingia rostrata 11, **127**

ribesii, Syrphus **140**, 141

Riponnensia splendens **128**

Riponnensia splendida 11

rosarum, Platycheirus **122**

rosarum, Pyrophaena 122

rostrata, Rhingia 11, **127**

rueppellii, Sphaerophoria **135**

rufa, Callicera 7, 10, **23**

ruffipes, Cheilosia 39

ruficornis, Ferdinandea 10, **73**

rupium, Eristalis 10, 63, **65**

S

sabulonum, Eumerus 10, **67**

sahlbergi, Cheilosia 10, **37**

Scaeva albomaculata 6, **128**

Scaeva mecogramma 6, **129**

Scaeva pyrastri 6, **129**

Scaeva selenitica **130**

scaevoides, Chamaesyrphus 10, **25**

scalare, Melanostoma **90**

scambus, Platycheirus **123**

scita, Tropidia **143**

scripta, Sphaerophoria 6, **135**

scutatus, Platycheirus 9, **123**, 124

scutellaris, Brachyopa 10, **20**

scutellata, Cheilosia **38**

segnis, Xylota **149**

selenitica, Scaeva **130**

semifasciata, Cheilosia 10, **38**

sepulchralis, Eristalinus **61**

sepulchralis, Eristalis 61

Sericomyia lappona **130**

Sericomyia silentis 130, **131**

sibirica, Sphegina 5, **139**

silentis, Sericomyia 130, **131**

similis, Eristalis **65**

solstitialis, Chrysogaster 43, **44**

soror, Cheilosia 10, **39**

species A, Cheilosia **42**

species A, Eupeodes **72**

species A, Melanostoma 11

species A, Metasyrphus 72

species A, Platycheirus 119

species B, Cheilosia 10, **43**

species B, Sphaerophoria **137**

species C, Cheilosia 30

species D, Cheilosia 36

species E, Cheilosia 36

speciosa, Caliprobola 10, **22**

Sphaerophoria abbreviata 132

Sphaerophoria bankowskae **131**

Sphaerophoria batava **132**

Sphaerophoria fatarum **132**

Sphaerophoria form A **137**

Sphaerophoria interrupta **133**, 137

Sphaerophoria loewi 11, **133**

Sphaerophoria menthastri 133

Sphaerophoria philanthus **134**

Sphaerophoria potentillae **134**

Sphaerophoria rueppellii **135**

Sphaerophoria scripta 6, **135**

Sphaerophoria species B **137**

Sphaerophoria taeniata **136**

Sphaerophoria virgata 11, **136**

Sphegina clunipes 11, **138**

Sphegina elegans 11, **138**

Sphegina kimakowiczii 11, 138

Sphegina sibirica 5, **139**

Sphegina verecunda 11, 138, **139**

spinolae, Callicera 6, 10, 13, **23**

splendens, Orthonevra 128

splendens, Platycheirus 13, 123, **124**

splendens, Riponnensia **128**

splendida, Lejogaster 11, 80

splendida, Riponnensia 11

sticticus, Platycheirus 11, **124**

strigatus, Eumerus **67**

superbiens, Arctophila **17**

sylvarum, Xylota 11, **149**

Syritta pipiens **140**

syrphoides, Eriozona 5, **60**

Syrphus albostriatus 51

Syrphus annulatus 103

Syrphus annulipes 59

Syrphus arcticus 83

Syrphus auricollis 92

Syrphus balteatus 59

Syrphus barbifrons 84

Syrphus bifasciatus 56

Syrphus cinctellus 93

Syrphus cinctus 84

Syrphus corollae 68

Syrphus diaphanus 56

Syrphus eligans 56

Syrphus ericarum 85

Syrphus euchromus 91

Syrphus glaucius 81

Syrphus grossulariae 57

Syrphus guttatus 91

Syrphus lapponicus 69

Syrphus lasiophthalmus 86

Syrphus laternarius 82

Syrphus latifasciatus 69

Syrphus latilunulatus 70

Syrphus lineola 103

Syrphus luniger 71

Syrphus lunulatus 52

Syrphus malinellus 104

Syrphus mecogramma 129

Syrphus nigritarsis 104

Syrphus nitidicollis 58

Syrphus punctulatus 105

Syrphus quadrimaculatus 87

Syrphus ribesii **140**, 141

Syrphus torvus **141**

Syrphus triangulifer 92

Syrphus tricinctus 53

Syrphus umbellatarum 87

Syrphus venustus 53

Syrphus vitripennis **141**

Syrphus vittiger 105

T

taeniata, Sphaerophoria **136**

tarda, Xylota 11, **150**

tarsalis, Platycheirus 11, **125**

tarsata, Lejogaster **80**

tenax, Eristalis 6, **66**

tenur, Neoascia **99**

tibialis, Paragus 5, 11, **102**

torvus, Syrphus **141**

transfuga, Anasimyia 15, **17**

transfuga, Helophilus 17

triangulifer, Syrphus 92

triangulifera, Melangyna 11, 92

trianguliferum, Meligramma 11, **92**

Trichopsomyia flavitarsis **142**

tricincta, Pelecocera 11, **107**

tricinctus, Dasysyrphus **53**

tricinctus, Syrphus 53

Triglyphus primus 11, **142**

trivittatus, Helophilus 6, **76**

Tropidia scita **143**

tuberculatus, Eumerus 5, 67, **68**

U

umbellatarum, Melangyna **87**

umbellatarum, Syrphus 87

uviformis, Cheilosia **39**

V

variabilis, Cheilosia **40**

varipes, Pipizella 111

velutina, Cheilosia 10, **40**

venustus, Dasysyrphus 52, **53**

venustus, Syrphus 53

verecunda, Sphegina 11, 138, **139**

vernale, Chrysotoxum 10, **48**

vernalis, Cheilosia **41**

verralli, Chrysotoxum 47, **48**

verrucula, Cnemodon 79

verrucula, Heringia 11, **79**

verrucula, Neocnemodon 11, 79

versicolor, Helophilus 107

versicolor, Parhelophilus **107**

vicina, Cheilosia **41**

viduata, Pipizella **111**, 112

virens, Pipizella 11, **112**

virescens, Chrysogaster **44**

virgata, Sphaerophoria 11, **136**

vitripennis, Cnemodon 79

vitripennis, Heringia **79**

vitripennis, Neocnemodon 79

vitripennis, Syrphus **141**

vittatus, Helophilus 81

vittatus, Lejops 11, **81**

vittiger, Parasyrphus **105**

vittiger, Syrphus 105

Volucella bombylans **143**

Volucella inanis 11, **144**, 145

Volucella inflata 11, **144**

Volucella pellucens **145**

Volucella zonaria 5, 11, **145**

vulpina, Cheilosia **42**

X

Xanthandrus comtus 6, 11, **146**

xanthocnema, Xylota 11, **150**

Xanthogramma citrofasciatum **146**, 147

Xanthogramma festivum 146

Xanthogramma pedissequum **147**

Xylota abiens 11, **147**

Xylota coeruleiventris 5, 11, **148**

Xylota florum 11, **148**

Xylota lenta 21

Xylota meigeniana 148

Xylota nemorum 24

Xylota segnis **149**

Xylota sylvarum 11, **149**

Xylota tarda 11, **150**

Xylota xanthocnema 11, **150**

Xylotomima lenta 21

Xylotomima nemorum 24

Z

zeneggenensis, Pipizella 111

zonaria, Volucella 5, 11, **145**